Management by Compulsion

Management by Compulsion

The Corporate Urge to Grow

by Rolf H. Wild

Houghton Mifflin Company Boston
1978

Library of Congress Cataloging in Publication Data

Wild, Rolf H
    Management by compulsion.

    1. Corporations.   2. Industrial management.
3. Big business.   I. Title.
HD2741.W54   658.4   78–4964
ISBN 0–395–26467–7

Printed in the United States of America

P 10 9 8 7 6 5 4 3 2 1

For "Lucy,"

who asked all the questions
this book tries to answer

Contents

Management by Compulsion

Introduction

Large corporations are often perceived as a menace to the public.

They are blamed for a multitude of ills that beset contemporary life. They are held responsible for abusing their large economic power to eliminate competition, impose prices, defraud customers, exploit the working masses, pollute the environment, exert undue influence on government, and commit all sorts of unspeakable crimes in the boardroom to enlarge their size, power, and profit. The misdeeds imputed to corporations by vociferous crusaders are legion.

Unfortunately, these attacks on big business rarely shed much light on the subject. The controversy does not reveal how corporations actually operate or how they are in fact controlled. And since we do not understand very clearly the incentives and threats to which corporations must respond if they are to survive, or the nature of this response, we tend to see them as tightly controlled monolithic organizations dominated by millionaire capitalists and using their large resources to extract the last ounce of profit from a hapless public, by means fair or foul. The image of the large corporation is thus formed to a considerable extent by ignorance, prejudice, and distrust, seemingly confirmed by frequent exposures of real or alleged corporate misdeeds.

We see the effects of corporate growth strategies and attribute them to the dark manipulations of powerful shareholders, or perhaps to bureaucratic management structures avidly enlarging their activities. Yet these growth strategies may simply be the natural response to a business environment in which growth has become a condition for survival.

We perceive a lack of true competition and deduce that the corporate giants control prices in a fiendish collusion to maximize profits. It does not occur to us that there may be another explanation for the similarity of many supposedly competing products sold with almost identical price tags.

We are outraged to learn of corporations that use devious ways to influence government, at home and abroad. But we never seem to consider the fact that corporations have no open and legal means to defend their interests. Any hobo on welfare can vote; General Motors cannot.

Out of this tissue of prejudice and distrust has grown the widespread impression that large corporations are evil, a menace to the public, giant structures that increasingly escape from outside control, economic monsters imposing their will on the helpless populace.

This somewhat stereotyped view of large corporations prevails not only among opponents of capitalism, but also in a large part of the general public as well as among political leaders, exponents of the mass media, and even distinguished economists. More surprisingly, perhaps, the image of the big bad corporation is encountered even among bankers, stockbrokers, and corporate managers — persons involved professionally in corporate activities.

Yet despite these widely held views, consumers go right on buying the products and services of the corporate giants. And since people have a reasonably free choice in selecting the products and services they buy, large corporations must offer the consumers certain advantages. If they did not, there would be at least a sharp reduction in the number of large corporations. Thus, corporations cannot be all bad and it is conceivable that their reputation is worse than they deserve.

However, one thing is clear. The activities of large corporations are of considerable importance to all of us in our roles as breadwinners, consumers, small investors, taxpayers, and prisoners of the environment. For this reason, it may be useful to set aside preconceived notions in order to develop some understanding of corporate activities.

To do so, we will have to consider the particular environment in which corporations operate and the incentives to corporate growth inherent in this environment. From this we may be able to understand the strategies that have been developed in response to these incentives, and the totalitarian methods that have been adopted to cope with the problems of managing large and diversified organizations. Finally, we should give some thought to the consequences of corporate growth and the concentration of business power in large enterprises.

Obviously, a subject this vast and complex cannot be treated exhaustively without going into voluminous technical detail. A certain amount of simplification and perhaps exaggeration has been necessary to sketch the broad outlines of the problem. However, this book is not intended as a scientific treatise on corporate economics, or as a textbook on corporate practice. It advances no complex theories, and its language has been kept simple and devoid of professional jargon. It is addressed to the broad public rather than to corporation presidents or management trainees.

While this book criticizes certain corporate practices, it is not meant to be yet another scorching exposé of corporate misdeeds. In fact, no corporation is named in connection with what may be considered dubious practices, mainly because it would not be just to single out any particular organization for procedures that may be common practice in a certain industry or among corporations of similar size, or even in the whole corporate community.

Rather, this book is intended to explain certain facts of modern corporate life. It is based largely on my experience as a senior executive in a diversified multinational corporation and as a consultant on acquisitions for various large corporations. I have thus been exposed to corporate activities from the inside, from the semidetached view of the consultant, and also from the position of a small investor and outsider.

My work on the manuscript has stretched over a number of years and during this time my point of view has subtly shifted. What was initially conceived of as a critique of certain corporate strategies and management techniques has led to an examination of the economic conditions that prompted the adoption of these strategies and practices. My involvement in the management of a very small company has contributed some specific insights into the problem of operating scale, which are perhaps less appreciated when dealing with large corporations only. From this broader point of view, it became apparent that the seeming menace of the large corporations is less the result of devious plans to enlarge corporate power than it is a logical reaction to economic circumstances.

And there lies a problem.

Is the giant corporation, with all its threatening aspects preferable to a revolution of our economic system, which makes the ever-increasing concentration of economic power in large enterprises almost inevitable?

1. Defining the Problem

A Fantasy

Let us indulge for a moment in a fantasy tinged with paranoia. Early in 1953, Stalin called a meeting of the Supreme Soviet to discuss certain matters of grave importance.

After whatever amenities were customary at top-level meetings in the Kremlin at that time, Stalin exposed the problem.

"Comrades," he said, "we are faced with a situation that threatens not only the future of our country and the development of socialism. It also presents a danger to our form of government, or, more specifically, to our jobs. Unless we cope with this threat, we may become scapegoats for our successors and end our days as traitors and revisionists."

He looked around and slowly filled his pipe. He rather enjoyed such ominous opening gambits, and as far as he could see, the impact of his words had not been lost. Anxiety was an important factor in keeping people in line and in getting results.

"There can be no doubt," he continued, "that the future decisive battle with capitalism will not be fought with armies, tanks, and missiles. Nuclear weapons have made all-out war too dangerous. Of course, we will continue to make use of our allies in minor wars and build up our own military organization.

Military power is still important, not only for our own security, but also to incite the other side to waste productive capacity on defense spending. A threat here, a small war there, will maintain an atmosphere of danger and insecurity in the capitalist camp. But the real battle is no longer military; it is a matter of economics, industrial production, worldwide competition, prosperity, and the ability to buy friends with money and equipment. And in this area the capitalists are way ahead of us. Look how the Americans bought Western Europe by giving away billions of dollars under the Marshall Plan. And they can do it again whenever they choose. They have the productive capacity, the technical knowhow, the economic growth, and the prosperity.

"And this is where we fall short," he continued. "We may boast of the success of our industrial development and our five-year plans and quote reams of figures to demonstrate our progress. But these statistics are misleading. Our industries produce huge quantities of unattractive and shoddy goods that nobody really wants. The only reason we can sell most of our products is because the state has a monopoly. If we opened our borders to imports, nobody would buy our homemade junk, and we would have an economic crisis on our hands, something that is supposed to happen only in capitalist countries. We could not exist in an open economy.

"This is a problem we have been trying to solve for years. We have five-year plans with targets that can only be met by poor quality and massive cheating. We have centralized management of entire industries and have used every means of coercion to get results. We have shot poor managers by the thousands and sent armies of underachievers to the new frontier in Siberia. And still the results are not very satisfactory.

"And since we have not been able to solve the problem, even with these drastic methods, of which not all of you approve, there is only one conclusion possible. Our inefficiency is not the result of human faults but is built into our system. Our methods of management are no good, and we may as well admit that we have made a terrible mistake."

The old man finally lit his pipe. Nobody moved. Long experience had taught all those still present that the rash expression of an opinion after such an opening statement could have dire consequences. People who jumped to conclusions too quickly and talked before the drift of the chairman's thoughts became absolutely clear had a tendency to leave suddenly for long trips. Keeping one's mouth shut was an important factor in improving one's chances for survival in the Soviet Union in 1953. Once it became clear just exactly what Stalin had in mind, there would be plenty of time to show the right kind of enthusiasm.

Stalin just sat there, fingering his pipe. Not a very inspiring team, he thought. Still, that was the way he had trained them. And there had been the purges. Too bad some of the best brains had had to be blown to bits because their owners had lacked loyalty. He had had no choice; now he would have to rely on the leftovers. He wondered if the plan was going to work. He was pretty certain he could do his part, but would his stooges be able to do theirs?

"No matter what we may have thought, or what Marx may have written, or Lenin may have said, the centralized management of state-owned industry does not really work. It is better than the unspeakable mess resulting from direct control by the workers, as we found out in the twenties, but not much. We are simply bogged down in a morass of bureaucracy. The failure of our system is not the fault of incompetent managers, but of the strait jacket of five-year plans and production quotas, of centralized administration by incompetent bureaucrats without experience in running anything, of blaming operating people for planning mistakes, of politicians setting targets without regard for reality. And then there is the ridiculous idea of producing everything on a larger scale than anybody else has ever done.

Mindless gigantism in planning new factories. The coercion to produce, or else. And the fear of the operating managers that one honest mistake may quite literally kill them. And the suppression of any new ideas by rigid plans and theories.

"Now, we can go on as before and lose out to the capitalists," he continued, fiercely puffing on his pipe. "Or we can admit our mistake, not to the public of course, but to ourselves, and change our system. To win the new game of economic warfare, we will have to change our strategy.

"To start with, we need better management. Now, this we will not find in our official doctrines. We will have to look elsewhere. We will have to learn management techniques from the Americans. They are the world leaders, as we all know."

"For pure materialistic efficiency without consideration for the dismal condition of the suppressed and impoverished proletariat, the Americans are hard to beat," someone said.

"Oh, stop this nonsense," Stalin glowered. "You are not addressing a party rally and you are not fooling anybody. We all know that the impoverished American workers drive the sort of big cars we reserve for senior government officials and eat better than we do. But we will have to beat them at their own game.

"And here is what we will do. I have worked out a plan in three phases, and I am sure you will all agree to this plan." Heads nodded silently.

"First of all, we will copy their management methods as best we can. Needless to say, we will pretend that these new methods are the logical outcome of socialist theory, and somebody had better start working on this angle. Propaganda, or what we will henceforth call public relations, is very important in carrying out our strategy.

"Borrowing the management methods ought to be simple. There appear to be hundreds of books and thousands of reports and other documents that can be bought anywhere in the

United States. Only the Americans could be stupid enough not to keep secret the knowhow that is the very strength of their system. The collection of this material ought to be well within the capacity of our overrated secret services. A special bureau will then be set up to sift though this material, translate the important parts, and work out the textbooks and training manuals. In about two years, we can then start introducing the new methods."

"We may also have to change our image, as they say over there," somebody suggested timidly.

"Of course, we will have to do that," Stalin grinned, emptying his pipe. At least some of the boys seemed to be catching on. Maybe he had underrated the qualities of his entourage. "Since I am the image," he said, "the answer is obvious. I will leave and let you fellows carry out the new strategy. And this brings me to the second phase of our plan. I intend to bring the curses of our own methods to the capitalists. I plan to convince them that they need five-year plans, impossibly large organizations run by bureaucrats and politicians, rigid organization structures, quotas, and so on. There may be some problems, particularly since the Americans have no really satisfactory substitute for Siberia, but I am sure we can think of something just as effective. We — that means Comrade Beria and myself — we intend to leave together and take a small group of sharp young people along to carry on after we are gone.

"All this may seem impossible to you, but we have looked very carefully at this problem. We have made an in-depth feasibility study, as the Americans would say, and the results are very positive. The old experienced managers in America are dying out. Business has become too complicated for them since corporations have become inflated by the war effort. They are rapidly being replaced by younger men who lack operating experience. These young managers are apt to buy any likely package of theories to teach them how to manage. We will have the money to promote our system, and once we have hooked a few customers, the others are likely to follow. And this is phase two of the plan," Stalin concluded.

Complete consternation filled the room. He could not be serious. Stalin and Beria leaving, just like that? Inconceivable. Must be one of his horrible jokes.

Stalin looked around. Just as he thought: stony faces trying to hide reeling minds. But once they got used to the idea there might be trouble. Better nip it in the bud.

"Just so you will not get any awkward ideas," he continued, "I will leave on my own terms. If anybody is inclined to disagree, let me remind you that Comrade Beria is still in full control of his fascinating organization. All necessary measures have been taken to prevent any upheaval, inside or out, as a result of our change in organization."

He watched the message sink in and nodded.

"Part three of the plan will come much later, say, ten or fifteen years from now. By that time we should be doing well and the Americans should be vulnerable because they will be tangled up in our old unworkable system. This will be the time to destabilize their economy by various measures. We will start cutting them off from important raw materials, Arab oil and African metals, for instance. It will not take much diplomatic skill to persuade backward countries with resources that they can gain a great deal from blackmailing the Western world. We will encourage currency and gold speculation. We can step up and scale down the cold war climate to cause fluctuations in their defense spending and upset their industrial balance. There will be small wars by our satellites, and so on. It will not take much to keep the capitalist countries in an almost continuous state of crisis and recession with which they cannot cope once they have adopted our inefficient management methods. And that is when we will bury them. Their governments will have no choice but to become more and more socialistic or risk being overthrown. Either way the ultimate result will be the same. Socialism will triumph, and we are the leaders of socialism.

"If we all do a good job, we should have them in difficulty in fifteen years, in trouble in twenty years, and out of the race by 1980. I know that is a long time, but believe me, it is the only way to beat them short of a nuclear war, which would wipe us all out. Few of us can expect to see the ultimate results, but in the end our system will win. And that is certainly more attractive than playing games with nuclear weapons."

The argument was so convincing that the leaders in the Kremlin adopted the new plan with considerable enthusiasm. Stalin and Beria disappeared shortly afterward, and with the help of substantial funds deposited in Swiss banks, they started their work of subverting American business.

And it came to pass that American corporations wholeheartedly espoused rapid growth strategies and became ever larger and more diversified. And to cope with their sprawling growth they adopted five-year plans, teeming bureaucracies, quota systems, and management methods closely patterned on the Russian model. Pretty soon, the United States started to lose its leadership in the markets of the world and began to suffer balance-of-payment problems, currency debasement, rampant inflation, shortages of critical materials, and large-scale unemployment. And the government had to resort to all sorts of measures to cope with these problems, interfering more and more massively with what used to be a free economy and restricting the freedom of its citizens to do business as they pleased.

The second and third phases of Stalin's game were a great success. On the other hand, the Russians did not prove very successful in taking over the methods that had, until quite recently, given American business a dominant position in the world. The reasons for this failure are not very clear. Perhaps the Russians misguidedly went on copying American practices after the dastardly work of subversion had been accomplished. Or perhaps the gentlemen left behind in the Kremlin changed their minds. Or Russian bureaucracy was not up to the problem of collecting, sorting out, digesting, and adopting the right kind of American management knowhow. All these are possibilities.

But there are two more plausible explanations.

First, it is quite possible that all the publications by experts in management science, with all their well-chosen case histories and complex theories, failed to reflect the true secrets of down-to-earth management. This need not be surprising. Well-paid and competent corporate executives rarely write books and invent theories. They are too busy plying their skills and making money. The books emanate mainly from those on the outside who make a living from teaching, consulting, and writing books, which is not quite the same thing as actually managing a corporation or a corporate department. Their books may reflect certain aspects of management, but they are not necessarily its substance.

The other explanation which comes to mind is that the successful management methods which propelled the United States to world leadership may simply not be suitable to run very large diversified organizations, be they state-owned industries or publicly held multinational corporations. If this were true, the similarity between the methods used to run monster state corporations in Russia and the management techniques adopted by large diversified enterprises in the United States would no longer be surprising.

Of course, our whole fantasy is obvious nonsense. There never was a dark devious Communist plot to subvert our business activities.

But the results are almost the same as if there had been.

So let us consider the factors that brought about this transformation of American business and its effects on both our economy and our lives.

Economic Reality

As the events of the last few years have shown, we live in a highly vulnerable economy. After years of growth and prosperity, we have suffered the worst recession since the thirties, and there is no guarantee that similar, or worse, recessions will not occur again.

Yet until quite recently, the United States had the healthiest economy in the world. The American standard of living was unsurpassed. American industry was the unchallenged leader in technology and productivity. American business methods were so manifestly successful that they were considered unique and widely copied. American wealth paid for a large part of the defense of the Western world and for economic aid to many countries. And the dollar was as good as gold.

Of course, there were economic fluctuations, booms and recessions, but they were temporary. In some years business would be great; in others there would be some slack and business would not be quite so good. But the overall trend was toward economic growth and increasing prosperity, not only in the United States but in the whole Western world. Everyone was basking in the pleasant expectation that the next year would almost inevitably be better than the last one.

Then — all of a sudden it seemed — things changed.

We found ourselves confronted with the sort of problems we used to associate with third-rate foreign nations. The dollar had to be devalued, not once but twice, and even then it kept losing ground against stronger currencies. Inflation was no longer a gradual thing, a creeping nuisance; it became rampant and painful. Unemployment became a political problem. There were sudden shortages and scares. And then the oil crisis triggered a severe recession, the effects of which are still felt today.

The fact that few countries fared any better and many of them much worse, offers little comfort. After years of good living, we were not prepared for the shock of a long and deep recession.

Even the gradual recovery that followed has not restored full confidence. The suspicion remains that the recovery is only a temporary interlude before the next crisis. If it happened once, it can certainly happen again, in spite of all the desperate measures taken by governments worried about their survival.

The most disconcerting fact which emerged during the recession is that there seems to be no practical solution to the economic problems of the highly developed modern industrial state. Even at the height of the recession, nobody seemed able to present a plausible plan for coping with the situation. Leading economists argue endlessly about their usually conflicting theories. Political leaders posture bravely and declare solemnly that recovery is imminent in order to calm disturbed voters and to discourage rioting in the streets. Various and sundry spokesmen chime in with their views, as do the mass media. And everyone is quick to claim credit when the awful situation shows some signs of improvement. But all that emerges from the din and confusion is that the causes of the economic sickness are uncertain and the cure is unknown.

If anyone had a sure-fire solution to the problem, no government worth reelecting would hesitate to hire, bribe, or even kidnap the genius with the magic wisdom. But there seems to be no plausible remedy, or at least none that can be applied without the risk of political upheaval.

All this illustrates the difficulty of the problem. In fact, the problem may not have a solution at all. Any economic theory has to assume that there is a state of equilibrium which either occurs naturally or can be made to occur through government action. However, if this equilibrium required that 40 per cent of the working population lose their jobs and the other 60 per cent work at half their customary wage, no government would dare to strive for this objective. Nor would 50 per cent annual inflation be compatible with political stability. The room to maneuver in solving the economic problems of a modern industrialized democracy is quite limited.

And within these limitations, the economy may well be inherently unstable, in the sense that unemployment and inflation can be held at tolerable levels only during periods of substantial economic growth. If growth flags, ceases, or becomes negative, unemployment and inflation soar and the instability of the economy becomes manifest. Unfortunately, growth has its limits. Markets become saturated, and the power of government to create work for idle hands is ultimately restricted by its capacity to tax and borrow. And the nearer the limits of growth are approached through measures to produce synthetic growth, the more vulnerable an economy will become.

As a result, even slight losses of public confidence can produce an economic crisis. At this point, governments can take all sorts of measures. They can change their spending, alter the supply of money, restrict imports, change taxation, subsidize exports, and tell the citizens there really is no crisis. But there is one thing they cannot do. They cannot convince, or compel, the citizens to buy more cars, build more houses — spend more money. The man who fears that he may lose his job is not about to spend his savings to redeem the economy, particularly when he notes that prices have been increased as a result of the decreasing demand.

Once public confidence in continuing prosperity is shaken, no act of government, short of perhaps starting a war, can restore the delicate balance of an economic system that appears reasonably stable only so long as there is substantial economic growth and that is, in fact, unstable.

Thus any comparatively minor event can upset the applecart. The action of the oil-producing countries threw the whole Western world into a deep recession. Yet this action involved a price increase of only around 25 cents per gallon of crude — steep, but surely survivable. However, nobody ever quoted the price increase per gallon. The public was given the alarming news in dollars per barrel, which made the price increase seem enormous.

In fact, the oil crisis may have triggered the recession, but it did not cause it. There had been signs of economic instability long before. The dollar devaluation had occurred years earlier, inflation had made severe inroads, and unemployment was not exactly at comfortable levels — at least not in the United States — long before the oil crisis materialized. Four years later, the same problems persist, hence the suspicion that similar crises of confidence will provoke major recessions again and again.

Meanwhile, attacks on big business tend to become more frequent and louder. The oil companies made large profits from the oil crisis, and there is a widespread suspicion that the business giants as a whole survived the recession far more comfortably than their small competitors or the average citizen. How else could they increase prices when business is bad instead of marking down their products to stimulate demand and give the public a break? Whatever happened to the mechanism of supply, demand, and price we were taught about in school? Where are the forces of competition to protect the customers? Are large corporations a law unto themselves, free to set their prices as they choose, exploiting the public in times of feast and famine?

Of course not. They are subject to the same economic conditions and restraints as their smaller brethren or the tiny Ma and Pa grocery store around the corner. But there is a difference. Because of their size, they are in a much better position to weather a storm, to adapt themselves to changing conditions, to exploit new opportunities, to reorganize their structures to cope with new problems. And the advantages of large size provide corporations with a compelling incentive to grow rapidly.

Corporate Power

Big corporations loom large in the American economy.

Exxon, the largest corporation in the world, had a sales volume of $42 billion in 1974. This is equivalent to the gross national product of Switzerland — all the goods and services produced by a highly industrialized country with a population of six million.

In the same year, the combined sales of the ten largest corporations in the United States amounted to $230 billion, or somewhat more than the GNP of Great Britain. It is interesting to note that the top ten include the two largest car makers and no less than five oil companies. The automobile and its source of energy play a dominant part in our economy.

Also, in 1974, the twenty largest corporations in the United States had combined sales of about $323 billion. This was equal to the federal budget for that year, or about 23 per cent of the gross national product of the United States; i.e., twenty corporations controlled almost a fourth of the U.S. economy.

But this is only one aspect of the economic power of the corporate giants. Employment is another. Between them, the top twenty corporations employed over 5 million people in 1974. This represents about 6 per cent of total employment for that year. However, if we consider all the jobs that depend directly on the activities of the twenty giants, and the families and dependents of the holders of these jobs, we can estimate that perhaps 25 million people derived their incomes and livelihood from the activities of these twenty large corporations.

The American Telephone and Telegraph Company alone employed just under one million people in 1974, making AT&T the largest corporate employer in the world. But there is another important human factor. AT&T has also around three million shareholders who own 560 million shares of the company and to whom the fate of the corporation is of some importance. Among these owners are some seven hundred institutions, which hold 24 million shares, or about 4 per cent of the total. The remaining 96 per cent of the share capital is owned by various and sundry investors with an average holding of less than 190 shares each. This average is misleading, for there are bound to be some large individual investors among the masses of little fellows with 50 or 100 shares each. Nevertheless, the ownership of the company is widely spread.

This ownership structure is fairly typical of many large and medium-sized corporations: a few per cent of the shares in the hands of institutions; the rest are owned by an assortment of large and small shareholders. Thus, millions of people are directly involved in the activities of very large corporations. But the influence of the corporate giants extends far beyond employees, stockholders, suppliers, and all those who feed on the scraps from the table of the giants. The fate of the large corporations affects virtually all of us. If anything truly drastic were to happen to any one of the largest corporations, serious repercussions would be felt by the whole economy; if disaster were to befall several of them, we would have a full-blown economic crisis.

But the giants are only the very visible peak of the corporate structure. Below them lie hundreds of smaller, but still quite large, companies. In 1974, there were more than three hundred corporations with sales above $1 billion. These lesser giants may not be as conspicuous as the top twenty, but they still enjoy very substantial benefits as a result of their size and scale of operations. They can get the financing, enlarge their markets, deploy their resources on a multinational scale, diversify, get the best managers and the top lawyers and lobbyists, pay for huge promotion campaigns, spend millions on research, and comply with all the government regulations — without going broke.

These substantial advantages of large size offer considerable incentives for corporate growth. And as smaller corporations implement the urge toward increasing size, gobbling up markets, resources, and other companies in the process, their rapid growth becomes a menace to their more staid and stable competitors. Once the race toward larger size is started, standing still becomes dangerous. Those who lag behind will tend to languish and ultimately lose out — for they become acquisition candidates for more aggressive corporations.

There lies a basic problem. The corporate environment becomes unstable in the presence of predatory growth strategies. Rapid growth ultimately becomes a condition of survival.

As a result, rapid growth strategies have been widely adopted, not only by companies controlled by aggressive promoters bent on pyramiding their holdings, but also by corporations whose managements are largely independent of shareholder pressures. The result of these strategies is a proliferation of mergers, diversification, and multinational expansion, and these in turn have spawned new management techniques to cope with sprawling and often unrelated activities as well as methods of motivation carefully designed to imbue every manager down the line with an irresistible urge to maximize profit and growth. In their more developed forms, these techniques tend to become totalitarian in character — they become management by soviet.

It is perhaps no coincidence that the manifestations of an unstable economic system are occurring at the time when growth strategies and management techniques that tend to destabilize the corporate environment have reached full bloom.

Is a destabilized corporate environment the result of an unstable economy or vice versa?

Are the large corporations culprits or victims?

One thing appears certain. Corporations did not adopt rapid growth strategies as a result of decisions based on dark, ulterior motives. They simply reacted to the exigencies of their environment.

To understand these growth strategies and their conse-quences, we will have to consider the nature of the environment in which corporations operate and the differences between this environment and the more popular models of economic thought.

2. The Corporate Structure

The Basic Idea

Any business activity involves resources, knowhow, risk, and the expectation of a profit.

The proportion of these ingredients depends on the nature of the business, which in turn determines the organizational structure of the business activity.

A simple business may require few resources, little specialized knowledge, and involve only a modest risk. This kind of business is open to anyone, but its profits are likely to be small.

Anyone can get into the shoeshine business. No technical knowledge or long experience is required. The investment is small — a box, some brushes and rags, shoe polish, and an apron. Work can start at once, and since customers pay cash there is no need for working capital. On the other hand, the profit potential is limited. Few professional shoeshine operators become millionaires.

Further, there are no problems with liquidating the business if success proves elusive. Supplies are bought for cash; there are no debts to settle. There are no employees to pay off, no rent, no commitments for advertising, no supply contracts. The unsuccessful owner/operator of the business simply walks away and starts looking for a new job. The risk is small.

But few businesses are that simple. Some may involve little in the way of investment and only a moderate risk but require skills that can only be obtained through long years of study and experience. This is the case with independent professions — doctors, lawyers, accountants, and consultants. Their investment is mainly in the long period spent acquiring the necessary knowhow and in the lean years of badly paid work until their practice finally becomes profitable.

Apart from such professional activities, most businesses not only require fairly substantial investments but also involve certain fixed costs and liabilities that must be met no matter what happens. And this changes the rules of the game. Rewards must be commensurate with the risk.

Suppose we want to open a small, traditional business — a restaurant, a small supermarket, or a garage. We will have to lease or build premises, buy equipment and merchandise, hire people, pay for advertising, and incur all sorts of obligations long before the grand opening of our establishment takes place and the first sales dollar is rung up on the cash register. We are now involved in a considerable risk. If the business turns out to be a ghastly mistake, we cannot simply walk away. We still have to pay the rent, the salaries of employees, and the bills of suppliers. The exposure may be large, even in a small business.

It is thus necessary to weigh this risk against the rewards of success. A high risk may be acceptable if the rewards are potentially vast — a million dollars for a risk investment of $20,000, for instance. But business opportunities of this kind are rare. So we usually have to accept less attractive odds for the same risk.

We may accept the risk and invest not only our money but also borrowed cash, gambling on our ability to succeed as independent businessmen. If the venture is a success, we may be able to pay back the loan, or better yet, borrow more and expand. Our business will prosper and our courage and hard work will bear fruit.

But not all businesses are successful. Sales may be less than expected, inflation may eat away profits, costs may be higher than anticipated, or some unforeseen disaster may wipe out the business altogether. If that happens, we may lose not only our investment, but everything else we possess. Our financial liability is unlimited. If our business fails, we too may go into bankruptcy.

This prospect is unattractive. It discourages investment in business ventures that involve substantial risk. Spreading this risk over several people in a partnership does not help much because the partners are still personally liable for the business debts incurred. They get rich together or go broke together. Professionals usually operate in partnerships because their risk is modest and they save on taxes. People in high tax brackets may invest in partnerships carefully designed to create attractive tax losses — but these are special cases.

Ventures with unlimited liability to the owners are not a practical way to raise money for business activities on more than a small, local scale. However, spurred by the twin incentives of greed and prudence, smart businessmen solved this problem hundreds of years ago. The solution was a formula that limited the risk of the owners to a fixed amount of capital invested in a business venture. If the business ended in disaster, the owners would lose their investment and nothing more. On the other hand, if the venture was successful, there was no limitation on the profit the lucky owners could split among themselves.

Because the risk of the owners was limited to the initial investment, these organizations were called limited companies. Once formed, a limited company could carry out all sorts of transactions on its own without implicating the fortunes of the owners. If it rolled over and died, its creditors had no way of getting their money back from the owners; their claim was against the company.

The limited company made it possible for large numbers of investors to share in a large or particularly risky enterprise. At the same time, the individual investor could spread his own risk and invest in several companies. Some of his investments might turn bad, but others might do better and still leave him with a profit.

But there was another important advantage. The investors were not locked in. They could sell their parts, or shares, in a particular company at any time at whatever price reflected the value of the company in the minds of buyer and seller. If the seller made a profit or a loss on the sale of the shares, that was his own problem and had no repercussions on the company itself. The company had obtained its capital when the original investors put up their money. Any subsequent trading of shares would neither add to nor subtract from the assets of the company.

The trading of company shares soon became a normal, everyday business transacted in certain places which ultimately developed into our modern stock exchanges, where millions of shares are traded every working day. The modern investor does not have to form his own company to put his money to work. He simply buys stock certificates of companies he particularly fancies at whatever price is quoted on the stock exchange. The choice of stocks is large, and a phone call to the stockbroker is sufficient to launch the transaction.

That is capitalism in a nutshell.

The concept of the limited company made possible the growth of very large business organizations capable of assuming risks far beyond the means and the courage of the wealthiest individual owners. And so the limited company of yore developed into the modern corporation, with thousands or even millions of owners. As we shall see, this wide diffusion of ownership, and the fact that this ownership continually changes as a result of stock trading, have important consequences for the activities of modern corporations.

The corporate form is obviously not limited to large multibillion-dollar enterprises whose shares are listed on the stock exchange. It is equally applicable to much smaller companies whose owners wish to limit their risk. The main difference is that the trading of shares tends to become more difficult when small companies are involved. It is always possible to find someone who will buy or sell shares in General Electric at a certain price. Shares in a small hardware store or a local cab company have no such ready market.

Clearly, the corporation is the mainstay of our industrialized society. At one end of the scale, it permits the backers of a new business to limit their risk exposure and perhaps gamble on the success of a new product or business concept that would never see the light of day if the backers had to assume full personal liability. At the other end of the scale, it makes possible the combination of vast resources to pursue activities that smaller enterprises could not carry out effectively.

Yet the corporate charter is not a license to do as the corporation pleases. Like the private citizen, the corporation has to comply with the rules and regulations imposed by the government. These restrictions on corporate freedom are not only intended to protect the public from a variety of real and imagined abuses, they are also meant to encourage investment, economic growth, and prosperity.

In fact, governments understood long ago that corporations play a key role in the life of a nation. They are the essential base for the development of trade and industry on which the economic strength of a nation depends. Prosperous business creates the wealth for financing public works, be they canals or superhighways, fortifications or airports, mercenary armies or foreign aid.

Moreover, corporations provide the industrial structure that is essential to any designs for national greatness and military strength. It takes an industrial base to produce muskets, battleships, or missile systems. The overwhelming importance of industrial capacity in warfare has been amply demonstrated since the days of Eli Whitney.

Finally, corporations provide large-scale employment, which in turn is a condition of political stability.

For these reasons, enlightened governments have all along encouraged corporate activities as a tool for developing business and industry, and they continue to do so, whether in highly developed nations or in every tiny country of the Third World.

To provide this economic development, the means for financing manufacturing and trading activities must be found. In totalitarian states, this merely involves the allocation of resources by government decree. Production capacity for tanks or power plants is created by diverting money, manpower, and machinery from other parts of the national economy. The choice between guns and butter is made by the government.

In a free capitalist society, the problem is more complex. People have to be encouraged to invest their money in business ventures rather than keeping their gold pieces stuffed into a mattress or their cash in a numbered bank account in Switzerland. Moreover, to create a broad financial base for investment, the game must be made attractive not only for the wealthy but for the less affluent as well. And to lure the small investor into the game, some regulation is necessary to protect the shareholders. Before the small speculator buys shares, he wants to be reasonably certain that he is dealing with respectable corporations which know their business and that his investment will yield some sort of a profit.

To protect investors from rapacious promoters and unethical practices, laws and regulations have been established setting forth in considerable detail the kind of activities that may be undertaken by corporations and the people involved in them.

As a result of these rules, the investor is largely protected from the grosser forms of corporate mischief.

While this protection is extended to shareholders, it also covers all others who deal with corporations — creditors, suppliers, customers, and to a certain extent the public at large. And as time goes on, the regulations become more refined and more complex — all of which delights the legal profession.

The rules of the corporate game, established and enforced by government agencies, do not always accomplish their purpose, but they do provide an orderly environment for corporate activities. They also make investment in corporate stocks attractive and easy. Moreover, many governments have enacted special tax benefits for shareholders; speculative gains made in trading stocks are more lightly taxed than ordinary income, presumably to encourage investment. In passing these laws, the legislators seem to have forgotten that trading in stock certificates generates no new investment capital except in the comparatively rare cases when corporations sell new stock. Yet this preferential treatment of speculative capital gains has had a very large effect on the activities of modern corporations.

The Mechanics

To understand the workings of the corporation, we must set aside popular images and clichés and consider the mechanics of the corporate structure.

Basically, a corporation is a collection of people and resources brought together to carry out certain activities in order to make a profit. The people involved are the shareholders, the management, and the workers and employees. The resources are the capital paid in by the original shareholders to start with and, later on, whatever assets the corporation may develop or acquire.

These assets include cash, receivables, real estate, equipment, materials, techniques, ideas, rights, patents, and the goodwill of the customers. Against these assets the corporation will also have liabilities — debts to suppliers and others, borrowings, and perhaps other commitments. The difference between assets and liabilities represents the net worth of the corporation, or the book value of the shares. Assets and liabilities belong to the corporation; the corporation belongs to the shareholders.

Setting up a new corporation is a simple matter. The founders decide to form a company for a particular purpose and determine the amount of capital needed. The articles of incorporation are then drawn up with the help of a lawyer. This document, which sets forth in appropriate language the name, purpose, capital, and rules of the new company, is then registered with the authorities, and the capital contributed by the original owners is paid in. The company is then ready to do business.

In a small company the founders may arrange all these transactions among themselves and put up the entire capital. If the venture is larger and more ambitious, they may sell some of the stock to outsiders, either directly or through intermediaries.

Once the incorporation formalities have been completed, the corporation can carry out in its own name any transactions consistent with its articles of incorporation and the laws of the land. It has to pay taxes, keep proper records, and provide its owners with sufficient information to permit them to judge how things are going. The corporation acquires its own legal personality.

With luck, the corporation will prosper and return large profits to its owners. It will develop and expand, and its stock may ultimately be listed for trading on a stock exchange. Or it may fall prey to the many dangers that stalk a young corporation and expire, to the chagrin of its owners.

Whatever happens, the shareholders have no further obligation to the company after they have paid for their shares. If the corporation needs more money, they are under no compulsion to contribute more capital. They may choose to do so anyway to protect their initial investment, but they cannot be forced to put up more cash.

On the other hand, the shareholders cannot demand repayment of their investment unless the company goes out of business. When that happens, everyone else is paid off first, and the owners receive whatever money may be left over. Their investment is risk capital, and they carry this risk as long as the corporation exists.

Since the shareholders own the corporation and carry the financial risk, it is only logical that they should control the corporation's destiny.

In a closely held company, this presents no problem. If the shares are held by a family, Dad may become president, Uncle Bill the treasurer, while young Charlie handles sales and Mom is in charge of personnel. There may be disagreements, but there is no doubt about who runs the company. The owners have full control.

This simple arrangement is no longer practical when there are more than a handful of owners, since they all cannot run the corporation. A more formal system of control is required. The owners have to elect from among themselves a board of directors, which will be responsible for actually running the corporation. The board reports to the shareholders; if the owners are not happy with the results, they can get rid of the board and elect a new team.

Unfortunately, this logical system of control tends to become somewhat unsatisfactory as companies get larger and shareholders become more numerous. When there are hundreds of owners, the individual shareholder does not know the candidates for board membership or what special interests they may represent. Nor does he have much choice in voting; there is usually only one slate of nominees. There are no opposition candidates, nor is there a way to vote against the official slate or against individuals on that slate. The voting options of the run-of-the-mill shareholder in a large corporation are the same as those of the citizens of the Soviet Union.

The shareholders have only three choices. They can vote for the official slate, rubber-stamping the nomination. They can withhold their vote in ineffectual protest. Or they can sell the stock.

The board members elected by this unusual procedure are important people. They set the policies of the corporation and manage its activities on behalf of the shareholders. But no matter how badly the corporation may be managed, or how suspect the abilities and ethics of the board members may be, the shareholders have no practical means to impeach the chairman, fire the president, or get rid of the board — not the large and diffused mass of small shareholders, anyway, no matter how much of the corporation they may collectively control.

Consequently, the seemingly logical structure of control through ownership does not work very well when the number of owners is large. When ownership is dispersed among many shareholders and changes frequently because of stock trading, effective control of the corporation reverts to the board itself or to dominant shareholder groups that may control only a few per cent of the stock; the rights of the small owners become purely symbolic.

Strangely enough, the small shareholders do not seem very much concerned over this lack of effective voting rights. The reason will soon become clear.

Checks and Balances

Business is conflict.

Success in any business activity is a matter of judicious compromise in bridging the gap between conflicting profit motives. Buying cheap and selling dear is the cardinal objective of any commercial activity. But unless the trader enjoys a monopoly, some restraints will limit the amount of profit the business will yield.

Even the humble chestnut vendor has to strike a balance between the dictates of his own greed and the realities of what the traffic will bear. When he buys chestnuts he wants the lowest possible price, but his supplier wants to maximize his own profit. The buyer can shop around and haggle, but somewhere along the way he and his supplier must strike a compromise and make a deal that cuts across their basic conflict of opposed interests.

The price at which the vendor can sell his chestnuts again requires some judgment. If he asks too much, the customers will buy elsewhere or not at all. If he sells too cheaply, he will throw away part of his profit or even lose money.

In a more sophisticated business the basic problem is the same, but conflicts multiply in number and complexity. The chestnut vendor has only one product to sell; a corporation may have dozens of product lines and hundreds or thousands of different products selling perhaps in several entirely different markets. The chestnut vendor is accountable only to himself; a corporation has to contend with both external and internal conflict situations. The internal conflicts reflect the strongly diverging interests of shareholders, managers, and workers at various levels of the organization.

The shareholders want to obtain the maximum benefit from their investment. This means high profits, high dividends, and increasing stock prices so their shares can be sold for capital gains.

Management's tendency is to create high profits but to keep dividends low in order to retain earnings for expansion and high management compensation. This conflict between owners and managers must be resolved somehow. If management pushes too far, the owners could, in theory at least, get a new management with a more generous dividend policy. If the shareholders are too greedy, management may quit and leave the company floundering.

The interests of owners and managers are, in turn, pitted against those of workers and employees, who want to earn as much as possible and who may be supported by labor unions that thrive on the exploitation of this theme. Unhappy workers can resign, and training replacements can be expensive. Worse yet, they can go on strikes, which are even more costly and can be fatal to the company if pursued long enough.

Then all the countless other conflicts of interest within the corporation have to be continually resolved. Which departments should be expanded? Which product lines should be pushed? Which activities should be abandoned to the distress of the people involved? How should research money be allocated? Where should new investments be made, in new product areas or in upgrading older products and plants? Who gets the carpeted office and who may use the company airplane? And so on, endlessly.

All these internal conflicts essentially revolve around the problem of splitting the profit cake. This assumes that there is a profit to be split, which leads to the external conflicts that have to be successfully resolved so there may be a profit.

Again, these conflicts are numerous and complicated. How does the corporation best take advantage of competition among suppliers without jeopardizing the flow of essential materials? How far can it beat down the price of a subcontractor without driving him out of business? What products can be sold to whom and how and at what price? How are important customers kept happy at minimum cost? How does the corporation stay competitive? Where is the crossover point between product innovation and promotion cost effectiveness? How should the corporation react to a sudden surge in demand or to a recession? How can it best cope with government interference or with noisy meddlers? How can corporate interests be reconciled with conflicting public interests?

Thus, thousands of conflicts of all sizes and shapes have to be worked out on an ongoing basis, month after month, year after year. Failure to do so effectively will ultimately put the corporation out of business.

The compromises necessary in the interest of survival and profit constitute some sort of a balance. Competition keeps competitors from making excessive profits and results in continuous improvements in the goods and services provided by the corporation. Reasonable rewards for shareholders ensure a continuing flow of investment money. Attractive wages reward employees and generate purchasing power.

As a result of this balance, corporations could be expected to gravitate to the best size for any particular business, the public would benefit from each corporation's efforts to outdo its competitors, and the inevitable weeding out of the unfit, or unlucky, would make room for new companies with new ideas to enter the market.

But this is not exactly what happens. The balance between opposing interests exists, but it is distorted by a number of important factors, and this distortion has some rather important consequences. It leads, among other things, to corporate giantism, to symbolic rather than real competition, and to the elimination of small businesses in many fields of activity.

3. The Distortions

Theory and Reality

A free economy is supposedly self-regulating.

As long as every individual pursues the dictates of his own greed with diligence and logic, the balance between conflicting interests is supposed to result in maximum benefits for everybody. Consequently, the best interest of every member of the public would best be served by avoiding any restrictions on business activities. Free enterprise means happiness for all.

This pleasant theory goes back to the intellectual models conceived when businesses were small. It assumes that economic man will pursue his interest with sublime logic: moving anyplace to get the highest wages, transferring the business unfailingly to whatever activity offers the best advantage, and investing in whatever enterprise offers the highest profit.

These models were based on an idealized view of the small business of long ago. They probably never were very realistic, but they provided a plausible and consistent theory. However, they hardly apply at all to modern business and the modern corporation.

There is, of course, a balance of conflicting interests, but this balance is distorted by a number of factors. Some of these factors have existed all along but were neglected by the founders of economic theory because they were too messy to fit into a logical pattern. Presumably they were considered the result of human imperfection rather than an indication that the theory might not be entirely correct. Other factors have gradually evolved and gained in importance as the scale of business activities became larger, widening the chasm between theory and reality. Yet the simple ideas of the merits of a free economy still linger on, finding their reflection in the belief that all would be for the best if business were freed from all outside restrictions in a laissez-faire economy.

Actually, it is not only the outside interference by government regulations, taxation, and other restrictions that upsets the supposedly benevolent balance of the free enterprise system. Other distortions of the economic environment are equally important, and perhaps even more so.

For one thing, every business inevitably involves real people, with all their imperfections and idiosyncrasies. And real people not only determine the fate of an organization; they are also formed, or deformed, by the organization and its usages, history, and taboos. The internal rules, written and unwritten, the policies, procedures, and experience accumulated within the organization — all have their effect on every decision, and even the most humdrum daily activities of a corporation.

The strike two years ago, the policy statement issued by the executive committee last summer, the development project that failed so disastrously in 1971, and even the offhand remark by the chief executive officer over lunch last Tuesday are all part of the corporate atmosphere that permeates the decision-making process throughout the organization. For this reason, different corporations are bound to react quite differently to the same problem. They have their own personalities, which may be hard to define, but which are very real all the same.

But the reaction of the people within the corporation to

problems, challenges, and dangers is not simply a matter of the corporate atmosphere. It also depends very much on the individual's interpretation of what the situation means to him personally. With all the best intentions and the most loyal frame of mind, the assessment of what is best for the organization will always be tempered by personal considerations. Closing down a department may be a perfectly logical step in the interest of the corporation as a whole. But the people who will be losing their jobs will not necessarily share this view. They will fight for their personal interests, and with luck they may be able to block the move for months or even years.

On the other hand, a new project of doubtful merit may be warmly applauded by managers who certainly know better because they sense that the chairman has his heart set on it. To oppose the chairman's pet project would be bad politics and might adversely affect the next raise or the next stock option award for the opponent.

Moreover, the reactions of the people involved in corporate problems are not always entirely rational, even from the point of view of pure self-interest. A worried manager may react quite irrationally to a perfectly harmless situation because he may see it as a threat to his position. Emotion may prevail over logic. Power struggles, in the boardroom or in the typing pool, may interfere with the orderly conduct of business and bias decisions in unexpected ways. Yet it is from the fabric of countless large and small decisions, made in the realm of the corporate atmosphere and reflecting the real or perceived self-interests of the individuals involved, that the tapestry of corporate history is woven.

And since corporations of substantial size dominate a large part of contemporary business activity, the difference between the rational man of economic theory and the member of a large and complex modern business organization becomes rather important.

But the inability of the human being, within or without the organization, to pursue his self-interest in a rational manner is only one of the many reasons why the subtle balance stipulated by classical economic theory does not work. Other factors play equally important roles in distorting the economic environment.

As noted earlier, the influence of the owners decreases as the number of shareholders gets larger, and becomes negligible in a big corporation with broadly dispersed ownership. Moreover, the economics of mass production and of capital-intensive operations, the structure of the labor market in the presence of unions and collective bargaining, the nature of competition in a mature technology, the advantages of sheer corporate size, modern methods of management compensation, and certain quirks in our tax laws all combine to distort the equilibrium of what we still fondly, but perhaps not very accurately, call the free enterprise system.

Production and Profit

When beans are plentiful, their price is generally lower than when beans are scarce. This is exactly what economic theory says ought to happen. When supply exceeds demand the sellers will lower prices to get rid of excess production. Conversely, when there are not enough beans, the buyers will pay more to get some of the precious vegetable. And when prices are high there is a strong motive to increase production, and vice versa. The production changes triggered by price changes then tend to bring prices back into line.

All this implies that competition in a free market is self-regulating through the interaction of demand, supply, and price.

However, practical experience shows that this theory does

not always work. The prices of manufactured goods tend to increase when business is bad. When car sales fell to disaster levels during the oil crisis, there were no large price cuts to get rid of excess production. There were some discount schemes, but nobody sold cars at half the normal price to clean out inventories and keep the production lines going. Experts, as is their wont, coined new expressions to explain the weird phenomenon and talked knowingly about stagflation, the combination of economic stagnation and inflation. And everybody deplored the failure of the large corporations to respond to falling demand by lowering prices. Obviously, the big bad giants were once again interfering with the free market mechanism through their insensitive and malicious policies.

In fact, the explanation may be quite different. Constant or rising prices during a recession are not so much a matter of evil design as of economic necessity.

A medieval bootmaker may have produced five pairs of boots in a week. If he could sell this modest production at a reasonable price, all was well. But there may have been times when he could not sell his production, or even weeks when he was unable to sell any boots at all. Since boots are not edible, he may then have been compelled to lower his prices in the hope of attracting at least enough business to survive.

On the other hand he might have been lucky. There may have been no competitor in town and he may have enjoyed a monopoly on boot production. Or his boots may have been so superior that people would line up in the street to buy his unique products. In that case he could have raised prices and charged whatever the traffic would bear. Obviously, there would be some limits to these price changes. If the boot business became too profitable, word would get around and competitors might move in and cut prices. Conversely, if prices dropped so low that nobody could make a living, some bootmakers would throw in their lasts and quit. The supply of boots would then be reduced and prices would increase.

This is a perfect example of a situation where supply and demand regulate prices. Yet even in medieval times this situation was probably the exception rather than the rule. Trade guilds restricted competition, and the bootmakers probably fixed prices among themselves over a tankard of ale in the back room of the tavern.

Nevertheless, the seeming logic of this mechanism for balancing supply, demand, and price has fascinated economists for a long time and remains part of what we are taught in school. The fact that the mechanism is not very evident in contemporary life is then usually attributed to the restraint of competition and the control of prices by large corporations operating in a planned environment rather than in a free market economy. If only we had real competition, the popular complaint goes, the market would be self-regulating again and we would all benefit from lower prices.

This is wishful thinking.

Price fixing and restraint of competition may occur in certain businesses, but there are other reasons why the cherished theory does not work. In fact, the theory implies four important assumptions. Workers must be prepared to accept wide fluctuations in their income; investment must be small; fixed cost must be negligible; and everyone involved in the whole process must behave in a perfectly rational fashion. These conditions do not apply to modern industrial production — nor to any other business activity of any importance. The following crude example illustrates this point.

As a counterpart to the medieval bootmaker, consider a small factory making boots with simple machinery. The machinery is old and written off, and we will neglect for the moment the need for working capital to finance work-in-progress and inventories. There are no shareholders and no dividends have to be paid. The owner is the manager, and he is prepared to accept large fluctuations in his income. He likes his work and believes in classical economics. As long as he can make a reasonable living, he is prepared to accept an unpredictable sequence of periods of feast and famine.

For the sake of argument, say that the company employs fifteen production workers who can produce 12,000 pairs of boots a year. Each worker earns $12,000 a year, including all fringe benefits. Material costs average $5.00 a pair. If the company works at normal capacity, the direct production cost of a pair of boots is $20.00.

However, the small company also has some indirect costs, such as rent for plant and office, insurance, office expenses, utilities, taxes, packing materials, supplies, and all the other expenses incurred in running a small business.

And then there are also people who are not directly involved in production but fulfill essential functions. There may be a foreman who plans production operations and supervises the work force, a stock keeper who also helps with packing, a shipping clerk who doubles as inspector of finished goods, and a secretary who runs the office and types invoices. There may also be a part-time accountant, a cleaning woman, and maybe a styling consultant who designs new models. We will not count the manager, who runs the company and acts as salesman, because he is paid out of profits, but we should note that profits have to be high enough to permit him to defray his living expenses. All these people produce nothing that could be sold to a customer, but they are all necessary to carry out the business activity.

Some of these indirect costs may change, depending on the actual volume of production, but most of them have to be paid whether business is good or bad. To keep the numbers simple, let's say these indirect costs run to $120,000 a year.

It should be noted that these figures are based roughly on a small boot factory that unfortunately succumbed to high costs and disappearing markets a few years ago and went out of business. However, the trends indicated by these figures must be fairly typical of many other small manufacturing activities. Using the above figures, the annual cost of staying in business — labor and indirect costs — amounts to $300,000. With material at $5.00 a pair, the total cost of a pair of boots is $30.00 if the company produces at its normal capacity of 12,000 pairs a year. On this basis, the sales price might be set at $32.50 a pair, and the owner-manager would make a profit of $30,000 a year before taxes. But there is no certainty that the company will operate at normal capacity. It may sell and produce more boots than the target figure, or it may not be able to reach the 12,000 pairs a year to achieve full utilization of the plant and its workers.

If business is better than expected, production can be stepped up. There may be overtime for the workers, more people may have to be hired, and perhaps a second shift will be necessary. The production cost per pair will probably stay the same, but the fixed cost of doing business is now spread over a larger volume. As a result, the total cost per pair of boots will drop. If production is increased from 12,000 pairs to 16,000 pairs, the cost per pair will be reduced from $30.00 to $27.50.

The company could now drop its price and pass at least part of the savings on to its customers. However, this would be foolish as long as the company can sell all the boots it can make. The windfall profit of $50,000 goes into the corporate treasury as a nest egg for rainy days or into the owner's pocket.

But if production is less than normal capacity the cost of the boots increases. Even if the actual production cost per pair can be kept the same, which implies firing some of the production workers, the fixed cost of doing business has to be carried by a smaller production volume. If only 10,000 pairs are made, the cost per pair will no longer be $30.00 but $32.00, and profits will almost disappear if the boots are sold at $32.50 a pair. And if production drops to 8000 pairs, the cost becomes $35.00 and the company loses $20,000 that year.

In reality, the situation will probably be worse. The above figures assume that some of the production workers can be laid off when business is bad. But once the skilled workers are laid off, they may no longer be available if business picks up again later. And since the workers are skilled artisans, it may not be possible to find qualified replacements.

Also, in a company this small it may not be practical to lay off enough workers to make any real difference because essential skills have to be retained, even though the people possessing these skills may no longer be working at full capacity. The skilled cutter cannot be laid off because there would be no one to cut the leather; the sole maker is equally essential, as is the worker who assembles uppers to soles. In the end, one or two sewing machine operators may be redundant, but the savings in labor cost will not be in proportion to the lower volume.

If the small company had to retain all its workers, the cost of a pair of boots would rise to $42.50 if production dropped to 8000 pairs a year. And even if some cost reductions were possible, the loss per pair at that volume might be around $7.00 or $8.00. But a loss on the order of $60,000 would probably spell the end of the small company.

The economics of a small artisanal manufacturing company thus show a reverse relationship between cost and business volume, which is illustrated in the following chart. Unit cost increases if volume falls off, and vice versa.

Consequently, when a small company with limited resources is hit by a recession it has no choice. It has to raise its prices to cover the higher unit costs due to the lower production volume. Even with our small artisanal boot shop, and an owner prepared to accept large fluctuations in profit, the self-regulating mechanism of supply, demand, and price does not work.

This poses a basic problem of survival. The small company has to protect itself against drops in demand that can easily be fatal.

Large corporations are accused of imposing their prices on

the hapless public. Strangely enough, our small boot factory has to do the same thing. It has to provide its customers with a firm price list, and once this price list is handed over, the manufacturer is stuck with the prices he has quoted, for that particular ordering season at least. The manufacturer has to set his prices before he knows how much he will actually sell, since the customers will place their orders on the basis of this price list. If he guesses wrong, he is in difficulty. An overly conservative volume estimate may price him out of the market. If he is too optimistic and sets his price too low, his company may incur substantial losses if the actual volume is lower than expected. And there is no practical way to recoup these losses. The price

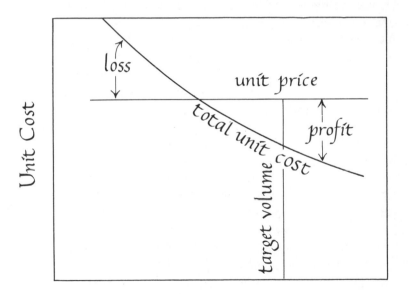

Production Volume

ECONOMICS OF SMALL-SCALE PRODUCTION

cannot be dropped to stimulate demand, and customers, not to mention the government, would not look kindly on a policy of charging different prices for the same product.

The dealer who sells the boots to the public does not have this problem. The dealer probably sells boots of different makes and maybe shoes and socks as well. He can drop the price on some items temporarily without jeopardizing his whole business. If the price cut brings in enough additional business to make it worthwhile, he can continue his low-margin, high-volume policy and expand. If it does not, he can increase the price again; nobody will sue him because he is charging $30.00 for a pair of shoes that sold at $19.98 two weeks before. The dealer thus can experiment with price changes with limited risk.

The manufacturer does not have this option. He has to charge the highest price the market will bear in case he has to operate at less than capacity. If market conditions prevent him from setting a sufficiently high price for his product, he will be vulnerable. Any temporary recession may drive him into bankruptcy.

As long as all competitors are of comparable size, they all have the same problem. Given the reverse relationship between cost and volume, they all try to protect themselves against the dire consequences of operating below normal capacity. For this reason, competition between fifty small boot factories will not necessarily result in competitive price reductions. There is more likely to be a gradual increase in prices, and wherever possible price fixing and production quotas, as each company tries to improve its chances for survival in a fluctuating market.

And the same problem exists in any business activity that involves fixed costs and the payment of wages. As volume decreases, the cost per unit of production increases, and this inhibits price reductions to stimulate demand. This is true even for very small businesses. The mechanism of self-regulating competition does not really work, not even for the one-man business or the one-horse farmer.

As a result, small businesses are not necessarily more competitive than large corporations.

Anyone who has doubts about the veracity of this statement need only go to France. French retailing is still largely in the hands of very small shops operating on very generous trading margins. Price competition is notably conspicuous by its absence, and so is competition by superior service.

The surly French shopkeeper may demonstrate in the streets and petition the government for aid against big bad competitors, but he will not lower prices and seduce his customers with winning manners. This lack of competition between small enterprises means that retail margins and prices in France tend to be notably higher than in countries where competition by large retailing organizations is more pronounced.

Small business is not inherently more competitive, as its proponents would like us to believe. The natural urge to survive among the unpredictable fluctuations of the market is not conducive to price competition.

Yet there is price competition, perhaps not in every field of business and not all the time, but it does exist. However, this price competition is not based on the willingness to work harder or to forgo profits to stimulate business. It is based on the economics of investment and scale of operations applied to the enlargement of market shares at the expense of competitors.

Return on Investment

Competition is a conflict over market shares.

The attempt to take business away from a competitor usually involves lower prices, better products, more persuasive promotion, or a combination of these weapons. And their effective use in the struggle for market shares requires resources and investment.

The boots made by our small factory offer only limited

scope for competition. By the time the wholesaler and the retailer have taken their markups, the customer will be paying close to $70 a pair. At that price, the market is bound to be limited. Nor does the company have the means to enlarge its market.

The boots are largely handmade, and there is no practical way to reduce costs and maintain quality. The company is too small to invest in expensive labor-saving equipment, to develop unique new products, or to carry out effective marketing campaigns to capture a larger share of the boot business. If it grows at all, it will have to grow gradually and painfully. Its base of operation and its resources are too small to permit the company to compete effectively.

However, if the company could produce twenty times as many boots, the business would be large enough to justify a certain amount of capital investment — in machinery and tooling to reduce labor cost and in the development of products which are easier to manufacture and employ perhaps less expensive materials. The resulting cost reductions would then provide the basis for some real competition. Prices could be lowered to capture a larger part of the market. Customers would rejoice, and smaller competitors would be in trouble. No small, artisanal outfit could achieve a 30 per cent price reduction to keep up with a large competitor. The small companies would lose part of their market and be forced to subsist by selling their goods to affluent customers who believe that high prices inevitably mean high quality.

To compete along these lines requires two things: the money to invest in cost reduction and the means to generate enough sales to make the investment worthwhile. The following, entirely fictitious example illustrates this point.

The management of a large corporation has looked at the fragmented boot market and come to the conclusion that the mass production of an inexpensive boot of good quality might be a good investment. To back up this hunch, a detailed market study is carried out.

Competitors, competitor products, prices, distribution methods, buying habits, and possible promotion strategies are investigated in considerable detail. The market study is not cheap. In fact, it may cost more than what a small boot company earns in a good year. But this expense is necessary. The investment in the new business will amount to several million dollars, and the possible risk and profit potential have to be determined as precisely as possible.

The study concludes that an annual market for half a million pairs of boots of a certain style and quality selling at $20 can be developed if $1 million is invested to create the necessary demand.

Management decides that this opportunity looks attractive, and a development project is launched. This is not merely a matter of designing several different boot models, making prototypes, working out production methods, and calculating costs and prices. The corporation is not in the small-time boot business; it designs for mass production and profit. This is a $10-million-a-year game, and there is no room for guesswork. A mistake could be altogether too expensive.

The boot is designed for a specific volume and a specific price: 500,000 pairs of boots a year at $20 each. But the operation must not only be profitable; the profit must be sufficiently large to make the investment worthwhile.

As the project proceeds, materials and production methods are investigated in great detail to find the best approach for meeting the target price. Styling and features of the new boot are developed in conjunction with the planning of the promotion effort necessary to sell the target quantity of boots. Obviously, at that price there will be no hand sewing, no saddle stitching, no expensive leather, and no unnecessary frills. But there may be sophisticated automatic machinery and perhaps exotic manmade materials to produce a handsome boot, which looks almost handmade.

There may also be some novel features of negligible cost to provide catchy promotion arguments and create an exclusive image for the boot. The boot has to be inexpensive, but it must not be cheap. Tooling cost, of course, will be high because of the diversity of the human feet the new boot will have to protect and cuddle. Different sizes will have to be produced in varying quantities, and for every size there has to be both a right and a left boot. To ensure that the statistically correct mix of sizes will pour out of the machinery, production may have to be computer controlled.

In the course of the development work, careful balances may have to be struck to satisfy many requirements. What is the best compromise between the cost of labor and investment? between appearance and ease of manufacturing? between product quality and the cost of possible product failures in the hands — or rather on the feet — of customers? between styling, cost of features, and additional promotion? between imaginary, promotion-created advantages and real quality?

The development of the product, its manufacturing process, and its marketing campaign to yield the proper profit objectives at the target volume is neither easy nor inexpensive. But the payoff is large. A five-cent difference in cost per pair translates into $25,000 more or less profit a year, more than $100,000 over the probable production life of the new boot.

For the sake of our example, we will assume that the investment to launch the new product amounts to $5 million. This includes market studies, product and process development, plant, equipment, tooling, initial promotion, and working capital. This investment must earn an adequate return over the life of the product.

Management may decide that an adequate return on this particular investment is 20 per cent net after tax. This amounts to a net profit of $1 million per year. Since corporate income tax is 50 per cent, the boot production operation has to generate a pretax profit of $2 million per year. Each pair of boots, sold at $20 at the factory door, must produce a pretax profit of $4.

At first glance, this profit rate may seem high, but it is not unreasonable. It reflects not only the size of the investment, but also the risk of the project and the fact that the product line will not live forever. It may go out of fashion or lose the market to a better or cheaper competitor product. Thus the investment must pay off as quickly as possible.

One very important point emerges from this reasoning. If a production activity — or, in fact, any other business activity — requires substantial investment, profit is no longer a matter of arbitrary choice, or something that can be left to accident. Profit level is determined by the size of the investment.

The return on investment becomes like an item of fixed cost to be built into the production process. The target return figure may in the end prove too optimistic when production actually gets into full swing, but the success or failure of the product will be measured by the return actually achieved. An investment that does not produce a better return than the interest rate on borrowed money is obviously a mistake. And if the product has a limited life, the investment has to be recovered before the product succumbs to competition or obsolescence. If a corporation does not earn an adequate return on its assets, it is not likely to have a promising future.

The operating economics of our industrialized boot production might now look as follows:

	PER PAIR	PER YEAR
Net Sales	$20	$ 10,000 000
Material	$ 4	$ 2,000 000
Labor	$ 3	$ 1,500 000
Plant Overhead	$ 4	$ 2,000 000
Production Cost	$ 11	$ 5,500 000
Gross Profit	$ 9	$ 4,500 000
Operating Expenses	$ 5	$ 2,500 000
Total Cost	$ 16	$ 8,000 000
Pretax Profit	$ 4	$ 2,000 000
Net Profit After Tax	$ 2	$ 1,000 000

These figures are purely imaginary and bear no relation to actual boot production. But they are typical of a mass production operation.

The investment represents about half of the expected annual sales volume, and as a result of this investment the labor cost per pair has been reduced from $15 to $3. Moreover, this is not the same kind of labor as that in the small boot factory. These are not skilled craftsmen but machine attendants, pushers of buttons and feeders of hoppers. Product quality has been built into the production equipment and is no longer the exclusive result of worker skill.

But the productivity of the semiskilled workers in our mass production operation is much higher because of the large investment in equipment. In the small factory, 15 production workers made 12,000 pairs of boots a year, or 800 pairs per worker. In our high investment plant, about 125 workers will produce 500,000 pairs annually, or 4000 pairs per worker. Productivity is five times as high as in the artisanal factory.

However, this high productivity is geared to a particular volume. If production drops below this target volume, it may not be possible to lay off workers unless part of the production line can be shut down or a shift can be eliminated. As long as the equipment operates it has to be attended to, and labor cost may be largely the same whether the plant works at normal capacity or 20 per cent below. Within a certain range of production volume, labor tends to become a fixed cost.

Of course, the same holds true for overhead and operating expenses. If business is bad, we may be able to get rid of a few packers, helpers, and floor sweepers, but we may also have to step up sales promotion to keep the production line going. In our hypothetical example, this means that three fourths of the total costs are fixed; only material costs are directly affected by changes in production volume.

As shown in the following diagram, the reverse relationship between production volume and cost is very similar to that of the small boot factory. If production drops by 20 per cent, profits almost disappear. A 30 per cent drop in production means a loss of $400,000 a year.

If sales do not reach the target figure on which the original investment was based, the corporation has a serious problem. At a volume of 400,000 pairs a year, the pretax profit will be only $400,000, or one fifth of the target figure. Return on investment after tax becomes 4 per cent, which is obviously unsatisfactory since the life of the product may only be around five years. Something must be done to improve the situation.

The first step is to increase promotion efforts to improve sales. If this does not work, there are only two practical courses of action to restore the profitability of the product: the corporation can drop prices in the hope of increasing volume, or it can raise prices to increase profits and hope that the price increase will not cut too deeply into the already low volume.

Dropping the price of the boots by 10 per cent — from $20 to $18 a pair — might stimulate sales. But it will also turn the small profit at the existing volume into a net loss. Merely to restore the unsatisfactory return that existed before the price cut, sales would have to increase from 400,000 to 460,000 pairs. And to obtain at least a 10 per cent return on investment, the price reduction would have to produce an increase in sales to 500,000 pairs. Unless management is quite certain that a substantial increase in sales will in fact

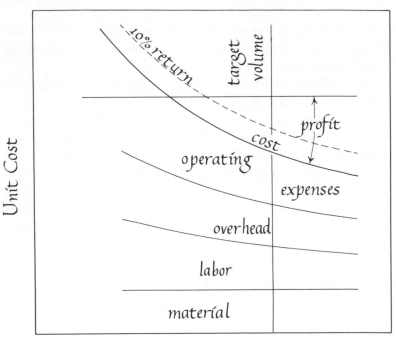

Production Volume

MASS PRODUCTION ECONOMICS

result from price reductions, this course of action is too risky to contemplate.

The safer approach is to increase prices at the earliest opportunity to restore at least an acceptable return on the invested money. In our example, a 10 per cent price increase would restore at least an acceptable, although not exciting, return. And management will learn its lesson. The next time around it will aim at a larger return at the target volume to have more leeway if actual sales fall short of expectations.

The problem is simply that the corporation is locked in. Once it decides to make the investment to produce a certain annual volume for sale at a certain price, it is committed to that volume and price. If the target volume is reached or exceeded, all is well. But if sales fall below expectations, price increases are almost inevitable.

This is why large corporations have to maintain their prices when all is reasonably well and raise them if business falls off. Economists may scold them for imposing their prices on the public, but the corporations have no choice. The investment requires a particular price and volume to produce the necessary return; once the investment is made, the die is cast.

While these prices may be called an imposition on the public, two important points are worth remembering. The investment in mass production usually results in a drastic lowering of prices compared to low-investment artisanal production. And the public is under no compulsion to buy the less expensive mass produced goods. The customer who does not like the idea of the price imposed by the large boot factory is perfectly free to buy handmade boots at $70 a pair and do his share to support small business.

However, the fact that there are large corporations tends to prove that their products and services must be attractive to a great many customers. Otherwise, these large corporations would not exist. It is not the large corporations that kill small enterprises, but the preference of the public for the products offered by large companies.

Competition by investment has its limits. Certain activities do not lend themselves to exploitation on a scale large enough to justify major investments. Markets may be too small or too dispersed to be worth exploiting, or the products themselves may offer insufficient scope for cost reduction or improvement. Or the market may already be dominated by a few large corporations, and any attempt to capture a larger market share would be ruinously expensive or not worthwhile.

The example of our boot production plant, crude as it may be, shows some of the effects of investment on production economics. And the same effects exist in all business activities involving substantial capital investment.

Investment can provide many competitive advantages. But once the investment in a new product, or a chain of hotels, or a fleet of airplanes is made, it must earn an adequate return. If business is bad the corporation may be able to lay off people, cut expenses, and save on postage stamps and telephone bills. But it cannot lay off part of the investment or drop prices drastically in the hope that this will improve business volume.

And since return on investment is usually very sensitive to volume and a major error in forecasting volume can have disastrous results, there is a strong trend toward conservatism. Prices will be set as high as competitive conditions permit and costs held as low as possible to provide from the start a large profit span. This is not to allow for possible price reductions in a recession but to enlarge the space for survival — the span between the forecast volume and that lower volume where profits disappear and disaster threatens. The natural urge to survive permits no other course of action.

The Mousetrap Fallacy

Every now and then a unique, new product beats all competition and sweeps the market.

But this does not happen very often. Not if we mean genuine product innovation rather than the phony novelty that is often touted as a technical breakthrough by glowing advertising copy.

Yet the temporary monopoly created by a new product that is superior to anything else on the market can be the source of the kind of profits corporation presidents dream about.

This scarcity of genuine innovation seems rather strange. There are thousands of corporations with large resources at their disposal looking for ways to increase profits. Huge amounts of time, effort, and money are spent on research and development. But there are no floods of new concepts and streams of truly novel products.

In spite of all the technical effort, there is in fact a surprising similarity between the products and services with which corporations compete with each other. And in many fields competition seems to consist mainly of flamboyant advertising claims lavished on products with only marginal differences in styling, performance, quality, and price. This is synthetic competition, a matter of promotion rather than better mousetraps.

There are exceptions, of course. There is genuine innovation in certain fields, such as electronics and office equipment, but in relation to the scope of research or the size of the overall market for technical products, the results in terms of really new items are rather meager.

What keeps the manufacturers of consumer goods, for instance, from developing better products to beat the competition? Lack of ingenuity? Mental inertia? Collusion to suppress product competition? Of course not.

Nor is the apparent lack of competitive product innovation necessarily the result of corporate decisions to restrain new development and maximize profits by selling the same old products in different packages, year after year. It is mainly a matter of economics.

The primary purpose of a corporate activity is not the blazing of new trails at the outer edges of technology for the benefit of mankind. The purpose is to make a profit.

Any investment in research and product development must have a reasonable chance to return an adequate profit within a reasonable time. If it does not, then the development effort is not an investment but a useless expenditure of corporate funds. A corporation that floods the market with new products but fails to make a sufficient profit on the development investment is liable to become extinct.

When development cost is modest in relation to the expected profit of a new product, a corporation may be able to take a chance and gamble. But in a well-developed product technology, the cost of creating new products can be very high, and mistakes can become ruinously expensive.

The technical development of a product or a product family, or even a whole new technology, generally involves three distinct phases.

In a young technology, progress tends to be rapid and relatively inexpensive as ingenuity is applied to reduce a new concept to practical utility. Investment in development is modest and can yield large returns in technical improvement. Small companies, even individuals, can create new products as long as the product itself does not require a large investment. We might call this the inventive phase of development.

Once all the more obvious improvements have been made,

the game becomes more difficult and more expensive. This is the phase of refinement, of cost reduction and gradual improvement. Research still leads to progress, but major advances become more costly and less frequent. More money has to be spent to develop improvements not already made by competitors. Progress is no longer simply a matter of ingenuity, willingness to take risks, and inspired courage to pursue a vision, but also of money. It becomes a matter of deploying resources in a judicious manner, of carefully weighing risks against probable rewards, of specific objectives and limited exposure.

Finally, in the mature phase of technical development, the returns diminish and ultimately become insignificant. More and more money has to be spent to push technical progress just a little further. The curve of progress against development cost becomes increasingly flat, or asymptotic. Development investment is worthwhile only if markets are particularly large and lucrative, or if the development can be subsidized by money or technical advances imported from other fields of activity. Ultimately, a point is reached where further technical advance becomes impractical, no matter how much money is spent.

Long before this point of zero return is attained, economic considerations and common sense will dictate that the search for technical perfection be abandoned because it no longer pays off. As financial returns from product improvement diminish, there will be a gradual shift toward cost reduction rather than product improvement, superficial styling changes, and perhaps the incorporation of gimmicky features to provide synthetic innovation.

Work on real technical improvement may continue on a low-key, low-budget basis just in case a competitor should be foolish enough to pursue further technical advance. At the same time, a search may be started for more profitable alternatives to a product technology that is approaching the limits of practical development potential.

Where this transition happens depends mainly on market size, profit potential of the product, intensity of competition, and the resources of the companies involved. Some highly ingenious products never get developed because the cost of development could never be recovered from the subsequent commercial exploitation. Others may take a very long time to reach even the refinement phase because their narrow market inhibits development investment. On the other hand, some products zoom rapidly from concept to maturity because the market is important enough to provide substantial rewards for major development investment.

Thus, the span of development may take decades or just a few years. The airplane took more than half a century to progress from bamboo and fabric contraptions of uncertain performance to supersonic flights, while pocket calculators were brought to maturity in just a few years because their development borrowed technology from other fields and their market potential is almost unlimited.

Real better mousetrap competition is most pronounced in the inventive phase, when almost anyone can play. This is where the small company with two scientists and three helpers operating out of a garage can turn new ideas into exciting new products. However, the success of these products is bound to attract competition from larger companies. With luck, the small company will grow fast enough to stay in the development race as the stakes become more important.

As technology becomes more sophisticated and development costs increase, the size of the corporation becomes an essential factor. A company with large resources and access to large markets can spend more on product development than a small competitor operating in a narrow market. But even the large corporation will have to place its development bets with care.

Before committing large chunks of corporate funds for the development of new products, management has to be reasonably certain that the investment makes economic sense. What are the chances that the development will be successful? Will the new product appeal to the market? Can it be sold at a price and in quantities to permit the rapid recovery of the development investment? Does the corporation have the resources to market the new product effectively? Will the project require financing beyond the means of the corporation and can this financing be obtained? Will the new product conflict with existing product lines? How will competitors react? Could the new product lead to competitive developments and a technical race the corporation cannot afford to follow?

Obviously not all these questions can be answered in a definitive manner when a new product is being considered, but they have to be kept in mind. And if there is a strong suspicion that the new project will run into difficulties on several of these counts, a reappraisal of the situation may be indicated.

But even if the project looks good by itself, certain other points must be considered. No company has unlimited resources, and as a result internal competition for investment money is inevitable. Management thus has to decide where the money will do the most good.

Should a million dollars be spent on a high-risk development project which, if successful, might double the size and profits of the corporation but which might also fail and turn the investment into a dead loss? Or should the money go into a more pedestrian project with a far more modest, but almost certain return? Or would it be better to invest in some face-lifting of existing products and a major promotion campaign? Or on new plant and machinery? Or should the money be used to pay off a high-interest loan?

The problem is complex, but it boils down to a careful analysis of the profit potential of alternate investment opportunities. Product development is no longer a matter of faith in the commercial merits of better mousetraps, but of carefully hedged investment.

To launch a new product in the fond hope that it will be a success in the marketplace may be reasonable when the investment is small. If the investment is large, the same course of action could be economic suicide, no matter how revolutionary the new product might be.

The careful assessment of risk versus profit potential does not exclude mistakes. Market studies have been wrong on occasion, research and development are frequently more expensive than expected, and sometimes the technical breakthrough so proudly predicted in requests for development money fails to materialize.

How much risk in new development can safely be assumed is mainly a function of company size. A large corporation has the resources to make major development investments and the marketing organization to cash in rapidly on a successful product. It can move with some audacity where the small company has to be careful. The large corporation will not go broke if a particular project does not pay out as expected.

The options of the smaller company become more limited as the cost of technical progress and product refinement grows steeper. It cannot place multiple bets or incur large risks. And even if it comes up with a winner, it may lack the marketing clout to cash in before competitors move into the market with similar products.

Yet, as a technology progresses, even large corporations may have to proceed with prudence, and somewhere along the way real product innovation may become too costly to be worthwhile, even for the giants, unless some special considerations are involved.

A corporation which dominates a large and lucrative market may pursue product development far into the mature, asymptotic phase that is beyond the reach of its less affluent competitors merely to maintain leadership and keep the little fellows out of the more attractive parts of the market. Wresting yet another ounce of improvement out of a technology, even at almost prohibitive cost, pays off because it ensures the domination of the market.

More common is the pursuit of asymptotic product development as a result of direct or indirect subsidies that reduce the effective cost of the technical effort. These subsidies may take many forms.

To start with, there are internal and external subsidies. Internal subsidies involve the shifting of resources between different activities inside a corporation. Profits made by the fast foods division may be used to finance a battle for market share in camping equipment.

Employing internal subsidies, a diversified corporation may undertake a very costly product development effort in a particular field to gain leadership and capture a large part of the market. The immediate financial return on this development may look disastrous, but the long-term benefits of a dominant position in the market may justify the temporary loss. This strategy is particularly attractive if business has to be taken away from smaller competitors who cannot afford to make similar development investments with little or no immediate return. In diversified corporations, internal subsidies applied to product development can be an important tool for outresourcing competitors.

Another form of development subsidy is the transfer of know-how and techniques originally developed for other uses. Applying outside technology often stimulates development in fields where the basic technology has become quite mature. Since the outside technology has been developed for other uses and been paid for by someone else, it subsidizes in effect the development activities of the borrower. Military and space programs, paid for with taxpayers' money, are an important source of technical advances that can be applied to commercial products.

Government contracts can also play an important role in subsidizing the development of new products for the commercial market. They not only provide the contractor with a base load of business and profit from which ambitious commercial development activities can be pursued more boldly than if the corporation had to rely on nongovernment business alone: they may also subsidize the operation of highly competent research and development organizations that can provide important services in developing commercial products for the corporation.

Finally, there are direct subsidies to finance the development of commercial products. The most conspicuous example of this type of direct subsidy is Concorde, a supersonic airliner, the development cost of which amounted to some three billion dollars, paid for by the British and French governments. So far Concorde has not been a commercial success. Only nine airplanes have been ordered by the airlines owned by the two governments involved in the project. In the first year of Concorde operation, both airlines incurred heavy losses because of the lack of suitable routes.

Yet even if Concorde were a great success in airline service, the market for the SST is quite small. The densest network of long-range routes is the North Atlantic, and about ten Concordes could handle comfortably all the first-class passengers on these routes. If all the other long routes with low traffic were added, at best perhaps thirty airplanes would be needed to carry all the premium priced supersonic traffic in the Western world. This market is woefully inadequate to justify the development investment.

Concorde is perhaps a somewhat extreme example of the risk of asymptotic development. Yet similar risks prevail in the development of subsonic airplanes. It has been shown that the cost of developing and launching an airplane of a given size doubles every six or seven years, even if constant dollars are used and the erosion of the value of money is discounted. The launching cost of a new transport plane might have been $200 million in 1960; launching a similar plane in 1977 would have involved an investment of around $1 billion. Yet the market for the aircraft might be only fifty or maybe one hundred units a year — if the new model is significantly better than the planes it is to replace. Years will pass before the launching investment is recovered if the new product is successful, and profits will largely depend on sales made late in the production life of the airplane.

The high investment necessary and the long period required to recover the launch investment show the risks in pursuing technical development in a mature technology. In fact, these risks may become too large for any single company to assume, and development risk may have to be split between different corporations in the field. This problem has led to a joint-venture approach in the development of airplanes and aircraft engines and, in Europe, to direct development subsidies for airliner development paid with taxpayers' money.

The payment of development expenses by governments is a result of the desire to maintain a viable aerospace industry and to provide employment for workers who would otherwise become redundant. The fact that the market for some of these subsidized projects is too small to permit recovery of the launching investment is then attributed to dark and despicable conspiracies by the industry leaders in the United States, aided and abetted by their government.

The fact remains that the cost of asymptotic development can be very high indeed, and there are few genuine markets that can support this kind of investment in a mature technology, even with direct and indirect subsidies.

All this illustrates the economic limits of better-mousetrap competition once the inventive phase of development has been left behind. Unless subsidized, technical advance becomes strictly a matter of economic return. The criteria for development thus become the same as those for any other kind of capital investment. Unless the market is large and profitable enough to permit the recovery of the investment within a reasonable time, the investment is a mistake. And the mistake has to be paid for by somebody — the shareholders, the creditors, or the taxpayers.

Real Competition?

The need to restore real competition is a popular theme song of economic crusaders, politicians, consumerists, and many other people who really ought to know better.

They point accusingly to a seeming lack of dog-eat-dog competition in the marketplace and attribute this lack to control of prices and markets by large corporations.

So there ought to be a law to curb the monopolistic power of large corporations to restore competition in all its glory. Prices would then presumably drop and products improve as competitors fought tooth and nail for survival and the public would reap vast benefits. No longer would big corporations impose their will on prices and markets to the detriment of small enterprises, which are supposedly the last bastion of real competition in the present world.

This is nonsense.

Competition is alive and well. But it does not follow the popular images based on yesterday's theories of small business. These images do not even apply to today's one-man businesses operating on the principle of self-exploitation.

What are today's small businesses? The very small merchant, the plumber, the doctor, the lawyer, and the public accountant, for instance. Yet price competition seems to be singularly lacking in most of these occupations.

Some practitioners of small business may do an excellent job and others may be less skillful; some may be terribly busy and others less so; some may be making lots of money while others scrape by at the subsistence level. But they all charge pretty much the same prices for their work.

This is not surprising. They all work for material gains, and while they may compete through the quality of their services, they all want to make as much money as possible. And since they are not assured of a steady flow of income or a steady sales volume, the only practical way to achieve their objective is to charge what the market will bear.

The only doctor in town may be on to a good thing and net $50,000 a year from his practice. Attracted by the prosperity of his colleague, a new doctor may move in and hang out his shingle. Now there is competition and prices ought to drop, but they do not. The established doctor knows he will lose some of his business volume no matter what happens. So he maintains his fees and hopes that most of his patients will stay with him. Lowering fees would not necessarily keep more patients in the fold but would definitely cut into his income.

The new man knows it will take some time before his practice really gets going, and he is prepared to live modestly during this time. But he will not offer cut-rate fees, which would cut even further into his initially meager income and which his patients might consider a sign of lack of competence. He might charge a little less than his established competitor and lift his rates as soon as business really gets going. After all, he too would like to earn $50,000 a year as rapidly as possible.

Similar reasoning probably applies to most small businesses that involve self-exploitation. What with the going market price, the need to survive, and the desire to make as much profit as possible, the ability to compete on price is very limited. The small businessman does not know how large his sales volume will be, and he has no means to determine how much additional business a price cut might generate. If he cuts prices and the expected additional volume does not materialize, he may not be able to survive. It thus makes more sense to stick close to the prevailing prices charged by competitors and hustle to bring in customers.

When the enterprise involves hired hands, fixed costs, and capital investment, the room for maneuvering becomes even smaller. Even if the owner is willing to work for free, the difference in total cost would be small, and dropping prices by 3 or 5 per cent is not likely to result in a stampede of customers. Reducing profits is not a very practical way for a small business to compete — unless profits happen to be indecently large to start with. But indecently large profits usually attract competitors who will spoil the game, not necessarily by lowering prices but by taking away some of the business. And when volume shrinks, so do profits, no matter how high the margin on each transaction may be.

Small businesses will thus not necessarily result in real competition. In fact, no business — small, medium-sized, or enormous — particularly welcomes competition because real competition is expensive and detrimental to the competitors. Nobody in his right mind wants to give up profits or spend money on developing new products unless it is absolutely necessary.

The necessity to compete arises only when at least one competitor wants to take market shares away from other competitors and is willing and able to spend money or sacrifice profits to attain this objective.

The reason for competition is thus that at least one corporation wants to grow in that particular market. And since corporations have as their main purpose the generation of a profit, this growth must be both worthwhile and attainable. A corporation may thus make a large investment — in product innovation, cost reduction, and promotion — to capture a larger market share because the return on this investment will be more attractive than merely plodding along with the original market share.

However, if all other competitors make similar investments to defend their market shares, the exercise will be self-defeating. Everybody will invest in better products and lower-cost production and promotion, and nobody will gain, except perhaps the customers, who may rejoice in new products offered at lower prices. This may provide some moral satisfaction to the managements of the participating companies, but it will also leave them with the unpleasant task of explaining what may be a sharp drop in earnings.

On the other hand, competition becomes more attractive when there is a reasonable certainty that at least some of the competitors will not have the resources to fight back. And this is why real competition becomes most pronounced when there are substantial differences in operating scale and resources between competitors. For the company bent on enlarging its market share, the existence of weaker competitors as a source of these market shares is essential. If there are no weaker competitors to be outresourced, the battle is likely to result in a costly stand-off.

The entry of a large company into a new field dominated by small enterprises is likely to result in a major competitive battle as the intruder deploys his resources to capture a share of the market sufficient to justify his investment. Once the battle is over, prices and product standards will settle down to a new level, determined by the intruder's need to maintain or further enlarge market shares and his desire to maximize profits. This level will then prevail until the intruder's market share is challenged by a competitor with a better product or larger resources or both.

Not all businesses are amenable to this kind of competition by resource differential. In some fields of activity, resources fail to provide an effective basis for competition. The opportunities for reducing labor cost or improving service through investment in repair businesses and in many service activities are strictly limited. Other businesses have too limited a market to make investment on a major scale worthwhile. At the other extreme, there are vast markets, in consumer goods, for instance, that can justify very large investments.

To tap these markets effectively, products have to be standardized for low-cost production. The ideal situation from this point of view is a single product in one color and style, carefully designed to appeal to the greatest number of customers. Unfortunately, however, customers want variety. The next best thing are product families with as many common parts as possible but differentiated in styling, price, and promotion. In the automobile business, a large choice of options and gimmicks provides the customer with an illusion of variety. The customer can then personalize his jalopy so it will look different from that of his neighbor and from the 100,000 other identical cars that have rolled off the assembly line.

However, since mass-production goods are designed for the same market, or the same segment of the market, and their makers are subject to similar economic restraints, the products tend to be largely identical except for differences in styling, packaging, and promotion. Moreover, they are sold at the same price. This is not really surprising.

To succeed, the product has to be competitive. In practice, this means a price as close to that of the nearest competitor product as is practical. The price does not have to be identical. It may be lower because the new product has to steal part of the market from a competitor or because it may lack a few features of the competitor product. Or it may be higher because it includes some minor innovation and is backed by a more classy promotion campaign. But the basic measure is the price of the competitor, and on this the whole economics of the product will hinge — cost, investment, promotion, and profit. There is no need to meet with competitors to fix prices in criminal collusion. Common sense dictates that the price for the same product should be the same. To charge more might limit the market for the new product and upset the carefully designed balance between volume, investment, and profit. To charge less would be squandering profits unless there is a clearly defined requirement to enlarge market shares.

This is why we are deluged with consumer products with almost identical features and price stickers. Price negotiation is then largely left to the contest between the distributor's greed and the customer's talent for haggling. Other than that, competition is strictly a matter of advertising imagery. Which car is most appropriate to the buyer's self-image? Which detergent washes whiter? Which airline provides better service? Which toaster toasts more gently?

Customer preference then becomes largely a matter of susceptibility to a particular advertising image, tempered perhaps by the consequences of random exposure to faulty products, surly clerks, and the inability of an authorized car dealer to fix a dragging brake.

All this indicates that large corporations operate in the same manner as very small businesses. They charge the going rate as established by their competitors as long as everyone is happy with his market share. Competition only exists if one or more competitors decide to enlarge their share of the market at the expense of someone else. And this decision makes sense only if the battle has a reasonable chance of success because there are significantly weaker competitors who can be outresourced.

Yet even in fields dominated by large corporations of similar size, competition seems to persist. Bitter battles are fought with advertising campaigns, special promotion deals, selective price cutting, and bold claims to superior products and services. In fact, the battle may be more apparent than real, since it involves similar organizations striving for similar goals, and subject to similar operating conditions.

The customer may be delighted when a battle over market shares erupts and he can reap the benefits. But his joy is bound to be short-lived. When the struggle over market shares has been won or abandoned, prices will return to their normal level as victor and victims lick their wounds and try to recuperate the losses incurred.

Competition limited to conflict over market shares and based on resource differentials is not quite the same thing as the continuous free-for-all price and product competition on which our economy is supposedly based. Competition is the life of trade and the death of traders, as the old adage says. And since no business enterprise wants to commit economic suicide, nobody wants to compete unless he is quite certain to win. And victory goes to the one with better products, lower costs, better promotion — in short, more resources.

However, another kind of competition is based not on resource differentials but on different cost structures and different product characteristics. This is competition by imported goods.

The competitive edge of imports may be due to lower production costs, which permit lower prices, or better quality than domestic products selling at the same price. Or these products may differ from what domestic mass production has to offer. Or both these aspects may combine to yield products that can capture a substantial share of the market. Radios, television sets, and small cars are examples of the successful penetration of U.S. markets by imports.

The small company has no effective means to fight competition by imports; it suffers or may even have to go out of business. The large corporation whose market shares are threatened by imports has somewhat broader options. It can move its own production to low-cost countries. It may be able to fight imports on their own territory; for example, General Motors, Ford, and Chrysler are among the largest producers of automobiles in Europe. It may also be able to abandon business areas that have become unpromising as a result of imports and diversify in other directions.

Finally, the large corporation can complain to the government and demand import restrictions to preserve employment in domestic factories. When a small textile mill that employs fifty people is wiped out by cheap imports, the government is not likely to be as concerned as when a larger company employing 20,000 workers is in jeopardy.

Thus the advantages lie rather heavily with the large corporation. It has the resources to continue product development long after the smaller outfits have run out of steam; it can make large investments because it has, or can capture, the market shares to make the investment worthwhile; it can hire the best managers, extract the best deals from subcontractors, dominate its dealers, survive temporary setbacks that might ruin companies with more limited resources, and shift its activities to take advantage of changing business conditions. And if it has to compete for market shares, either because it needs to grow or because it is being challenged by someone else who does, it has the resources to exploit the situation or to survive the crisis. Security lies in large size.

However, since real competition among large corporations is a costly activity that may include substantial risks, it might be thought that annual model changes, in cars, for instance, represent a mindless waste. If all the manufacturers of consumer goods agreed to freeze their models and split the market among themselves, the elimination of the substantial investment in annual restyling, tooling, model changeover shutdowns, and costly promotion campaigns might save billions of dollars, and some of these savings could be passed on to the customers.

Almost everyone would seem to benefit from this arrangement. The manufacturers would have a reasonably stable and predictable business and benefit from long production runs and reduced investment needs. The customer would save money in buying a product which would no longer have to bear the cost of the annual model change and, since it had been in production for years, would be thoroughly reliable. The customer would also get better service because mechanics would always be dealing with the same model, and be assured of a continuing supply of spare parts.

Yet the concept is impractical for several reasons.

For one thing, it is illegal. Collusion to fix prices or to establish market shares would impair competition, and this is a criminal offense, no matter how synthetic competition may actually be.

Second, the model changes create artificial obsolescence and help sell products the customer does not really need. Eliminating this artificial obsolescence, even by replacing it with products carefully designed for limited life, would cut down on essential replacement sales and hurt the manufacturers. Lacking the attraction of new styling, users would be tempted to keep the limited-life car until its life is exhausted. They would be left with a heap of useless junk without any trade-in value.

Limited life is thus not a very practical solution, and the elimination of artificial obsolescence would cut down sharply on automobile sales. And since automobile manufacturers are very large corporations, this would cause unemployment and hurt the national economy. Consumerists may clamor for better products and the elimination of costly waste, paid for by the consumer, but when better value to the consumer implies an economic crisis, the cost of improving the world comes rather high.

But there is a third and very important aspect to the seeming waste of frequent model changes. Customers tend to view with concern a price increase on an existing product which represents inflation, pure and simple. Model changes make it possible to hide this inflation, or at least a part of it. The model change enables the manufacturer to carry out a steady program of cost reduction through design simplification and the substitution of cheaper materials and less costly production processes. At the same time, restyling and the addition of new gimmicks of dubious value and low cost permit price increases under the pretext that the new model is a vast improvement over last year's product.

This illusion is carefully nurtured by expensive promotion campaigns designed to persuade the customer that he gets much more value for a nominal increase in price. Nor will the customer necessarily notice that various cost and quality reductions have been incorporated under the gleaming restyled paneling. His first inkling of the nature of these "improvements" may come when he discovers that the new design includes weaknesses in parts almost inaccessible for servicing and that costly assemblies may have to be replaced because of the failure of one small component.

But model changes are not limited to consumer goods. They are employed in many other fields where products are being replaced for two major reasons.

One reason is to improve profits while sweeping visible inflation under the rug. The other is the capture of market shares from weaker competitors who cannot afford the cost of the model change. The new, more expensive product, backed by convincing promotion, replaces the cheap old product that may have been just as effective but lacks the advantage of novelty.

That, too, is competition.

A Fair Day's Pay

One does not have to be a rabid socialist to believe that workers should share in the wealth they create. But it helps.

Once this principle is accepted, it is only reasonable to propose that workers should be paid for their productivity. The more they produce, the more money they should receive.

Unfortunately, this perfectly reasonable idea tends to lead to conclusions that are no longer quite so reasonable. And the unreasonable consequences of a reasonable idea are often overlooked.

A worker who produces, by skill and diligence, twice as many boots as his colleague should obviously receive some sort of reward for his performance. Perhaps he should not be paid twice as much as the slowpoke next to him, but he should get more money. How much more is open to debate and negotiation, but the difference should be enough to make the extra effort worthwhile.

This kind of negotiation of rewards for individual performance assumes a free labor market where employer and worker arrive at some sort of a bargain, balancing out their conflicting greeds, where workers compete for jobs and employers compete to attract the best workers.

But this free competition in the labor market rarely exists. It has been replaced by collective bargaining, standardized wage levels, seniority rules, and minimum wage laws. Wages are settled by collective agreements, and this limits the freedom of the employer in rewarding good workers. And as a result of the action of unions and the government, this freedom is becoming ever more restricted. Today, discrimination against race, color, creed, and sex is illegal. Tomorrow, discrimination against age, incompetence, and sloth may be illegal because such acts would impair the worker's right to a job.

But the most important problem in modern wage negotiations concerns the custom of rewarding, on a collective basis, workers for productivity not of their own making.

A man who operates a machine worth a hundred thousand dollars may produce as much as twenty skilled craftsmen working with simple tools. Compared with the craftsmen, his productivity is enormous. The machine, once set up, does all the drilling, milling, grinding, and polishing while the worker pushes buttons, keeps the feed hopper filled, and places the finished products on a rack. As far as effort, experience, and skill are concerned, his work is probably far less strenuous than that of the skilled artisan. Yet productivity is an important factor in setting wage levels.

It is usually not possible to determine the effective worker productivity of a company from the outside because neither the number of workers nor the investment in production machinery is known. However, a rough idea of productivity can be gleaned from the relation between assets per employee and sales per employee, and this relation follows some fairly distinct patterns for different areas of business.

In large manufacturing and processing industries, a rough approximation is that each investment dollar yields about $1.35 in sales. If there is little subcontracting and the products sold are made inside the company, this ratio may fall to $1.00 in sales for $1.00 in investment. If subcontracting is extensive, $1.00 in investment may produce $1.50 in sales.

Investment per employee again follows certain patterns. In the garment industry, which is not highly mechanized, investment per employee is perhaps around $18,000 and sales per employee $24,000. On the other hand, large oil refining companies may have assets of $180,000 per employee and obtain $240,000 in sales per head. Apart from these extremes, typical large-scale manufacturing activities yield

sales of between $30,000 and $50,000 per employee and involve assets of $25,000 to $40,000 per man.

These figures are of course very rough approximations, but they
illustrate the relation between investment and productivity.

Other fields have different assets-sales characteristics. In railroads, sales tend to be about half the asset value; in airlines the
ratio is about one to one; while in the trucking business assets
are typically half of sales. The American Telephone and Telegraph Company's assets are about three times sales, and in
utility companies even higher ratios are common. These figures
reflect, of course, the cost of sophisticated installations. Telephone companies, utilities, and railroads have to pay for their
installations. Truckers do not have to build highways.

Productivity is thus a function of investment. If productivity
per worker is high, the impact of wages on total cost is lower
than when labor costs account for a large part of the total cost
of production. The employer can thus be more generous in
rewarding his workers. An oil refinery employee accounts for
ten times the sales of a garment worker and can be paid on a
more lavish scale than the woman who runs a sewing machine
eight hours a day.

A certain differentiation in wages between different industries is thus to be expected, not because employees work more
or less diligently, but simply because high-productivity industries with large investments can afford to pay more. But whatever the prevailing wage level, wages can hardly ever be rolled
back, no matter how bad business may become. In fact, wages
are subject to an almost automatic escalation.

Unions are financed by the contributions of their members.
In return for the payment of union dues, the workers expect to
receive certain benefits. To keep their jobs, and all the perqui-
sites that go with them, the union leaders have to produce these
benefits. They have to campaign for higher wages, better fringe
benefits, more job security, and a bigger slice of the profits for

their members no matter what the economic situation. That is what union leaders are paid for. If they fail to obtain a steady increase in worker benefits, they risk being replaced by more aggressive leaders.

In this battle with labor unions, company size plays an important role. A company with high investment and high productivity is usually in a better position to accede to union demands. It is also more vulnerable to union blackmail. If labor is only a modest part of the total cost, a wage increase may be far easier to accept than a strike, which would leave costly investment idle and fixed costs piling up. A plant shut down by a strike no longer earns a return, and there is no way to lay off assets for the duration of the strike.

In our earlier example of a small artisanal boot factory, a 20 per cent wage increase would boost the cost of a pair of boots from $30.00 to $33.00, and there is no way for the company to absorb this increase. It would have to be passed on to the customers. This price increase might in turn cut into sales and further raise costs, necessitating even further price increases. From $32.50 a pair, the price might have to be raised to $37.00 a pair to provide some margin for falling volume.

By contrast, the same 20 per cent wage increase in our hypothetical large boot factory would raise costs only from $16.00 to $16.60. This increase is easier to pass on to the customer if necessary. It might even be absorbed by the company, if business is good, or compensated by some additional investment or an increase in volume.

On the other hand, a strike would cost the large boot company more than $350,000 a month in fixed cost and over $160,000 in lost pretax profit if the plant had been operating at normal capacity. A month's strike would thus be far more expensive than the annual cost of the wage increase. Moreover, the wage increase provides a good explanation if and when the cost has to be passed on to the customers. But there is no way to recover the cost of a strike from anybody when the plant is shut down.

There is another aspect to this problem that is not quite so obvious. Wage increases granted by large corporations usually trickle down to smaller competitors, and this can be useful. The small company may not be able to afford either the higher labor cost or the investment necessary to make up for this increase by reducing the labor content of its products. It may be faced with a problem that has no solution. No amount of ingenuity and competitive spirit can overcome the problem of being priced out of the market by escalating labor cost when a company does not have the resources to invest in labor-saving equipment.

And whenever a smaller company fails, the survivors have a chance to inherit its market share.

And here lies yet another distortion of the economic environment: the existence of powerful unions inhibits competition in the labor market. And this tends to penalize the smaller companies with limited resources.

The Government

The government plays an important part in distorting the corporate environment by interfering massively in the activities of the corporation. This interference takes various forms, and no matter how reasonable and well intentioned its purpose may be, compliance is costly and cumbersome.

Tax laws require every corporation to keep proper records and to file tax returns. This is only just and reasonable. But it involves the corporation in activities not related to its business.

Even the tiniest company usually retains the services of an accountant to prepare its tax return and to ensure that its records are kept in an order that will satisfy a tax audit. The large multinational corporation often spends millions just to keep the revenuers happy. It, too, has to keep proper records and file proper returns, but its activities may be sufficiently complex to involve the corporate tax department in long-drawn-out negotiations with the tax people to haggle out the size of the annual tax bite. And its tax specialists continually have to keep abreast of new rulings and regulations in all the countries in which the corporation operates.

Whether the company is large or small, the cost of complying with tax regulations — as distinct from actually paying the tax — is substantial. And this cost has to be borne whether business flourishes or flounders.

But this is only the beginning. If the company has employees, the government also insists that it calculate, withhold, remit, and account for their withholding taxes and social security payments. The company thus serves as a tax collector for the government. And the work and bureaucratic fuss involved are entirely at the expense of the company.

The fledgling small company will find the cost of these services performed for the government harder to bear than the corporate giant, which has access to computers and specialists and can talk back to the government bureaucrats.

However, while the government extorts money and unpaid work from its citizens and corporations, it also provides certain services. Ever anxious to protect the public from various real, potential, and imagined dangers, the government passes laws and establishes regulatory agencies for the specific purpose of making the marketplace, the factory, and the office safe for the populace. And from this laudable principle have sprung vast bureaucracies to conceive and enforce vast and growing arrays of regulations.

Presumably, every regulation has its roots in a perceived need to curb certain abuses or to eliminate certain dangers that have attracted the attention of the public, perhaps as a result of the agitation of a noisy minority led by self-styled reformers and crusaders. Once established, each regulation tends to gather momentum as a result of the natural desire of a regulatory agency to expand its size, importance, and budget.

As regulatory agencies go about developing and refining their activities to protect the public, corporations are compelled to keep more records, provide more reports, request more permits and authorizations — thus spending more time and money on such bureaucratic demands. And the more these demands develop, the larger the resources required to comply with government red tape while still producing a profit.

The cost of obtaining government approval for a new pharmaceutical product or a new small airplane is such that it can only be recovered if the corporation has a substantial market. For this reason, there are no small drug companies of any significance left, and a newcomer has virtually no chance to break into the light airplane field, no matter how interesting his product might be. In fact, the cost of government measures to improve product quality can become a heavy burden even for corporate giants, as the case of automobile safety requirements and pollution standards has shown.

The environmental craze in the early 1970s spawned its own breed of regulations and enforcement agencies. Environmental protection is obviously desirable, but can also involve substantial costs. These costs are related not only to meeting the government standards, but also to proving that these standards are being met. And even here the small corporation is at a disadvantage. An environmental impact statement for a small plant may be much more costly in relation to the investment involved than the same document prepared for a large facility.

If a government agency, in its ultimate wisdom and deep concern with the public interest, decides that a product is unsafe, or that a production activity is dangerous, unhygienic, or a menace to the environment, or that the business methods of a corporation are not acceptable, the large company has the expertise and the resources to cope with the problem. It can hire topnotch lawyers to fight the ruling; it can redesign the product, modify the manufacturing equipment, move the plant elsewhere, and agitate public opinion over the hardships and unemployment problems caused by the ruling.

And if everything fails, it can simply close down the plant and fire all hands if the cost of compliance is too heavy, and it will still survive. The one-plant company with limited resources does not have these options. It may be badly hurt or even driven from the field by the zealous enforcement of rules to protect the public interest, even though the demands of the government minions may be madly inappropriate in its particular case.

So the key to survival in an environment of strong and growing government regulation is, once again, corporate size. The pursuit of the public interest by government agencies thus makes its own contribution to the trend toward concentration of corporate power.

The Need to Grow

The scale of an activity can have important effects on its yield.

Teaching one child at a time may be pleasant and effective but tends to be rather expensive. Teaching one hundred children in one class greatly reduces the cost per student, but the results are probably not very satisfactory. The optimum scale of classroom teaching — the best compromise between cost and effectiveness — probably lies somewhere between ten and twenty students, the exact number depending on the subject, teaching method, teacher's salary, and the ability and willingness of the parents to pay.

By the same token, business activities also tend to have an

optimum scale that offers the best results in terms of profit. This optimum scale also depends on a variety of factors, among them costs, market conditions, competition, management talent, and form of organization. Beyond the optimum scale the returns from further growth will diminish, until finally further expansion becomes inefficient and perhaps even impractical. The sheer size of the organization may become too ponderous, additional markets may be too expensive to capture, additional sales may no longer yield any worthwhile profit.

On the other hand, there is also a minimum practical scale of activity. Below this critical size a company will languish because it no longer generates adequate profits.

The critical size of a particular business activity is determined mainly by the level of fixed costs and investment in relation to the profitability of the business. A business involving neither fixed costs nor investment could, in theory, be of any size. As long as everybody is engaged in production, the product cost would be the same; that is, twenty carpenters would produce roughly twenty times as much as one carpenter working alone, and the unit cost of the product would be independent of the size of the operation. Profit per unit of production would be the same, and the scale of the operation would be immaterial.

But businesses involving neither fixed cost nor investment are rare. Even the one-man business usually involves some fixed cost, and when several people are employed fixed cost and investment become an important consideration. Once there are more than a handful of carpenters, somebody has to coordinate their work, go out and drum up business, write bills, keep accounts, and calculate withholding taxes. These activities, while necessary, contribute nothing to production. Their cost has to be recovered from the work of the carpenters, and the enterprise has to be large enough to carry this indirect expense. It may take seven carpenters a-working to pay for one boss a-managing.

In a more sophisticated business it may take hundreds of productive people to pay for managers, salesmen, researchers, paper shufflers, and lawyers. The company has to be large enough to bear these costs and still produce an adequate return on investment. A corporation that needs an investment of $1 million to operate has to be large enough to produce a profit of around $100,000 to make the investment worthwhile. The minimum scale of activity will thus be determined by fixed cost and investment.

This is why ten-room hotels are no longer very practical. They do not generate enough income to pay for operating expenses and the capital tied up in building and equipment if the room rates have to compete with larger establishments, which benefit from the economies of larger scale.

Scale is thus an important factor in business life. But scale is not a constant thing. The minimum practical size for a particular business may increase rapidly as a result of inflation, technical progress, and competition based on resource differentials. To keep up with these changes, growth is necessary, and sometimes rapid growth can become essential to survival.

The need for fast growth is not really a new development. Even in pre-industrial times there must have been certain activities that required rapid growth to remain competitive or even to survive.

A limited company operating a whole fleet of stagecoaches probably had certain distinct advantages over the one-horse, one-coach operator. It could draw traffic from a larger area, organize its activities more efficiently, and perhaps even monopolize certain kinds of traffic. If one coach fell prey to marauding Indians, that was regrettable, but it did not put the company out of business. The larger scale paid off in lower risk exposure and higher profits.

As long as there was enough business to go around, nobody

had any particular reason for lowering prices, and the small outfits could survive, even though their profits were probably much smaller than those of the large company. But traffic might not be unlimited, and this might provoke a struggle for market shares, popularly known as competition.

The large company, being more profitable to start with, could drop prices to defend its market against hungry intruders or to take markets away from weaker competitors. It could trade off profits for additional market shares and recoup the lost profits later, either from the increased volume or by raising prices after bothersome competitors had been wiped out. The small competitor, caught in this kind of struggle, would either have to grow quickly or merge with other small fry in order to meet the larger competitor on a more equal basis.

. The existence of the larger competitor as such did not threaten the smaller operators. But if the large competitor chose to use his advantage of size to carve a larger market out of the business of the small outfits, life would become difficult. The critical size of the coach operating business would increase.

Changes in markets and technology can also escalate the critical size of a business. A railroad company working a ten-mile line with two locomotives and twenty cars may have been a paying proposition around 1840, in the early days of the iron horse. But as demand for the new mode of transport grew, the company's resources might not have been sufficient to build more track and buy more equipment. To stay in the game the small railroad would have to grow or merge with other small railroads. In this case, the need for larger resources to cope with expanding markets and advancing technology determined the critical scale for continued profitable operation.

In the case of railroads, another factor affecting scale became important. Smart operators discovered that monopolies could be established by judicious mergers. If all railroad companies in a particular region could be brought into one operation, competition could conveniently be eliminated. Fares could then be set at the discretion of the railroad and standards of service dropped to the lowest practical level to maximize profits.

These monopolies were so profitable that mergers and consolidations became popular in many fields. Large trusts were created that dominated, either as monopolies or in collusion with other trusts, a variety of major industries, such as oil, steel, and transportation. Competition was ruthlessly suppressed, and the complexity of many trusts permitted the exploitation of outside shareholders on a large scale for the benefit of the robber barons.

The stifling of competition by monopolistic trusts and the sharp practices involved in their formation have given capitalism an ugly reputation that persists to this day. They created the image of the malevolent Wall Street manipulators exploiting workers, customers, and small capitalists with unrelenting greed.

Ultimately, something had to be done to curb the excesses of mergers, consolidations, and monopolies. The government passed antitrust laws, which prohibit mergers or any other acts that tend to impair free competition; laws to dismantle some of the more obnoxious trusts; and measures to regulate the stock markets and curb excessive speculation.

Stock market manipulation and corporate fraud may still be with us, but on a far smaller and more discreet scale than in the age of the great trust builders. Moreover, government agencies are quick to crack down on any major transaction that smacks of monopoly or restraint of competition. No longer can dominant market positions be built by mergers between large corporations, nor can large corporations buy out their suppliers or otherwise gain an unfair advantage over their competitors. Some monopolies (such as the telephone industry) or near monopolies remain, but they are regulated and watched by government agencies.

Once the big bad trusts were broken up, restraint of competition declared a crime, and the millionaire stock market manipulators shoved out of the limelight, business ought to have returned to the idyllic state of free-for-all competition. Competitors should have been free again to fight tooth and nail for market shares and the public should have benefited enormously.

Of course, this is not what happened.

As we have seen, competition is worthwhile only when it promises an economic return, that is, when there is an opportunity to capture market shares from weaker competitors. Once all the remaining players have similar resources, competition becomes uneconomical. And since mergers with competitors are now against the law, the urge to grow must find other outlets.

These outlets are multinational expansion and diversification. Both avenues open new growth opportunities that can yield important advantages, the most important of which is that the size of the corporation is no longer tied to the optimum size attainable in any particular business area.

The multibusiness corporation, or conglomerate, can sprawl into any field it chooses to, spread its risk over different activities, and pursue the advantages of large size far beyond the limitations of its monobusiness competitors. And large size, regardless of the limitations of a particular business field, presents some rather compelling advantages.

The multibusiness corporation can strive to attain optimum size in several different fields. And even if its entry into one particular field is initially small, it has behind it the resources of the parent corporation, which gives it a substantial advantage. It can borrow money more easily because the parent corporation has a reputation and its size makes it an excellent credit risk. Even the small foreign subsidiary of a large corporation may be able to borrow money more easily than its local competitors because its borrowing is guaranteed by the parent company. And the large corporation can issue debentures to the public, not only at home, but overseas as well. Its small competitor serving a backwoods locale would find this route to financing impossible.

The pursuit of sheer corporate size thus offers many advantages. It also presents problems to smaller monobusiness competitors. The intrusion of a large corporation into a new field usually changes the rules of the game. Established smaller competitors may have to grow very rapidly to survive. The entry of large corporations into fields previously dominated by smaller companies destabilizes the whole corporate environment in these fields. And multibusiness corporations are ever anxious to exploit new fields where their large resources will give them a significant advantage over established competitors.

However, another important factor can change the minimum scale of a business activity. That factor is inflation.

As inflation erodes profits, model changes may be necessary to camouflage price increases. Thus, a pharmaceutical company may have to create new products which are not necessarily more effective than the old drugs, but have better profit margins and provide the medical visitors with new features to talk about when they go out into the field to badger the doctors.

But the model change will be expensive. A new substance has to be found or a new permutation of existing substances worked out. The new product then has to be tested, for effectiveness and lack of unacceptable side effects, and the company will have to prove to the health authorities that the new product complies with all regulations and obtain authorization for its sale to the public.

Several years and a large amount of money may have been spent between the "Eureka!" shout of the scientist who found the new substance and the moment when the product, duly tested and registered, is finally placed on the shelf of the pharmacist. This investment has to be recovered. The new product may be far more profitable than its predecessor, but unless the market is large, recovery of the launching investment may be slow.

As long as all competitors are of similar size, they will have the same problem of recouping model change investments in limited markets. New products will then be launched only at intervals that correspond to the development cost exposure, and prices will be raised during the intervals to make up for inflation. But if there are large competitors, the situation will be different. The competitor with half a billion dollars in sales can speed up the cycle of model changes to improve profits, secure in the knowledge that his larger market base will permit rapid recovery of the launching investment.

The small company may not be able to follow this trend to rapid model changes and may, for this reason, become an acquisition candidate. Yet the large competitor has made no particular effort to compete; he has not cut prices to grab a larger share of the market. He has simply used the equivalent of model changes to maintain profits in the face of inflation. And in doing so, he has raised the critical size of the business.

And to cope with the problem of escalating critical size there is only one solution: rapid growth.

4. Motivations

Tax Angles

The distortions of the corporate environment discussed so far affect mainly the business transactions and strategies of corporations. But there are also distortions that primarily affect corporate owners and managers. These distortions provide strong motivations for shareholders and for those who effectively control the destiny of corporations to behave in ways that are rather different from what economic theories might lead us to expect. And a key factor in these motivations is taxation and the manner in which corporate profits are taxed.

To governments, corporations are an important source of revenue. In the United States, corporate income taxes amount to about 15 per cent of the federal budget. In 1974 corporate income taxes yielded $39 billion. This figure corresponds to all the internal revenue receipts of the federal government in 1950. Growth in government is not negligible.

But these figures understate the importance of corporate activities to the government. Corporations provide employment for millions of taxpayers. They pay dividends that are taxed as shareholders' personal income. And corporations are taxed not only by the federal government; they also pay substantial state and local taxes. The corporate goose provides the various layers of government with many golden eggs.

Personal tax returns may be baffling to many of us, but they are simple in comparison with the work involved in preparing corporate tax returns. And tax problems can become very complex indeed if a corporation pays tax in several countries. As corporations and government haggle over the size of the tax bite, whole armies of specialists on both sides of the fence are engaged in a continuous battle of wits to protect the interests of their respective employers and clients.

Tax evasion is a criminal offense in the United States, but the payment of unnecessary taxes can often be avoided if a transaction is carefully planned. Tax avoidance may yield large returns and for this reason is an important consideration in corporate decisions. This, of course, introduces yet another distortion of the corporate environment.

As a result, normal business reasoning may have to be modified by tax-planning considerations. A certain project may look very attractive from a simple profit-and-loss point of view. However, tax considerations may dictate a seemingly less attractive and far more complicated transaction because the tax advantages outweigh the operating merits of the original project.

It is obvious that a small company with modest resources has far fewer opportunities to develop attractive tax structures than its large competitor, which can bring the knowledge of skilled and expensive tax experts to bear on the problem and follow their recommendations on a multinational basis.

Corporate tax rates vary from country to country. In some foreign countries they may be mild and avoidable, in others they can be almost confiscatory; and tax avoidance, or even outright cheating, may be a matter of survival. For multinationals the artful shifting of profits between countries to ease the tax burden opens broad avenues for creative tax structuring. The mononational company cannot play the same game; it has to live with the local tax situation.

In the United States the principle, if not the practice, of corporate income tax collection is fairly simple. After all allowable deductions for legitimate business expenses have been worked out, and after taxes levied by state, county, and township have been paid, the accountants arrive at the pretax profit for the year. Corporate income tax is then paid on this amount. The tax rate is 50 per cent, with minor fluctuations depending on the economic policies and reelection politics of the government. The federal government thus takes half of all corporate profits after state and local taxes have taken their toll.

But worse is yet to come. The same profit is taxed again when part of it is paid out to the shareholders. The owners of the corporation pay personal income tax on the dividends they receive.

An investor may buy one hundred shares of International Abacus for $10,000 and sit back to enjoy his dividends. If he does, he is not very smart. Under today's economic conditions, he will lose money as long as he holds on to his investment. The mathematics are quite simple.

If Abacus sold at ten times earnings, the hundred shares correspond to a pretax profit of $2000, or $1000 after the government has collected corporate income tax. But few corporations pay out all of their earnings in dividends. Abacus might pay out only half, or even less, and reinvest the balance. As a result, the investor will receive a dividend check of perhaps $500 a year, on which he has to pay personal income tax. With inflation rates of 6 to 10 per cent and high interest rates on borrowed money, a 5 per cent pretax return on an investment is terribly unattractive, particularly if the risk of a stock investment is considered. And after personal income taxes have been paid, the net return to the investor might be only something like 3 per cent. The investor is losing money, and the whole venture is really profitable only to the government. Out of $2000 in pretax profit earned by the hundred shares, the government has taken something like $1200, the company has retained $500, and the poor investor is left with $300. Still, the investor is lucky. He has bought stock with a modest price-earnings ratio. If he had bought stock selling at twenty times earnings, the deal would have been even more lopsided.

Buying stocks for income is thus an unattractive way of spending money. All the same, people who are fully aware of the poor yield and inherent risk of stocks keep right on buying corporate stock certificates. This seemingly irrational behavior is the result of a major distortion built into our economic system. Through its tax laws, the government encourages stock market speculation and punishes continued ownership of stocks. Earnings distributed by corporations are taxed twice, but profits made from trading in stocks are subject to a reduced capital gains rate if the stocks have been held for a certain time. Moreover, capital gains profits can be offset against capital losses suffered on other investments.

The reasons for this tax discrimination against continued stock ownership and in favor of stock trading are somewhat obscure. The usual explanation is that capital gains tax rates encourage investment. Actually, they do no such thing.

Buying a stock from a broker does not add one cent to the corporate treasury and provides no investment capital except if the stock is newly issued. But new issues by major corporations are fairly rare because issuing new stock dilutes equity and depresses stock prices. As a result, the bulk of shares now traded on the stock markets were issued twenty or fifty years ago. Since then the shares have passed through many hands, and their prices may have fluctuated over a wide range. Yet all these transactions have been strictly between the buyers and sellers of stocks, aided and abetted by stockbrokers trying to eke out a modest living.

Capital gains benefits, of course, encourage the original investors, who actually put money into the company when they buy shares. But the same rewards are also given to all subsequent speculators, who merely buy and sell ownership certificates between themselves.

The double taxation of distributed profits and the tax break on speculative gains have some important repercussions on the attitudes of shareholders and corporate managers.

Since continued ownership of stocks is unattractive, investor interest is firmly focused on stocks that promise speculative gains rather than on staid and stable companies with unexciting stock market prospects. The hunt for stocks expected to show "price appreciation," as the stockbrokers call it, is not just a matter of small individual investors looking for quick profits. It is also the concern of institutional investors anxious to impress their clients with a fine performance so the same clients will provide them with more money to play stock market games with.

But even when the market is booming, the number of stocks with a truly attractive speculative potential is limited. Investors thus tend to fall all over themselves trying to buy those stocks with more than average possibilities for quick profits. Stocks believed to be particularly attractive may thus be driven to ridiculously high prices while the shares of less spectacular companies are largely left in the hands of widows, orphans, estate trustees, and pension funds.

But speculators not only react to the market; they actually create it. Playing the stock market is a collective guessing game. The individual gambler's problem is to guess what all the other gamblers will do. When stocks advance, everybody wants to get in on the action; when they decline, there is a general desire to get out from under; and when the market is in the doldrums, nobody wants to play. Thus come about the swings of the stock market, which offer the chance of capital gains to the lucky, losses to the less fortunate, and important motivations to corporate managers.

Investor confidence in a particular stock is indicated by the price-earnings ratio: the stock price divided by earnings per share. A stock which looks interesting in the collective guesses of the speculators will command a higher price-earnings ratio than a stock that fails to attract any particular attention. And a high price-earnings ratio is bound to attract other investors because it offers a certain leverage. A ten-cent increase in earnings per share of a stock traded at a price-earnings ratio of ten corresponds to a one-dollar increase in the stock price. The same profit increase in a corporation whose stock sells at forty times earnings implies a four-dollar price increase. A high price-earnings ratio is thus an important attribute to distinguish the shares that may be attractive investments from the masses of dull stocks on the market. And the distinction of a high price-earnings ratio is usually associated with the promise of increasing profits implied by rapid corporate growth. This adds another facet to the advantages rapid growth can bestow on an ambitious corporation.

Some moves are now being made to eliminate the double taxation of distributed earnings and to lengthen the period over which stocks have to be held to qualify for reduced capital gains tax rates. These moves would no doubt be beneficial for shareholders and corporations, but they certainly would not eliminate the penalty imposed on continued stock ownership. As long as inflation rates are substantially higher than stock yields, the only way to avoid losing money on the stock market through capital erosion is speculation.

And speculators are not really interested in the company whose stock they temporarily own. They want to take their profits and get out. They are not investing in the proper sense of the word; they are simply gambling. Ownership of corporations has become largely a game of chance in which the individual players try to guess what the other players will do. Who cares how a corporation is being run as long as it offers a chance for quick capital gains?

The Shareholders

"Small shareholders are not only stupid; they are also a nuisance," a German banker once said. "They are stupid to give us their money, and they are a nuisance because they ask silly questions about what we have done with their investment." This particular attitude may be exaggerated, but it pretty much sums up the role of the small shareholder in Europe, where business is largely dominated by banks and financial trusts.

The shareholder naturally has certain rights, but all important decisions are made by insiders long before the owners of the company get a chance to voice their opinions. Actually, even board members representing substantial minority interests may not know very much about the real situation of the company. The shots are called by the group, or groups, which control the company.

The small European shareholder may thus have only a vague notion of the state of the organization in which he has invested his money. Nor will published financial statements be of much help, since they tend to be rather sketchy. Many European companies feel that no useful purpose would be served by revealing sales figures, and assets may be deftly hidden from the scrutiny of tax collector and shareholder alike. Moreover, even earnings figures may be distorted. The insiders simply agree beforehand what sort of a dividend should be paid, and the financial statement is then doctored to show a corresponding net profit.

The small European investor buys his shares — if he buys any shares at all — because his banker, who is also his stockbroker, suggests that a particular stock would be a good investment. And he is liable to hold on to the stock until his banker tells him to sell. Since banks are also stockholders in their own right, they thus have considerable opportunity to influence the stock market. This may not seem quite ethical by American standards, but it keeps the stock market game largely in the hands of specialists.

Any shareholder has the right to attend the annual shareholders' meeting and ask questions. However, since the shareholders have very little information to start with, they may find it difficult to get much meaningful information. Chairmen with great skill in handling hecklers tend to discourage any bold incursions by small shareholders that might disturb the solemn ritual of the meeting. Even a skilled and articulate shareholder will have trouble in stemming the flood of suave generalities and pinning the chairman down to specific issues.

Consequently, few small shareholders bother to attend the meetings. They provide their banks with blank proxies, usually on a permanent basis. The banks can then vote the stock as they please, and this arrangement provides a welcome addition to the bank's own voting power.

Yet even if the small shareholders succeeded in appointing their own men to the board of directors, nothing much would change because the board would still be dominated by insiders. This has been amply proven by the fate of worker board members required by law in certain European countries. Designed to give workers a participation in key policy decisions, such laws provide mainly worker votes and union support for political parties. But as long as the worker board members are in a minority, their effect on corporate policies need not be important.

What happens is that the board meeting itself is reduced to a meaningless charade. The insiders and "real" directors meet quietly beforehand and decide what should be done. The formal board meeting is then held for the benefit of the distinguished colleagues from the work force. The agenda is covered as quickly as possible while the insiders manfully hide their boredom and the views of the worker directors are frequently solicited with patronizing kindness. But any embarrassing questions are skillfully fielded.

The contributions of the worker directors pretty soon become limited to political speeches for the benefit of their fellow workers on the shop floor, usually accompanied by suggestions to repaint the locker rooms. These proposals are inevitably greeted as most constructive by an appreciative board. The important thing is that the worker directors shall not otherwise interfere with the theatrical performance held for their benefit. And that is certainly worth a new coat of paint in the locker room.

An independent board member representing small shareholders would find himself in a very similar position. He might have a better understanding of business practices and he would be independent, since he does not work for the company, but he would still lack any real inside information and power. And he might gradually be subverted as the insiders gave him glimpses of the real situation of the company as a reward for good behavior and a growing understanding of the insider problems.

Still, there have been some ominous developments in the European corporate world. For political reasons, several countries, among them Germany and the United Kingdom, are strengthening worker participation in corporate management with the general idea that the workers, or rather the unions, should have at least as much to say as the owners. This is bound to put an end to the amusing charades played for the benefit of minority worker delegations on the board. Instead, there will be bitter battles between trade unions pursuing the interests of their members and leaders and the insider groups defending their own interests. Once these battles get under way, the small shareholder will be completely lost in the struggle of titans.

Thus, it is not surprising that the small European investor looks at the stock market with a certain amount of well-founded suspicion, dimly sensing that his partnership with the large interests dominating corporate life might be somewhat one-sided. He may let the bank invest his money and hope for the best. Or he may shun the stock market altogether and put his money into savings accounts, government bonds, or real estate. And if he craves risk and excitement, he does not need the stock market. He gambles on horses, soccer pools, lotteries, and other legal and often government-sponsored games of chance.

In the United States, the situation is fundamentally different. Gambling may be popular, but with few exceptions it happens to be against the law. Playing the stock market is probably the only game of chance, played for real money, which is perfectly legal in all fifty states of the Union. Moreover, this game is highly encouraged by the government since successful stock market bets enjoy reduced tax rates as capital gains.

Unlike his European counterpart, the American stock market player is provided with a great deal of reliable information. American corporations have only one set of books, and their financial results are available to the public. The investors are thus largely protected against fraud. But a great deal of additional information is available to help the investor place his bets. Racetrack gamblers may study detailed reports of the past achievements of the horses in the race to back up their hunches. The stock market player can draw on the research services of his stockbroker and subscribe to a variety of tipster services that provide detailed recommendations on interesting situations.

Of course, past performance is no guarantee of future success. The horse that won all the races last year may no longer be in top form this season. Nor does the extrapolation of the past results of a corporation indicate how stock prices will be affected by the collective hunches of the stock market players. But that is the thrill of the game.

But the stock market has another important advantage over other games of chance. The roulette player places his bets and either wins or loses when the little ball stops spinning. The stock market goes on and on. The player can let his bet stand as long as he wants to — a week, a year, or twenty years. He can limit his losses when the stock dips too much for his comfort, take a modest profit and run, or wait for long-term gains. He can invest as much or as little as he chooses. He can buy one share for twenty dollars, or spend a couple of million dollars on thousands of shares. In fact, he does not even have to buy shares to play; he can buy options at a fraction of the cost of the shares and hope the shares will go up during the option period and give him a quick profit, or sell options on shares he does not own if he is quite certain that the share price will drop. The risk of option trading is naturally higher, and can become very high if uncovered options are called, but that need not be a serious deterrent to the skillful gambler.

The stock market game is very popular; in 1975 statistics show that stocks were owned by some 25 million people in the United States. Our corporations may not be owned by all the people, but they belong to a great many of us. Yet the influence of the large masses of small shareholders on corporate activities is negligible. The large diffusion of ownership precludes any effective representation of the shareholders' interests on the boards of major corporations.

The reasons for this lack of small shareholder power are quite simple. The ordinary shareholder meeting, held once a year, involves mainly the election of directors and auditors, and these are largely automatic. The shareholders vote for the proposed board or they withhold their vote. There are no opposition candidates, and there is usually no way to vote against the proposed slate. The vote for the auditors is equally symbolic.

And that usually completes the business of an ordinary
shareholder meeting. Of course, there will be inspirational
speeches by the chairman and perhaps some of the representatives of management. There will be benevolently condescending
responses to inoffensive shareholder questions. There may even
be resolutions introduced by maverick shareholders. Management usually recommends in no uncertain terms that these
resolutions not be adopted. And they rarely ever seem to be.

All this may be very entertaining and impressive, but it leaves
the shareholders with very few means to assert themselves.
They are not asked whether they feel the corporation is properly managed or whether they approve the financial statements.
The whole meeting is pretty much a formality.

The owner of a few or a few hundred shares will hardly find
it worth his while to attend the meeting in person. Most of the
voting is therefore done by mailing a proxy to appoint board
members to vote for the shareholder. The proxy may contain
voting instructions ("I withhold my vote on the election of
directors"), or it may be mailed in blank in the fond hope that
the board members will vote in the best interests of the shareholder. The result of this procedure is that most of the votes will
be cast or assigned to board members long before the shareholder meeting takes place.

The reluctance of shareholders to attend meetings can be
reinforced by holding critical meetings at some remote plant
location. The pretext is that the owners will have the opportunity to visit a particularly exciting part of the corporation's
far-flung activities. A shareholder meeting held in a remote
town in Illinois is bound to attract even fewer shareholders than
the same event held at corporate headquarters in New York.

Management, of course, dotes on old ladies in tennis sneakers
or grizzled foremen with thirty years of loyal service and ten
shares in their possession. They lend an air of folksy authentic-
ity to the event, particularly if they can be induced to make a

homely little speech about how much they love that beautiful corporation. So by all means let us have a few hundred small shareholders at the meeting. And if there are any troublemakers, let us hope they will clamor for minority rights, or environmental protection, or social responsibility, or some other issue not really related to the problems of the corporation.

But shareholder meetings are not always bland formalities. Every now and then some important business crops up and the owners may have to vote for or against a specific proposal. Management may propose a capital increase, or a merger with another company, or the spin-off of part of the corporation's activities, or a new incentive plan for key personnel. These proposals are carefully presented to sound like great ideas. They are also couched in legalese language that gives little indication of the practical implication of the proposal or the ulterior motives that have prompted it. Yet they can be tools for interesting transactions which may have a considerable impact on the future of the corporation or for rewarding the efforts of management on a surprisingly lavish scale.

The small shareholder may well be inclined to vote in favor of these proposals in the fond belief that management knows best. Yet even if he violently disagrees, he would not be able to organize any effective opposition to what he might perceive as a dastardly plot. To defeat a dubious proposal takes considerably more than a rousing speech at the shareholder meeting. To have any chance of success, the opposition would have to be carefully organized to explain to the masses of the small shareholders why the proposal is not in their interest. And this campaign would have to be carried out before the shareholders mail in their proxies. Since they usually receive their proxy forms at the same time as the proposal this task is almost impossible unless the objectors have prior knowledge of what is afoot.

Even a battle of proxies for board seats, where time is not

critical, is difficult and beyond the means of even the most irate small shareholder. A large shareholder who has the means, and enough of a stake to make the battle worthwhile, usually does not have to bother. The board will know about him and make sure he agrees before the matter is put to the vote of the docile masses of small shareholders. In fact, the large shareholder probably has his man, or men, on the board and becomes an insider to the transaction.

As a result, large shareholders may have an influence on the corporation out of proportion to the amount of stock they control. If ownership is widely dispersed, a few per cent of the stock may be sufficient to provide a large measure of control to the owner. The small shareholders are usually not aware of the identity of these dominant shareholders; they do not know who actually controls the corporation.

Yet the small shareholders rarely complain because their interest in the corporation is limited. They do not want to control it, or even get particularly involved in its problems. They have bought their shares strictly for capital gains and they will sell them as soon as there is a sufficient profit, or as soon as another investment seems to offer a better chance to make money. Getting involved in the problems of a particular corporation would be a mistake because it might interfere with the cool decisions necessary to maximize capital gains.

Of course, there may be some shareholders who hang on to a particular stock for sentimental reasons. They may actually believe the statements put out by publicity departments extolling the intrinsic goodness of the corporation. Or they may refuse to sell because they cannot think of a better investment opportunity. Or because Grandpa told them, a few days before he passed on, that this was a fine company and that they should never sell its stock. But these are exceptions.

In fact, the small shareholder does not give a hoot about the company whose stock he buys. As long as he thinks he can make money, he is content. And if he lacks this assurance he will not start a riot. He calls his stockbroker and tells him to sell the darn shares.

The Board of Directors

The board of directors manages the corporation on behalf of its owners. It controls the destiny of the organization.

This power is subject to certain restrictions imposed by laws to protect the interests of the shareholders and the public. The nature of these restrictions depends on the laws of the state in which the corporation has been established. However, there are three basic things the board of a corporation may not do. It may not commit illegal acts. It may not take on its own actions that require the approval of the owners of the company. Nor may it engage in acts which conflict with the articles of incorporation.

And whatever it does, the board must act with due care, in good faith, and be guided by the best interests of the shareholders. The board members are personally liable for gross negligence and any acts of bad faith committed during their tenure of office. They can be sued if they have acted against the interests of the company or its owners.

Board members are usually elected once a year by vote of the shareholders. Once elected, they are in full charge until their term of office expires. If the shareholders are dissatisfied with the performance of the board, they are free to elect a new and presumably more competent team when election time comes around. At least that is the basic idea.

While this sounds logical and reasonable, the arrangement is marred by several flaws. The main flaw is the assumption that the power of the board will be checked by the power of the shareholders to replace the board members. This is largely a fiction if the stock of the corporation is widely held. The diffusion of ownership gives the board a very large amount of power and freedom, which goes far beyond the responsibility of running the company between board elections. It also includes the power to decide what information shall be divulged to the owners and the nomination of board candidates for virtually automatic election. The board thus reelects itself.

Since shareholder approval is virtually a foregone conclusion, the board can run the corporation as if it owned it — at least as long as no major shareholders are involved. Of course, the board members will make every effort to protect the interests of the shareholders and lose no opportunity to proclaim their firm belief in this laudable objective. But the board remains the sole judge of what the best interests of the shareholders might be.

But who are the board members? Who does this small group with very broad powers actually represent?

The composition of the board of a large corporation depends on a variety of factors. If there are any important shareholders, some board members are bound to represent the interests of the dominant owners. Other directors may represent banks or insurance companies that have lent the corporation money. Then there may be apparent outsiders of impartial mien and impeccable standing. A partner of the corporation's law firm, for instance, or the president of a university or presidents of other companies make impressive board members. These people may be on the board because their special knowledge may be helpful in making major decisions, because their reputations add luster to the group, or because they are well-camouflaged representatives of special interests.

Then there may be board members who have been nominated for cosmetic reasons; their background and qualifications will help to improve the image of the corporation. Their appeal may be to certain pressure groups, to customers, or even to racial minorities. Female board members will proclaim their determination to create better career opportunities for female employees and perhaps their desire to make the corporation more responsive to social needs. Or there may be board members representing consumerism in its milder forms, defenders of oppressed racial minorities, or environmental crusaders. The role of these board members is to make the corporation appear open-minded, humane, and concerned with important issues of modern life. Of course, they will not be dyed-in-the-wool revolutionaries, but rather domesticated advocates of mild reform. The outsiders in the boardroom look good, generate favorable publicity, and may even be helpful in presenting minority points of view in boardroom discussions. And they are certainly vastly preferable to government-decreed industrial democracy.

But no matter what the qualifications of these board members may be — and their qualifications are always impressive — they cannot be considered representative of the large masses of small shareholders, who may between them own 90 per cent of the stock of the corporation. They represent special interests: big shareholders, creditors, law firms, the corporate establishment, consumerism, women's rights, and other fashionable trends. They have been coopted to the board, not chosen by the people who own most of the corporation. There are no representatives of small shareholders on the board.

But another group of special interests is usually represented in force on corporate boards — the members of top management. These are the corporate officers — presidents, vice presidents, and treasurers — who are employees of the corporation, appointed by the board, responsible to the board, and at the same time members of the board in their own right. And therein lies an important conflict of interest.

In some foreign countries, like Germany, managers are not permitted to serve on boards in order to avoid this particular conflict. The board then controls the managers who actually run the company and serves as watchdog for the shareholders. The German boards may be loaded with people representing large banks and other special interests, but they will not represent the special interests of the people who are being paid to run the company.

In the United States, management usually supplies a heavy contingent of board members. The appointment of such inside directors can be defended on many grounds. The managers are bound to have a far more intimate knowledge of the problems of the corporation than the distinguished outsiders who make up the rest of the board. The managers live with the corporation; they are familiar with the intricate problems of a complex organization dealing with complex problems. The outsiders may spend a few days a year dealing with these problems at the board level; even though they may work hard to fulfill their responsibilities, they may be out of their depth when major decisions must be made.

The outside directors will thus find the presence of their inside colleagues reassuring. Inside directors thus will make the board more effective. Yet by no stretch of the imagination can management directors be considered the representatives of the shareholders. By the nature of things, they represent management.

It is difficult enough to visualize management board members in the act of effectively judging their own performance when they step to the boardroom and don their director's hats. Neither can they reasonably be expected to oppose the desires of any large shareholders or to take up the defense of the interests of the small owners of stock. They can, however, be expected to take a very strong personal interest in board decisions relating to the appointment and compensation of corporate officers, one of the functions of the board. In substance, the management board members will help the outside directors set their own salaries.

For this reason, board and management have become almost the same thing in many corporations. And as long as the board-management group gets along with the major shareholders, it does not have to worry much about the little people with a hundred or five thousand shares. If there are no dominant shareholders happiness is complete: the board can largely do as it pleases. There is no way to impeach the board of a corporation except in cases of gross negligence, acts of manifest bad faith, or crime.

This does not mean that the board can ignore certain outside influences; it has to respond to public pressures and even to shareholder discontent. The response may not be timely or effective, but the board must pay some heed to what is going on outside the doors of the boardroom. But whatever the management-board group does will reflect its own interests rather than those of the people who own the corporation. However, the gap between these different interests is not necessarily as large as might be thought.

The main interest of the average small shareholder is a capital gains profit from share price movements. These price movements on the stock market do not necessarily have to reflect the actual performance of the corporation or the quality of its management. It suffices that a large number of speculators imagine that the stock will be worth more at some future time to produce the convenient and necessary price changes.

By some strange coincidence, the objective of the management of many corporations is exactly the same — stock price increases. And all of a sudden the lack of checks and balances between the shareholders and management becomes unimportant. What is good for management is good for the small shareholders.

The mechanics by which this remarkable conciliation of supposedly opposed interests has been achieved merits some examination.

Incentives and the Stock Market

Let us suppose for a moment that the net earnings of IBM were to drop to $1.00 per share. Moreover, we will assume that for certain reasons it has been established beyond any reasonable doubt that $1.00 per share is the maximum profit IBM could conceivably earn over the next ten or twelve years. What would happen then?

As this is being written, IBM earnings are about $16 per share and the stock sells at $270, or seventeen times earnings. In our gruesome hypothesis, the outlook for the company looks bleak, and this would obviously be reflected in the price of its stock. Clearly, the drop in earnings is not a temporary setback; low earnings will prevail for years to come. There is no hope of potential stock market profits except perhaps in the long-term future. Still, IBM is a large corporation with substantial assets. It also employs enough people that the government could hardly afford to let the company collapse, no matter what might happen.

As a result, the price of the stock might stabilize around $12, or twelve times earnings. This would be a disastrous drop from the present level. Each share would lose $258 from its present value. There are about 150 million shares and about 600,000 shareholders. Between them, the unfortunate owners would lose $38 billion. This is almost enough to make the whole stock market collapse.

But what would happen to the company itself?

There would probably be noisy recriminations between major shareholders and management over the causes of the catastrophe, and as a result there might be some management changes. But otherwise business would continue, although perhaps on a more subdued scale. The company still would have its assets, produce outstanding equipment, and make a profit of $150 million a year. The huge losses of the owners would have no direct repercussions on the company. No company money was involved in the tragedy. The shareholders gambled and lost, but that is their problem. The horse that fails to win does not pay for the losses of the people who bet on its victory.

Of course, the wailing of the afflicted would be very loud. The horrible drop of the IBM stock price would probably cause a major panic on the stock exchanges as investors woke up to the risk of the game. The Dow Jones would plunge. And stockbrokers would be wringing their hands in despair and lament the evil consequences of a setback that discourages investment to fill the capital needs of American business.

This is nonsense. The people who bought IBM stock and got wiped out did not put their money into the company unless they bought new stock. They merely bought ownership certificates from other speculators. The money went to the previous owners of the precious pieces of paper and not into the corporate treasury. They gambled, and gamblers must be prepared for the risk of the game.

A sharp decline in stock price has, of course, some indirect repercussions on the corporation. Raising money through the sale of additional stock becomes more difficult. More shares have to be sold to raise a given amount, and the owners of the old shares will not be happy about the dilution of their equity. Selling the shares resulting from a capital increase will depress earnings per share accordingly, and large capital increases can have a strong adverse effect on stock prices. For this reason, the sale of new shares is not a popular way to raise money. Corporations prefer to borrow rather than water down the value of their stock.

In the case of IBM, the number of shares outstanding rose by about 10 per cent between 1965 and 1974. Yet during the same ten-year period IBM sales more than tripled and so did profits. Thus, the importance of new stock issues as a means of raising money is not overwhelming.

On the other hand, a sharp drop in stock prices poses some problems when convertible bonds are involved. Convertibles pay substantially lower interest rates than straight bonds, but in return they can be converted into shares of the company, usually at a price somewhat above the market price of the stock when the bonds are issued. The lender accepts the lower interest in the hope that the conversion privilege will pay off. At current stock prices, IBM could borrow $30 million in the form of convertible bonds, and even if all the bonds were ultimately converted, the stock dilution would only amount to about 100,000 shares, which is insignificant. With a share price of $12, the same loan amount could dilute the equity by more than two million shares. This may be undesirable, and the money may have to be raised by straight bonds at higher interest rates. Borrowings would become more expensive.

These problems may be annoying, but they are quite survivable. The sharp drop in stock price would not have any major effect on the activities of the corporation. However, it would affect the management of the corporation to a rather important degree. In fact, it would represent a serious threat to the board-management group.

The most obvious danger is shareholder discontent. As long as the shares are widely dispersed the problem may be minor, but if there are important shareholder groups, board and management may be dismissed and replaced by a new team as the dominant shareholders search for a means to recoup their losses.

Another danger exists when the share price drops substantially below the asset value of the corporation. Somebody might then buy enough of the cheap stock to get control so as to exploit the idle assets for his own purposes. In a large corporation, this problem is not serious because the cost of acquiring effective control requires more money than any ambitious raider is likely to get his hands on. In our hypothetical example, the worth of all IBM shares at $12 each is still $1.8 billion. However, smaller companies have to consider this danger. But even a large corporation may not be safe from being acquired by another corporation when its stock sells at a low price. And for these reasons, stock prices are of considerable interest to management.

But the most important motive for focusing management attention on the stock market is connected with managerial compensation practices. And this motive has distorted corporate practices to a remarkable degree. Like many other problems, this distortion has at its origin a perfectly reasonable idea.

The idea is that outstanding performance should be rewarded. A manager who creates a substantial improvement in the profits of his corporation should to some extent share in the profits he has generated. He should get an extra reward for his superb performance.

Unfortunately, in this age of high inflation and high taxation, providing financial incentives worth striving for can get rather expensive. A senior executive may be paid $100,000 a year. He has done an outstanding job, and the board decides to award him a $20,000 bonus. For that kind of money he is bound to do even better next time.

This is where taxation raises its ugly head. The manager probably pays around $40,000 in taxes on his base salary, but on the bonus he will have to pay around 60 per cent tax. He keeps $8000 and the government gets $12,000. This is no longer a very compelling incentive. If the corporation wants to provide him with $20,000 after taxes, it would have to pay a pretax bonus of $50,000. This is very expensive, and since the compensation of key executives may have to be reported to the shareholders, someone might complain about the largesse of the award.

The solution to the problem of incentives being eaten away

by the Internal Revenue Service has been the development of stock-based incentive schemes. The stock option entitles the executive to buy a certain number of shares from the corporation at a fixed price over a certain period. The price usually corresponds to the market price of the stock on the day the option was granted. The option holder has the privilege of buying tomorrow at today's price.

A typical option may be for one thousand shares at today's price of $40 a share. The lucky recipient of the option then waits to see what happens. If the stock price dips and stays below $40 for the entire option period, he does nothing. The option is worthless since he can buy the stock cheaper on the market. However, if the stock price rises above $40, he will exercise the option and buy the stock from the corporation. He will then hold the stock as long as may be required for tax reasons and sell it for capital gains. His risk is limited to whatever price fluctuations the stock may undergo during the time he holds it.

The cost of the option to the corporation is modest, even if the stock has to be bought on the open market. If the stock is newly issued, the cost to the corporation is zero. Yet the corporation has provided the deserving manager with an attractive reward and a powerful incentive to do even better the next year. Similar reasoning underlies the award of stock as a performance bonus in lieu of cash. Originally these schemes were conceived as a form of tax-favored compensation. Tax laws have gradually been tightened and have taken some of the gloss away from stock-based incentive schemes. However, even if the stock awards and options had to be taxed at the full personal income tax rate, they would still remain popular because they provide powerful incentives at relatively low cost to the corporation.

Yet this incentive is somewhat lopsided; it only pays off if the stock price increases. The fortune of the option-holder is thus tied to the vagaries of the stock market rather than to improved performance of the company itself. And there lies an important difference. Managers are no longer spectators of the stock market game. They become participants, playing with the stock of their own company. Their interests become identical with those of the shareholders looking for capital gains.

But managers are also insiders. They run the corporation and create the events that provide stock market speculators with a basis for their decisions. The acts of corporate managers are therefore not without repercussions on stock market movements, which in turn are reflected in the personal fortunes of the members of management benefiting from options and stock awards. And since managers are, by definition, dynamic achievers, they can be expected to do something about this situation.

This is where corporate strategy comes in.

5. Corporate Strategy

Whose Strategy?

There are several popular misconceptions about the main objectives of corporate strategy. At one extreme, as noted before, there is the suspicion that corporate strategies are fiendishly clever plans to deceive the public, defraud the customers, exploit the workers, and corrupt the government in order to extort huge profits for the benefit of fat-cat shareholders.

This image may have had some justification in the days of robber baron capitalism, but it hardly applies to the modern corporation with widespread ownership. Still, the image lingers on.

At the other extreme is the pleasant notion that the main purpose of corporate strategy is the best use of available resources to ensure the long-term prosperity of the enterprise and to provide joy and happiness to owners, workers, customers, and the public at large. Although widely propagated by institutional advertising and in after-dinner speeches by prominent businessmen, this is not necessarily a realistic image either.

In fact, there are as many different corporate strategies as there are corporations. Some of them may be formal documents in hard-cover bindings, others perhaps a collection of memos, and some just informal understandings or mental images of the president of the corporation. Yet even the most explicit formal position paper on strategy may fail to cover certain important aspects of the grand design. There are bound to be objectives and concepts which are not recorded and left unsaid lest they fall into the hands of the profane.

Corporate strategy will naturally have to take into account the particular situation of the company — its resources, products, market conditions, competition, threats, opportunities, and all the other characteristics of the business, or businesses, the corporation engages in. It will also take into account the distortions of the business environment and their effect on the corporation and its long-term objectives. Corporate growth as a tool for attaining the advantages inherent in operating on a larger scale will obviously occupy an important place in strategic planning. And so will the advantages of diversification, multinational expansion, and the opportunities offered by tax laws, governmental regulations, financing possibilities, and ownership structure.

Needless to say, the strategy of a corporation is not a static philosophy. It changes with changing outside conditions, inside power constellations, and the changing images in the minds of the people who shape strategy. Thus, corporate strategies are bound to reflect the vast variety of different corporate environments and different reactions to these environments.

But all corporate strategies have one thing in common. They are developed by the board-management groups of the corporations involved. And no matter how objective and selfless the members of these groups may try to be, their strategies will inevitably reflect their personal interests. The self-interest and feelings of the strategy makers thus create objectives rather different from the formal organization goals outlined in corporate policy documents.

The nature and order of importance of these objectives will depend on the particular circumstances of the corporation and the personalities of the management group. But no matter what

the situation of the corporation may be, the objectives will
reflect the management group's instinct for self-preservation,
the desire for independence, and the attraction of personal
profits.

Neither these objectives nor the strategies for attaining them
are likely to be revealed outside the most intimate circles of top
management. In fact, they may not even be alluded to by the
highest echelon of management meeting in the privacy of the
boardroom. Corporate officers and board members are so
steeped in the tradition of making sincere statements about the
best interests of the public and the welfare of the corporate
family that the actual expression of selfish motives that would
contradict these homilies may be too much for them.

Nevertheless, the strategies to cope with the incentives and
dangers to which managements are exposed are not difficult to
reconstruct. Consider the men who have struggled for years to
reach the top of the corporate ladder. They obviously want to
derive some benefit from their position to make up for all the
toil, cunning, and patience that were necessary for the successful climb to the top. They want security, independence, and
material rewards. These personal goals will cast a long shadow
over the pursuit of the rational objectives of the organization.

Security

Unhappy shareholders are dangerous. If their holdings are
large, they may be able to make management changes, organize
ugly proxy fights, or even sell out to undesirables bent on acquiring control of the corporation. They do not actually have
to do any of these things. The mere fact that they could take
some unpleasant action if sufficiently provoked is a standing
threat to management. Dominant shareholders must be kept
contented if at all possible.

Small shareholders also pose a threat. They can sell their shares, and if enough of them do so, the stock price is bound to decline. This is a nuisance for two reasons.

Any large shareholders will be disturbed by the erosion of stock prices. They may then start asking embarrassing questions and wondering whether management is really doing an adequate job. And if the answer to these questions is doubtful, they may cause trouble and perhaps even push through changes in the management structure.

But even if there are no strong, dominant shareholders involved, the drop in share prices as a result of widespread discontent among small owners will affect the stock incentive profits of management. Some attention must thus be paid to the feelings of small shareholders. This does not imply that the little people should be given any real influence or, heaven forbid, real voting rights. Still, they ought to be kept reasonably happy.

Happy shareholders are people who open the morning newspaper and gleefully discover that their shares have gone up another notch in yesterday's stock market trading. They also love to see the little item announcing a new development, a new product, or better yet, a technical breakthrough made by the corporation whose shares they own.

If no breakthrough can be manufactured for publicity purposes and no new product held up for the multitudes to admire, the gap may have to be filled with synthetic news. An optimistic announcement by a corporate officer along the lines of "Smith sees large market for Abacus products in East Timbuktoo" may have to do.

Since the price of the shares is strictly a figment of the imagination of the stock market players, this opens the door to all sorts of gambits designed to make the corporation appealing to investors.

First of all, there is advertising. Companies spend millions of dollars of shareholder money on what is called institutional advertising. The purpose of this advertising is not primarily to sell the products and services of the corporation. In fact, products may not even be mentioned. Instead, institutional advertising extols the greatness of the corporation, its contributions to mankind, its lovable character, its concern with public welfare, or its superb and selfless research to give people the best things in life at competitive prices. The scope of such advertising is limited only by the outer edges of advertising agency ingenuity and the amount of money management cares to spend.

The purpose of institutional advertising is not merely the advancement of the fortunes of advertising agencies and media. The objective is to sell the corporation to the public — literally and figuratively. The glowing images of a dynamic and attractive company imply that a highly competent management will lead the enterprise to ever higher peaks of success.

All this may actually stimulate sales of airplanes, aspirins, or bathroom fixtures, but that is largely beside the point. The real message is an invitation to become part of this great corporation. Buy some shares and you, too, are likely to make capital gains as the company pursues its path to glory and higher earnings. Any stockbroker will be happy to take your order. And if enough small investors follow the call of the pied piper, there will be demand for the stock, and its price may increase. Not much, perhaps, but every little bit helps.

Then there are the security analysts who have to provide stock trading recommendations week after dreary week. These are the experts of the stock market game, the professional touts of the capital gains racetrack. They work with charts, balance sheets, projections of future earnings, and profound theories and communicate largely in a jargon incomprehensible to outsiders. All this serves to dress up in an impressive scientific manner what may in reality be educated hunches. The advice of the analysts is obviously based on more information than the individual investor has at his disposal or cares to digest. Of course, they make mistakes once in a while, but so do racing-tipsters who perform a similar service to mankind.

Stock analysts are condemned to produce a steady stream of recommendations. To do this they need, apart from figures and charts and theories, some special information, hot tips that can be passed on to the anxious masses. An occasional luncheon speech by the chief executive officer of a corporation to a gathering of distinguished analysts can benefit both parties. The talk will stress the sound financial situation of the company, play down the recent difficulties which have now been overcome, express serene optimism about the outcome of heavily publicized lawsuits against the company, and generally paint an attractive picture. There may be tantalizing glimpses of future breakthroughs and earnings forecasts to provide grist for the mills of the analysts.

Charming the analysts is not an amusing pastime but has a very definite purpose. A good recommendation by some well-known stock market experts as a result of the luncheon speech can send thousands of investors — small, large, and institutional — panting to the phone to buy the stock.

The stockbrokers who live on portfolio turnover, rather than on the profits of their clients, welcome analysts' recommendations. For one thing, no analyst will recommend the same stocks week after week. The changing kaleidoscope of recommendations will thus provide investors with an incentive to trade, and every trade means a commission. Also, by referring to the recommendations of distinguished analysts, the broker can encourage his clients to churn their portfolios without being directly implicated if the results are a disaster.

While the projection of exciting images can play a part in provoking short-term stock price movements, the real long-term appreciation of a stock requires growth in earnings per share. Maximizing profits — this year, this month, this week, no matter what may be happening — is thus an important ingredient of management strategy. Consequently, sophisticated management systems have been developed to extract maximum profits from all levels of the organization to provide a steady flow of good news to the investing public.

However, it sometimes happens that earnings fail to meet the pleasant pattern of rapid and sustained growth. When earnings dip, the frantic effort to increase profits urgently and immediately, no matter what the long-term cost to the corporation, is a good indication of the insecurity felt by management. The ruthless curtailing of activities, wholesale firings, milking of assets, and other desperate crash programs to restore profits may save the day for the management group, but they are hardly conducive to the long-term prosperity of the corporation.

Yet management has no choice. Its fate is largely tied to the day-to-day stock market quotations rather than to the operating prospects of the company itself. Management may not be able to take the long-term view and ride out the storm. It may be compelled to support the stock price today and tomorrow; otherwise, it may no longer be around when the situation improves if there are large shareholder groups with the power to make management changes. And even if there are no dominant shareholders, the economic motivation of management is tied to the stock market. A drop in stock price can mean an important personal loss to the members of the management team. A management that feels the tremors of an approaching upheaval may thus have to resort to the most radical means to save their own jobs or to protect their options.

Of course, some management teams have been known to systematically milk corporations of their assets and to build synthetic profits out of drastic cost-reduction programs. If a company has grown soft and flabby, these measures can have a salutary effect if used in moderation. But the same technique can also be used to produce a strong, although temporary, jump in earnings followed by an even more pronounced decline. If skillful timing is used, the top men will have moved on by the time the decline sets in and landed better jobs somewhere else on the strength of having turned around the company they left. It may then take several years and perhaps several managements to salvage the wreckage they have left behind.

While earnings increases are important, the leverage provided by high price-earnings ratios must not be neglected. And while earnings have to be worked for through tireless exertions to squeeze the last nickel of profits out of the organization, price-earnings ratios are a matter of investor confidence, which can be encouraged in various ways. And sometimes the games played to increase investor confidence tend to produce more attractive results than the tedious nose-to-the-grindstone battle to increase earnings from day-to-day operations.

The key to high price-earnings ratios is the expectation of increasing profits per share. And this is often considered synonymous with increasing size of the corporation. High price-earnings ratios are thus often associated with rapid corporate growth. And the key to rapid growth is the merger. But mergers have certain other strategic advantages which must not be overlooked.

Independence

Management does not particularly cherish the idea of outside interference. It wants to be free to run the business as it sees fit and to pursue its own interests in peace.

There are two basic threats to management independence. One is the existence of large shareholders who may exert considerable influence and impair management's freedom. The other is being taken over by another company through purchase or an undesirable merger. Management has to cope with both of these threats.

The power of important shareholders can be curbed by diluting their holdings through mergers, which involve the acquisition of other companies through an exchange of shares. The owners of the victim hand over their shares and in return receive an appropriate number of shares in the aggressor company. As a result of this stock exchange, the number of shareholders in the surviving company increases. If the victim was a small company owned by only a handful of people, this is not very important. But if the victim happens to be a large corporation the number of shareholders in the aggressor may rise enormously. This swelling of the shareholder ranks will reduce the importance of formerly dominant shareholders. A group that controlled 5 per cent of the stock may only control 3 per cent after the merger.

The only way to avoid this predicament is for the dominant shareholders to buy more shares of the aggressor or to buy into the victim before word of the merger seeps out. The value of inside information in such a case is obvious, but even so the transaction may be costly.

Mergers can thus be an important tool for curbing the influence of dominant shareholders. But mergers also provide the corporation with instant growth and the benefits of operating on a larger scale. For this reason they are not very likely to run into serious shareholder opposition. Growth, as we have seen, implies higher profits, higher share prices, and capital gains for people who play the stock market.

Still, if a merger does not look very attractive it is conceivable that some of the shareholders may raise objections. Important shareholders may even cause enough of a fuss to block the project. It is thus advisable to obtain the consent of the major shareholders before the merger proposal is officially announced. Even if there is some reluctance on the part of important owners, a friendly chat in the privacy of the boardroom may soothe their feelings or result in some mutually satisfactory arrangement to eliminate their opposition. At the least, this forewarning will give dominant shareholders time to take whatever measures they may deem necessary to protect their positions.

The rank and file of shareholders are far less likely to object. For one thing, they may only vaguely understand the terms of the transaction and blithely assume that whatever the board considers good for the corporation will also be good for the shareholders. And even if some small shareholders were to object, they would lack the means to organize any effective resistance. Knowing this, they will not get excited and waste their time in futile protests. If they do not like the merger they can sell their shares.

But it is conceivable that for some strange and unusual reasons there may be real opposition to a merger proposal. This may be a nuisance but is not necessarily fatal. Mergers can be structured so they will not require shareholder approval. This takes a little longer and lacks the attraction of reducing shareholder influence, but the method is quite practical and perfectly legal. The procedure involves several steps.

First, management and board decide to incorporate a part of the company as a separate corporation. The new corporation becomes a wholly-owned subsidiary of the parent. The shareholders are told that this arrangement will enable the new subsidiary to operate more effectively, and, not knowing any better, they are unlikely to object. More effective function, after all, implies higher profits and capital gains.

Once the subsidiary has been established, management is free to carry out a variety of interesting transactions without shareholder approval because the subsidiary is owned by the parent company rather than by the owners of the parent. The board of the parent company can thus make any decisions normally reserved to the owners of a corporation.

The board may decide to merge the subsidiary with another company. Or the subsidiary can be spun off and sold for cash. Or its shares may be sold to the public to raise money. All these transactions are entirely at the discretion of the board of the parent company.

In one particular case, a highly profitable division of a diversified corporation was spun off and merged with a somewhat mediocre partner. The shares of the new merged company were then distributed to the shareholders in the parent company and the former owners of the merger victim. As a result, the former owners of shares in a fairly attractive company now owned shares in two not particularly exciting companies—the truncated former parent stripped of its most profitable division and the company formed by the merger of beauty and beast.

The reasons for this unusual transaction were never revealed, and the shareholders of the parent company were simply faced with a *fait accompli.* They were not consulted nor given any meaningful explanation. And apparently nobody complained.

There is, of course, the chance that some particularly irate shareholders may sue the corporation if a clever transaction strikes them as detrimental to their interests. This may cause some minor headlines in the financial pages, and if the plaintiffs have the stamina and resources to persist there might even be some sort of a settlement, years after the fact. But the danger of shareholder suits is not substantial unless the board has really been careless.

All corporations of any importance have highly skilled legal departments and can afford the services of expert legal firms. This high-priced help makes quite certain that any major transaction will comply with the letter of the law, whatever its real implications and merits may be. It also stands ready to defend the corporation and its management against all comers.

Even very irate large shareholders with considerable resources may be reluctant to spend time and money to fight a case that may involve years of costly litigation before it is finally settled in court. They may make threatening gestures in the hope of extracting something from the corporation. But unless they have an ironclad case, they are likely to drop the matter quietly if a settlement does not appear probable. On the other hand, if the suit looks as if it will be decided in favor of the shareholder, the corporation will settle out of court while declaring its complete innocence. The settlement, the declaration will claim, was made merely to avoid the cost of protracted further litigation.

The joke in shareholder suits is that the defense of management is paid for out of corporate funds, that is, with shareholder money. And a successful suit may be detrimental to the reputation of the company and depress the price of its stock. This can make shareholder suits somewhat self-defeating unless the plaintiffs have taken the precaution to sell their shares before the litigation generates any publicity and stock prices drop.

But mergers are not only a means for increasing management independence through the dilution of the holdings of important shareholders. They are also a measure of protection against the corporation being taken over itself. Mergers enlarge the size of the corporation and thus make acquisition of a controlling interest more expensive. They also create the image of rapid growth, which encourages high price-earnings ratios. And this protects management against intruders from the outside.

Large investors will be more reluctant to buy several million dollars' worth of a stock that sells at forty times earnings and has a negligible yield, just to acquire control of a company, than when shares sell at ten times earnings, yield 6 per cent, and control can be achieved with half a million dollars. The transaction simply gets too expensive when the corporation is large and the price of the stock is high.

Large size and a high-priced stock also provide protection against unwanted mergers. A company with a lower price-earnings ratio would find the acquisition of a high PE company terribly expensive if made by cash, and unattractive by exchange of shares, because the earnings per share of the aggressor would be instantly reduced. And large size automatically limits the number of corporate suitors to companies of roughly similar size.

As a result, mergers can play an important role in protecting the independence of management against challengers, both within and outside the corporation.

Making Money

As we have noted earlier, senior managers not only want to keep their jobs and become as independent from outside influence as circumstances may permit, they also want to derive some tangible rewards from their diligent toil. They want to make money.

This desire to acquire a certain modest wealth is perfectly understandable. Equally understandable is the wish that the accumulation of this wealth not take twenty years. High corporate office can be a perishable commodity. In consequence, there should be some sort of protection in case the tenure of an exalted position is cut short because of some regrettable incident. Furthermore, the method of compensation should also provide some shelter from the ravages of progressive taxation, which can eat deeply into high salaries. This is where stock-based performance incentives come in.

Few shareholders would dispute the idea that ownership of corporate stock by senior managers is a desirable principle. Not only will the managers benefit as the corporation prospers through their ardent efforts; these efforts will also be slanted in the one direction that does the shareholders the most good. In their own interest, managers will strive for stock price increases conducive to capital gains.

Stock-based incentive plans can thus count on the enthusiastic support of the shareholders, who sense, quite correctly, that these incentives will benefit themselves almost as much as the managers. But few shareholders realize all the implications of the incentive plans they endorse with such glee.

For one thing, no matter what the fine print in the announcement of a new incentive plan to the shareholders may say, the plan will be largely administered by its main beneficiaries. The granting of incentive awards will be the responsibility of the board. And the senior managers of the corporation, who are likely to receive the fattest awards, also happen to be board members. Of course, there may be a board committee to administer the plan, and management-board members may be excluded from this committee to preserve appearances. But this artificial separation is not necessarily a guarantee that the committee members will boldly oppose the greed of their colleagues from management. A particularly striking example will illustrate this point.

The Nameless Corporation grew from $800 million in sales in 1967 to $1100 million in 1972. During this period, net income from normal activities dropped from $55 million to $30 million. But there were also some substantial extraordinary losses from the sale of unprofitable operations. As a result, earnings in 1970 were negligible and there was a loss of $50 million in 1972.

No doubt there were compelling reasons for these unfortunate setbacks, but still, the situation of the corporation did not look very good at the time. Did management tighten its belts and cut down on its own incentive awards until the situation improved? Of course not.

For their fine performance in 1972, resulting in a loss of $50 million, the officers of the company received $900,000 in incentives, and stock options for 174,000 shares were granted to officers and board members. The president alone received, in addition to his salary of $170,000, a bonus of $150,000 and options for 40,000 shares of common stock, which at the time sold for about $20 a share. This was in a very bad year.

It is of interest to note that the corporation's generosity toward its managers was not limited to the more successful parts of the operation. The worst results seem to have been produced by one particular division, which accounted for one fourth of the total sales volume but contributed only some 3 per cent of the operating profit — after taking a loss the previous year. The vice president and general manager of this division was still rewarded with $40,000 in incentive payments and options for 14,000 shares of the company that particular year.

There is no indication that any of the shareholders questioned this lavish distribution of performance awards when performance was somewhat less than exciting. Of course, the corporation went right on paying dividends; $21 million in 1970, when profits were half a million, and $25 million in 1972, when the company had lost twice that amount. Since there were no profits, the dividends were simply paid out of the substance of the corporation, and the net worth dropped accordingly. Obviously, this development was not very good for stock prices.

Yet, by some strange coincidence, the corporation spent $7 million in shareholder money in 1972 to buy 400,000 shares of its own stock. The purchase of almost 2 per cent of the outstanding stock on the market presumably was for shares to be used for future acquisitions and options. Still, the suspicion remains that this massive purchase may have been the means to support share prices in a particularly lackluster year.

The purchase of its own stock by a corporation is not an unusual thing. As this is being written, IBM has offered to purchase four million of its own shares at $280 each. The full-page announcements in the press explained the transaction in considerable detail, but failed to give even the slightest hint of its purpose. Yet the operation involved some very large amounts of corporate money. If enough shareholders tendered their shares for purchase, the company would pay $1.12 billion to acquire 2.7 per cent of its own stock. Since there are about 150 million IBM shares out, the purchase price works out to around $7.50 per share of all outstanding stock. If the purpose was to get rid of excess cash, the same result could have been reached by declaring a special $7.50 dividend, from which all shareholders would have benefited. However, since the purpose of the share purchase is not known to the public, it is difficult to assess the ulterior motives that may have prompted the operation.

There is, in fact, no compelling reason why a corporation should not be able, over a period of time, perhaps, to buy out the outside shareholders altogether, using its own cash or borrowed money. The company could then go private, with a few insiders becoming the sole owners. The stock would no longer have to be registered with the stock exchange authorities, would no longer be traded on the market, and would leave the insiders free to do as they pleased.

As far as options and stock awards are concerned, the example of the Nameless Corporation shows how management can acquire substantial fortunes by exploiting stock price fluctuations no matter what the situation of the company may be. And there is no practical way to stop abuses of incentive plans once the plan in general has been approved by the shareholders.

Yet even in corporations which do not abuse the opportunities offered by incentive plans — and we assume that few of them actually do — stock options involve a problem for the beneficiary. He may need large amounts of cash to buy the shares from the company when the time comes to exercise an option. And this money will be tied up until the shares can be sold for capital gains.

This can mean expensive borrowing from banks, which is not

particularly attractive at the sort of interest rates that have prevailed over recent years. In some corporations this problem was solved by financing option purchases with corporate funds, lent to the option holder at nominal interest rates. Borrowing money from the corporation at 4 per cent obviously made more sense than paying 7 or 8 per cent to the friendly neighborhood bank. Thus, shareholder money was in effect used to subsidize the personal option transactions of senior management people. However, it seems that the ethics of such company loans have been seriously questioned — not by shareholders, but by government agencies — and apparently the practice is now frowned upon.

However, there is another catch. In return for the award of an option, the beneficiary is usually required to sign an undertaking that he will not leave the corporation for a certain number of years. If he leaves anyway, he will not be able to exercise the option. Of course, the corporation has no reciprocal obligation; it can fire the bum anytime it chooses to. Senior managers thus accept something akin to the status of indentured servants when they receive options. But the potential rewards certainly make this small sacrifice of personal liberty worthwhile.

Even without company-subsidized financing, stock options and stock awards can create considerable managerial prosperity, assuming that the stock price moves in the right direction. After a few years at the horn of plenty, the management of even a smallish corporation with a good stock performance is likely to include a few millionaires. And there is no doubt that when the stack of chips reaches a certain size, management attention will be focused less on the long-term performance of the corporation than on the near-term fluctuations of the price of its stock.

This may create a terrible temptation for corporate managers to play games with the stock of their corporations. Determined managements may attempt to create synthetic growth stocks by rapidly enlarging the size of the corporation through acquisitions and mergers. The stock market players will see the rapid growth and jump to the conclusion, not always justified, that profits will increase accordingly, and bid up the price of the stock. The stock price changes generated by the outside investors can then be exploited by the insiders for their own benefit.

But convenient stock price fluctuations on a lesser scale can be produced by less drastic measures. Reports on the situation of the corporation emanate from management, and greedy managers lacking in ethics could presumably time these announcements to fit in with their own stock transactions. Thus, a drop in stock price is highly desirable when the time for the granting of new options comes around, since the option will be based on the market price on the date the option is granted. A high price is obviously desirable when members of management get ready to sell some of their shares.

Apart from such unethical practices as corporate news management tied in with managerial stock transactions, however, the mere knowledge that good news or bad news will be released on a certain date is sufficient to give mangement a substantial advantage in stock trading.

Insider transactions are, of course, illegal, but they are difficult to prove unless the transaction is conspicuously large and flagrantly triggered by insider information. But what happens if the president of a corporation sells 5000 shares in October because he knows from day-to-day reports that business is not good while the public gets the same information only months later when the quarterly earnings statement is published? Even the most ethical corporate officer cannot be expected simply to ignore the confidential information to which he is privy when he may have thousands of shares at stake.

What may be more worrisome is the role stock-based management incentives have played, and are still playing, in corporate growth strategies, indiscriminate mergers, profit extortion by totalitarian systems, and other manifestations of stock price manipulation. As this is being written, there is considerable talk about suppressing the tax advantages of stock options. But this would not solve the problem as long as management compensation remains tied, in some form or other, to the price at which the stock of the corporation is being traded on the stock exchange.

6. Implementing the Strategy

Recipe for Instant Growth

We have seen that mergers are one of the key weapons in the arsenal of corporate strategy. They produce instant growth and the immediate advantage of operating on a larger scale. They can also project the image of a dynamic management and attract the attention of the stock market, which may be reflected in higher stock prices. This can be of help to management in exploiting the benefits of stock-based incentives. And mergers can produce a welcome dilution of the power of important shareholders.

But that is not all. Certain types of mergers, arranged with a moderate amount of skill, may even increase earnings per share at the stroke of a pen. As a result, a good merger can increase profits far more rapidly than months or even years of toil and heartbreak devoted to profit improvement through growth from within.

Mergers, of course, are not a new idea. Companies have been gobbled up by other companies for a long time, and for a variety of reasons. However, the systematic pursuit of mergers between companies operating in entirely different fields of activity is a rather recent technique. And this technique is employed not only by daring entrepreneurs pyramiding control of one company into sprawling conglomerates by a sequence of skillful mergers. It has also become popular with corporations that are not under the influence of any particular dominant shareholder.

Growth by merger has simply become a way of life, a normal reaction to the environment in which corporations operate.

The ideal merger involves two companies in the same business. By pooling their markets, products, knowhow, and resources, the two merging partners will benefit from improved efficiency and a larger scale of operations. There will be less duplication of effort, better standardization of products and services, and operating costs are bound to be reduced when two similar activities are brought under one corporate roof. Moreover, the merger will eliminate a competitor.

And there lies the problem.

Antitrust laws prohibit the restriction of competition, and a merger between two major competitors does exactly that. If the merger partners are small and not very important in their field there is no problem. A grocery store can buy out, or merge with, another small grocery store, but a merger between Safeway and A&P would be a different matter. When the merger involves large competitors with important market shares, the government is likely to block the deal.

Next in order of attraction are mergers with suppliers or customers. Called vertical integration, such mergers make much sense because they provide the corporation with control over sources of supply or marketing outlets. Companies with captive suppliers or captive customers tend to have a distinct edge over competitors which are not integrated and operate only at one particular level of the business sequence. The oil company that owns wells, pipelines, tankers, refinery plants, and retail outlets is bound to have an advantage over the competitor whose business is limited to a refinery or a chain of filling stations. A steel company that controls mines, smelting plants, rolling mills, and fabricating plants has more room to maneuver than the competitor who operates only one link in the chain of steel processing.

Unfortunately, vertical mergers on a major scale may deprive other companies of free access to suppliers or customers and may, once again, be construed as a restriction of free competition. Thus the two most attractive forms of mergers are largely denied to corporations of any importance.

However, a corporation really determined to grow quickly need not be unduly hampered by these restraints. If growth from within is too slow and if mergers with competitors, suppliers, and customers are foiled by ambitious antitrust lawyers in the service of the government, all is not lost. The corporation will simply have to merge with companies in different fields. These mergers may not be quite as attractive as the forbidden transactions, but they still hold considerable charm. Antitrust legislation has thus given a large impetus to corporate diversification and the development of multibusiness operations.

The ostensible reason for diversification is the better use of resources through expansion into new areas of activity. These new businesses may be related to the corporation's existing operations — they may serve the same markets, use similar technology, involve knowhow already available, or tie in with the structure of the corporation in some other manner.

Diversification may provide scope for new growth and profits for a corporation that faces stagnating markets in its traditional business. It may also be a tool for leveling out what may be inevitable fluctuations in the existing business. By being active in several different fields, a corporation may become less vulnerable to recessions in any one business area.

As the road to diversification through mergers is pursued with diligence and zeal, the relation between the original business of the corporation and its new fields of endeavor may become very tenuous indeed. What started off as a diversification into related fields may become simply a matter of acquiring any new business that looks promising. Cigarette paper, housing developments, firearms, heavy chemicals, and specialty metals bear very little relationship to each other, but this fact may become unimportant in the pursuit of rapid corporate growth.

Once old-fashioned inhibitions have been shed, diversification in almost any direction becomes feasible, and the growth potential becomes almost unlimited. As long as the business of the merger victim looks reasonably attractive and does not compete with the businesses of the aggressor, there is no obstacle to a merger, no matter how strange the resulting hodgepodge of unrelated activities may appear to the outsider.

Having established the advantages of acquisition and mergers, the problem then becomes one of method. Corporate cannibalism can take many forms, but like any other investment, the transaction must show an adequate return to the investor.

Not too long ago, raids on companies with depressed stock prices were quite popular. This involved buying up the shares of companies whose assets were substantially larger than the market value of their stock. The general idea was to get control, usually over the screaming protests of the victim's management, in order to put the undervalued assets to better use. Once control was attained, the new rulers could exploit the situation to their profit. They could liquidate the victim's assets and leave the company an empty shell. Or they could reorganize the company, cut out the deadwood, put the idle assets to work, and finally sell the company at a profit after it had been "turned around." Or the assets could be employed to make other acquisitions.

None of these prospects was likely to fill the hearts of the doomed company's managers with joy. For this reason, raids often involved bitter proxy battles as management and raiders tried to rally the shareholders to their causes.

Today, predatory raids have become rather rare. Managements have learned that the best defenses against raids are high asset utilization, large company size, and high stock prices, all of which make raids unprofitable and expensive. The highly publicized raids of yesterday have thus made their contribution to the growth strategy of astute managers. As a result, buying up shares to acquire control of a company generally poses some problems, even if the intentions of the buyer are honorable and have the support of the victim's management.

If the victim is small and has only a few owners, a price is agreed upon and the owners sell all their shares. The buyer then becomes the sole owner and can do with the company as he pleases. When the victim is larger, problems tend to arise. The acquisition of control is more costly, and buying out all the shareholders may be almost impossible. There may be holdouts who want to prevent the merger of the victim with the aggressor. The holdouts may then have to be frozen out by disappearing dividends and other acts of corporate chicanery, but this can be tedious, take years, and cause bad publicity or even lawsuits.

There is also the problem of cost. If the stock is bought on the open market, the share price will inevitably rise, and the operation may become too expensive for the buyer long before he has enough shares to exert control. A public offer avoids this danger since the price the buyer will pay is fixed in advance. But the buyer has no idea of how many shareholders will accept the offer. He may get all the stock he needs — in which case his offer may have been too lavish — or he may get very little.

If the response to the offering is not sufficient, he cannot make a second offering at a higher price without paying the difference to those who accepted the original offer. The stock may thus have to be bought gradually on the market, which may be costly, particularly if smart speculators realize what is going on. But even if the transaction is successful, the aggressor has a problem, since the purpose of the acquisition was not only to get effective control, but also to show a good return on the money spent.

A millionaire operator, working alone or with a syndicate, may be quite content to buy enough shares to obtain effective control. If the ownership of the victim is widely dispersed and there are no other large shareholders around, a few per cent of the stock may suffice. The new major shareholder can then put his men on the board and exert his influence. Presumably he has a plan to exploit the situation to his own purposes before he starts buying the stock, and his benefits will accrue when this plan is implemented.

A corporate buyer is in a different situation. The purchase of the participation in the victim will be reflected in his financial statement and must be seen to be worthwhile. It should not depress the aggressor's earnings or the aggressor's stock will suffer and management stock incentives will suffer as well. The acquisition must show a reasonable return, not in ten years, but preferably right now.

If less than half of the victim's stock has been acquired, the buyer may in fact have control, but for accounting purposes he has only a minority participation. This means that only the dividends received from the participation can be shown in the books of the parent company. Since most companies pay out only part of their profits as dividends, the investment will show a poor return and appear unattractive.

To solve this problem, the aggressor may have to buy more than 50 per cent of the stock of the victim. The financial results of the two companies can then be consolidated. The parent corporation can show in its accounts a prorated part of the earnings, sales, and assets of the new affiliate, and the participation will therefore look much better than if only dividends could be shown. The investment results in higher earnings, sales, and assets for the parent corporation. But even so, an acquisition through the purchase of the victim's stock is not necessarily very attractive, unless the victim is small in relation to the aggressor.

If the victim is small, the corporate treasurer may simply dig into the company's piggy bank and pay up. For larger acquisitions, the piggy bank may not suffice, and funds will have to be found to finance the purchase. This means borrowing from banks or other financial institutions, or even from the sellers of the stock if the victim's owners can be persuaded to accept the aggressor's straight or convertible bonds. In these days of high interest rates, however, this borrowing can be rather expensive.

If the stock of the victim is bought at fourteen times earnings, the consolidated return on investment will be about 7 per cent. No matter what the other merits of the deal may be, a 7 per cent return on investment is not very exciting if the cost of the borrowed money happens to be 8 or 9 per cent. In this case, the buyer has to be quite certain that he can quickly step up the earnings of the new affiliate or otherwise generate enough benefits to make the acquisition worthwhile.

Finally, there is another snag. If shares are bought to make an acquisition, the profits of the parent company will be depressed by the need to write off what is known as good will. This quirk in accounting practice reflects the fact that the price paid for the victim's shares usually exceeds the value of the victim's net assets, unless the shares happen to be priced below the book value of these assets. The difference between the price paid and the book value takes into account the profit potential of the victim, and this difference will have to be written off until only the net assets of the victim — or a prorated part of these assets corresponding to the percentage of participation acquired — remain on the books of the parent company. But writing off the good will involved in a large and profitable acquisition can put a considerable crimp in the net earnings of the parent company.

This is undesirable. The purpose of the acquisition was to increase not only the size but also the profits of the aggressor. A drop in earnings after buying, or buying into, another company would depress share prices and possibly annoy shareholders. This does not mean that acquisitions based on stock purchases are impractical, but they do have certain drawbacks.

Fortunately there is a far better and more profitable way to acquire companies. This is the merger between consenting companies effected through an exchange of shares. The result is an attractive, inexpensive, and neat way to enlarge corporate size and to project the image of dynamic growth so cherished by stock market speculators. The advantages of such mergers can be quite substantial. They require no cash, involve little risk, avoid the problem of recalcitrant shareholders in either company, and are unlikely to cause fights or bad publicity. Nor need they adversely affect the financial statement of the aggressor, politely known as the surviving company. In fact, such mergers, if properly effected, can generate new profits in the surviving company.

And this is particularly important. The sudden growth of the survivor and the instant sleight-of-hand profits a judicious merger can produce may increase the price of the shares and provide handsome capital gains to shareholders and managers. And the transaction itself is tax-free. What more could one possibly hope for?

The perfect solution to the need for instant growth has been found by skilled corporate managers, ably assisted by highly qualified legal counsel. The whole method is so ingenious that it should be studied in some detail so we may fully understand its logic and beauty.

A Hypothetical Merger

A fictitious example may serve to illustrate how a pooling-of-interest merger works, how it is arranged and consummated, and how it affects the shareholders of the two merging companies. Needless to say, the transaction described here is purely imaginary, but similarities with actual mergers are not necessarily a coincidence.

Superior Drugs, Incorporated, a fast-growing corporation, is looking for new growth opportunities. The drug business is healthy and profitable. Sick people do not quibble over the cost of drugs; they buy whatever the doctor prescribes, and various forms of health insurance help defray the cost of medical treatment. An efficient team of medical visitors skilled in the arts of pharmaceutical promotion keep the doctors sold on SDI products. The company's able research team provides a steady flow of new products and product permutations that permit the replacement of older pills and capsules with flagging profitability by new and exciting drugs with better profit margins. The company is doing well in its traditional business.

But SDI's happiness is not quite complete. Research and promotion costs are high, the time needed to launch new products is long, and the chance of a major breakthrough that would sweep the field and drastically increase market shares is not very great. Pharmaceutical growth is satisfactory but not really spectacular enough to achieve the corporation's ambitious growth objectives.

To remedy this situation, SDI has developed a growth strategy to gradually restructure the corporation and, it is hoped, quadruple its size in six years. Mergers in the drug field are not possible in the domestic market because of antitrust problems. The expansion urges of the corporation are thus channeled into other directions. The first phase involved the development of

multinational activities. As a result, SDI has established overseas operations in the more important markets and bought out
several small competitors to acquire a local image and local
operating knowhow. This international development is being
pursued with diligence and zeal.

At home the new business development staff has already led
SDI into several fields that offer attractive opportunities for a
conglomerate. The overall development policy established by
SDI management specifies that the main thrust of diversification should be in the direction of products and services which
people are compelled to use all the time. Thus, the initial diversification into hospital supplies and medical equipment has been
rapidly followed by mergers that have led SDI into several new
fields. Dream of Passion, a cosmetics company, was taken over
some time ago. Then came a series of mergers that launched the
corporation into baby foods, convenience foods, airline catering, snack bars, and food substitutes. Further major progress
through mergers in these areas is now no longer possible, because the company has become an important factor in the food
field.

These acquisitions have given SDI a reputation for fast
growth, and as a result its stock sells at a high price-earnings
ratio. To maintain this reputation and the leveraged stock price
that goes with it, the company has to continue its rapid growth.

The next step is fairly obvious. People not only get sick, eat,
and love. They also die with a similar inevitability. And here
lies a large market not yet tapped by major companies. This is
a field where small, local, and relatively inefficient enterprises
prevail. A large corporation with substantial resources and considerable knowhow in promotion and management could revo-
lutionize the business. The idea finds considerable support
among the higher echelons of SDI's management, and an active
search for a suitable merger candidate is launched.

Word of this latest merger objective of SDI is passed on to

consultants, bankers, brokers, and assorted luncheon companions of senior management. After a while leads start dribbling in and are assiduously checked out. Most of the suggested candidates are either too small, badly run, too deep in real estate, or too close to bankruptcy to merit further study. But others look pretty good. Preliminary meetings are held with their managements, facts and figures are compiled, detailed reports are written assessing the merits and shortcomings of each proposed candidate, and many meetings are held internally to digest all this information.

The search finally boils down to one single prospect. The Heavenly Rest Corporation may not be perfect, but it does look much better than any of the other opportunities unearthed by the careful search. For one thing, Heavenly Rest is not a small, local operation; it is large enough to make the deal worthwhile. It operates a chain of some fifty funeral homes in the Northeast, sells plots in some forty private cemeteries, and has its own plants to produce tombstones, coffins, and mortician supplies.

Moreover, the company appears to have a good image, an efficient sales force, and is well introduced with doctors and hospitals. Further investigation reveals that while Heavenly Rest is profitable, its growth has been stagnating of late, there are some management problems, and the company is short of working capital. In fact, it has become somewhat overextended as a result of its own ambitious growth plans. Profits could no doubt be improved by reorganization and access to the resources of a larger corporation.

Superior Drugs decides to proceed with merger discussions. There is never any doubt about the mode of the merger. There will be a gentlemanly deal with the management of the victim, and the merger will be effected through an exchange of stock. The owners of HRC will hand over their shares and receive stock in SDI, with the terms of the exchange to be negotiated. The cost to SDI will be negligible.

Then follows a series of furtive meetings, held in hotel rooms away from the headquarters of the two companies, during which the representatives of the two managements discuss the terms of the possible merger. Once these two august bodies reach an agreement on mutually acceptable terms, the merger is practically in the bag. The lawyers will then set forth the terms of the merger in proper legal language, and the shareholders of the two companies will meet on the same date to ratify the deal. Shareholder meetings being what they are, there should be no problem in getting approval as long as the major owners have been persuaded that the transaction is in their interest. Heavenly Rest will then become a division of the surviving corporation.

To maintain the polite fiction of a genuine merger rather than an act of corporate cannibalism, the name of the surviving company may even be changed, perhaps to Heavenly Drugs International. The name change may be only temporary. In a couple of years a new name may be adopted, perhaps to soothe the feelings of the owners of the next major victim of SDI's diversification efforts.

As it is, the merger looks very promising. There will be no problems of cash, depressed earnings, taxes, or minority shareholders who might refuse to swap their shares. At the shareholder meetings the majority will decide for everybody. And there will be little time to organize effective shareholder opposition between the time the announcement is made and the date of the meetings. As long as the victim's management is really sold on the merger, there is unlikely to be any snag. HRC will be gobbled up by SDI, lock, stock, and barrel. The main objective is thus to procure the enthusiastic support of HRC's management.

During the intense courtship between the managements of the two companies that precedes the merger, a great many things will be discussed, among them the terms of the stock exchange offer. Agreement may be finally reached that the exchange should reflect the current market price of the shares. We will assume that SDI has net earnings of $20 million. There are ten million shares out. Earnings per share are thus $2 and the stock sells at $50, or twenty-five times earnings. SDI pays a dividend of 40 cents a share.

HRC earnings are $10 million. There are also ten million shares, and the company pays a dividend of 50 cents a share. However, since HRC is neither very glamorous nor a fast grower, its stock sells at only ten times earnings, or $10 a share.

Under the terms of the agreement, the owners of HRC will receive one share of SDI, worth $50, for five shares of HRC, worth $10 each. This appears very reasonable, and the negotiators then retire to the nearest bar to celebrate the successful and equitable conclusion of the deal.

The results of the exchange of stock will then be as follows: to acquire HRC 2 million new shares of SDI will be issued, bringing the total to 12 million. The post-merger company will have combined net earnings of $30 million: $20 million from SDI and $10 million from HRC. This means that earnings per share of SDI will increase from $2.00 to $2.50 as a result of the merger.

A miracle has been wrought. The merger has increased the profits per share of SDI by one fourth. Judicious negotiations, gentle persuasion, and a carefully presented proposal to the owners of the two companies have created not only a larger and more diversified corporation, which will be able to face the challenges of the future with greater confidence. They have also generated an instant increase in earnings per share of the surviving corporation. And the cost of the whole transaction has been negligible.

If we consider the toil and trouble necessary to accomplish a comparable earnings increase by slow, plodding growth from within, it becomes immediately obvious why mergers can be so attractive. The important factor is that proper attention must be given to the price-earnings ratios of the two companies. To generate a profit as a result of the merger, the aggressor's price-earnings ratio must be higher than that of the victim.

With some luck, the stock market players may even believe that the new post-merger corporation still merits the same price-earnings ratio as before. Applied to the instant jump in earnings per share, this would imply an increase in the price of SDI stock from $50 to $62.50, yielding handsome profits to the owners of SDI and its management.

But what about the management of the victim?

Pooling-of-interest mergers require not only the consent but the enthusiastic support of the victim's management. The board of the victim has to recommend the merger in unequivocal terms to its shareholders or there will be no deal. Why should board and management agree to lose their independence and perhaps even their jobs?

The answer is simple. By courtesy of our antitrust laws, most mergers involve corporations in different fields of activity. This means that the management of the aggressor company is not really familiar with the victim's business, so somebody who has the necessary knowhow will have to run the new business for the aggressor. Since the management of Superior Drugs knows next to nothing about the commercial exploitation of death, the managers of Heavenly Rest will be implored to stay on to run the new division of SDI.

The fact that there will be attractive jobs for the victim's key people will be made quite clear from the very outset of the merger discussions. These jobs may not last forever, but in the intensive wooing of the victim's management that precedes the merger, the negotiators for SDI are unlikely to dwell on this point.

Instead, they will develop attractive job packages for the managers of HRC to make certain that their invaluable talents will remain available after the merger has taken place. The generosity of these offers will, of course, be somewhat influenced by the knowledge that the chance of a merger becomes negligible if the victim's managers do not find these offers simply irresistible. For those who cannot or do not want to play with the new team, there will be generous settlements, in the guise of consulting fees, for instance.

These job packages may sometimes appear unnecessarily lavish and costly, but they are indispensable to the success of the merger. Compared to the amounts involved in the virtually free transfer of the assets of even a small company, the cost of the most exorbitant settlements for the top people of a victim is negligible.

It would be a nasty exaggeration to suggest that many mergers are arranged by the simple expedient of bribing the management of the victim. But the overwhelming importance of attractive personal arrangements for the people who decide whether a merger offer should be submitted to the shareholders of their company is rather obvious.

Thus the merger arranged by consenting boards seems to offer nothing but advantages. The two companies unite to form a larger and less vulnerable organization, earnings per share of the surviving company increase instantly, and everybody, from management to the lowliest shareholder, has a chance to make some capital gains. Well, almost everybody.

In fact, the beauty of the arrangement for instant growth and profit is marred by a few minor flaws. There is the problem of the people in the victim company who may lose their jobs as teams from the aggressor move in to streamline operations and mold the organization in the preferred image of the new masters. The lucrative job offers that are such an important part of merger negotiations obviously cover only the top people, those involved in structuring the deal. This means officers and board members.

The rank and file will have to fend for themselves as the operations of the two companies are integrated: as deadwood is cut out, redundant departments are liquidated, functions are centralized, and new policies are established and enforced.

The need for these drastic actions is implicit in the nature of the merger. In our example, SDI is a high-growth corporation. HRC is not, and its more pedestrian performance provides the differential in price-earnings ratio that made the merger so attractive to start with. Yet after the generation of instant profits from the merger between fast grower and dull victim, the victim can remain dull no longer or it will compromise the future growth of the surviving corporation. Its activities have to be stepped up to match, as far as possible, the pace of the rest of the organization.

Every effort must be made to improve the profitability of the new acquisition and to convert it from mediocrity to a state of dynamic progress. Unfortunately, these efforts do not always succeed, no matter what methods are employed. More mergers may then become necessary to hide the resulting slump in profits.

This is precisely why mergers tend to be addictive. The growth corporation that merges with less glamorous victims to produce instant earnings-per-share increases is almost compelled to keep on merging or it will lose its reputation for fast growth. And when this is lost, its price-earnings ratio may decline. Merger opportunities then become more scarce and less profitable, and the corporation may, in due time, even become a potential merger victim itself.

There is also a point of some slight importance to the shareholders of companies about to become merger victims. The windfall profits that accrue to the surviving company as a result of the merger are not an act of God. The money must come from somewhere. The instant profit is, in fact, paid for by the former owners of the victim.

In our example, the owners of HRC received one SDI share for every five HRC shares. Before the merger, HRC earned $1 per share. SDI earnings immediately after the merger were $2.50 per share. Since five shares of HRC were swapped for one SDI share, earnings per original HRC share have dropped by half.

Also, before the merger, the owner of 100 shares of HRC received a dividend check of $50. After exchanging the 100 shares for 20 shares of SDI, the shareholder receives a dividend of $8 if SDI maintains its distribution of 40 cents per share. Still, the former owners of HRC are lucky. As a fast grower, SDI might not have paid any dividends at all and reinvested all its earnings. In that case, the former owners of HRC would have lost their dividend income altogether.

Yet sharcholders never seem to consider this particular aspect of mergers. All they see is the chance of capital gains once they have exchanged their stock in a lackluster company for shares in a high-growth outfit. Greed and hope spring forever from the breast of the stock market player.

Going Multinational

The word "multinational" has acquired an almost sinister meaning. It has come to imply international corporate power defying almost any form of outside control in its pursuit of profits on a worldwide scale. It evokes the image of large corporations exploiting their vast resources to dominate foreign markets, in the process destroying competitors and competition, exporting jobs, evading taxes, speculating in currencies, and even tinkering with the economic and political structures of their host countries to reach their objectives.

The last twenty years have seen a large growth in multinational activities. However, the invasion of foreign markets on

a broad front has not been the exclusive domain of large corporations. It has also involved many medium-sized and even relatively small companies not normally thought of as big, bad
multinationals. This urge to build corporate colonial empires
has been the result of certain economic conditions, which
endow multinational operations with certain particular advantages. These advantages have resulted in a rapid international
sprawl of corporate activities.

Multinational activities as such are not necessarily new.
Some major corporations established operations in foreign
countries long before the recent wave of colonialism was
launched and long before multinational became a word with
unpleasant connotations. The original purpose of moving production plants overseas was primarily the exploitation of knowhow and products in markets that were not readily accessible
to imports because of the nature of the products or because of
the penalties imposed by shipping costs and import duties.
Moreover, foreign production often provided the advantage of
lower cost of labor and/or materials.

In many cases, the most important advantage of foreign production was the ability to adapt products and operating methods to local conditions. This enabled the foreign subsidiary to
meet competition effectively on its home ground while still
retaining the benefits of being part of a larger foreign-based
organization. The local operation was familiar with local conditions and could work within the market rather than from the
outside. And products could be designed specifically for the
local market requirements, which might be quite different from
the market needs back home.

The necessary product modifications might be minor changes
in style or packaging or major ones, to the extent that the
overseas product might have very little in common with its
domestic counterpart. An extreme example of the latter is
found in automobile production. The European subsidiaries of

the large U.S. car makers produce models that have little if anything in common with the tried and true cars sold in the United States. In countries where automobile taxes are high, gasoline is very costly and road systems may not be as fully developed as in the United States, and where the standard of living was, until recently, considerably lower than in the States, the market for American-size cars was bound to be limited. For this reason, the European plants of General Motors, Ford, and Chrysler have produced cars with characteristics that appeal to the European market. They have not exported jobs but created new products to conquer markets which could not have been reached with domestic models, whether imported or made locally.

The same principle applies to many other product areas. What sells like hotcakes in the United States does not necessarily sell in Europe or in the Far East. Thus, the detergent manufacturers have created their own special formulas for local markets. The name of the product may be the same, but its composition reflects local usage as well as differences in the local cost of raw materials. If the Dutch housewife likes to soak her laundry overnight, she obviously needs a different detergent than the German homemaker, who feels her laundry could not possibly be clean unless it has been boiled.

Furthermore, successful multinationals have managed to blend their domestic knowhow and experience with the operating requirements in foreign markets. The ability to adapt to widely varying business conditions has given the multinational corporations a broad outlook and the ability to handle problems on an international basis that mere national companies may find hard to match.

But while the original mainspring of colonial expansion was access to foreign markets that could not be developed through exports of domestic products, it was soon realized that foreign development also offers opportunities for rapid corporate growth when expansion of domestic operations becomes difficult.

A corporation may reach the stage where significant growth in market shares on the home front becomes awkward. At the same time, its importance may be such that growth through merger in the same field is inhibited by antitrust laws. It is condemned to what may be only slow, creeping growth, which may not be acceptable to corporate management. The company can diversify, but acquisitions in other fields may not show the same attractive profits, nor will they provide a broader base for exploiting the results of new product development in the main field of activity. The company is thus prevented from rapid growth in its primary field as long as its activities are confined to the domestic market.

But there is nothing to prevent the company from expansion overseas. It is free to buy up competitors in twenty foreign countries in a move that may ultimately double its size and profits. For this reason, multinational expansion can be an important tool for by-passing antitrust laws and overcoming limitations that would prevent rapid growth at home. This fact has no doubt been a major cause in the rush to go multinational.

By invading foreign markets, multinationals have often brought about important changes in the business environment of the host countries. They may have introduced aggressive marketing in fields where competitors had been comfortably dozing under cartel agreements, with fixed prices and sales quotas that permitted everyone to make a comfortable living. The intruders swept away the cobwebs with new ideas, new knowhow, and new practices, backed by the resources of their parent companies. They established important and even dominant positions in many business areas the world over. And wherever they set up their colonies, they tended to change the rules of the game. Local competitors had to play by the new rules, except where governments managed to stem the tide of the invasion by restrictive measures to protect the home-grown companies.

All this does not make multinational companies very popular, because the impact of their resources and methods has often jeopardized the fortunes, or even the continued existence, of their mononational competitors. In the battle for a local market, the subsidiary of a multinational corporation enjoys obvious advantages over its local adversaries. It can draw on the resources of the parent company, both financial and technical. It can obtain subsidies from other parts of the organization to cover temporary losses incurred while it builds up its market position or weathers a temporary storm. It can borrow money more easily and perhaps on better terms because its loans can be guaranteed by the parent corporation. It can draw on the parent's pool of expertise and personnel. And the parent corporation can spend more money on product development because its foreign subsidiaries provide a broader basis to recover the investment.

The purely national competitor who operates within a more limited market may not be able to match resources with the local subsidiary of the multinational against which he has to compete. In fact, the national company has little room to maneuver. It works in one market, and its economics are determined by the costs, taxes, regulations, and market conditions of one country. The multinational is not tied to any particular country, and it can take advantage of the differences in costs, tariffs, taxes, and government regulations that exist between the different countries in which it operates. These differences permit all sorts of sophisticated games for maximizing profits.

A corporation may have a product for which there is a large market in Ruritania, which is far away and has high import duties, but local cost levels are low. A manufacturing plant in Ruritania would thus offer obvious benefits. The product can be produced cheaply for the local market, and shipping charges and import duties are conveniently eliminated. Moreover, since production cost is low, part of the output of the local plant can be exported to other countries where manufacturing costs are higher. Unfortunately, these advantages are largely offset by the fact that Ruritania has confiscatory taxes on profits. There is little point in establishing a very profitable plant if the bulk of the profit goes to the local government.

The local competitors are stuck with this tax, and their prices have to be set accordingly. But the multinational can structure the Ruritanian subsidiary in such a manner that the tax bite will be sharply reduced. There are a number of ways to do this. The principle behind them is to move profits to countries with low taxation in one of a variety of ways.

To start with, the Ruritanian subsidiary may have to pay a royalty to the parent company for the use of its product technology. This technology has been developed at great cost, and it is only reasonable that the subsidiary pay some sort of a license fee in return for the use of products, patents, and know-how. The local government may limit the amount of profit that can be exported in the guise of royalties, but the local management of the company is unlikely to object to the terms of the license agreement. And even just a few per cent in royalties on net sales will help to reduce unwanted local profits.

If this is not sufficient, there are other ways to skin the cat. A crucial part of the product made in Ruritania can be made elsewhere. The parent corporation then sells this part to its subsidiary in Ruritania at an inflated price. Even though this part could be made much more cheaply in Ruritania or perhaps even be bought on the open market at half the cost, it is bought from the parent company to remove profits from the grasp of the Ruritanian tax collector.

Undesirable local profits can also be extracted through export activities. The local plant sells finished goods at carefully set prices to another part of the corporation. These products are then resold, perhaps at an exaggerated profit in other markets, which permits the parent company to accumulate profits outside Ruritania. There may also be management agreements under which the local subsidiary pays a retainer for important management services to a headquarters company located in another country. The permutations of such schemes are almost infinite. And since the Ruritanian company is a wholly-owned subsidiary, the parent company can control local profits to minimize overall taxation. The local competitor does not have this option. He pays the tax in full.

These examples are obviously crude and simplified, but they show how a multinational corporation can move its profits to the most convenient locations. But the flexibility of multinational operations is not just a matter of shifting profits between countries to ease the tax load. The multinational corporation can also move production plants and service establishments to keep pace with changing economic conditions. It has the means and the knowledge to change its structure to follow cost and market trends. It can produce in Africa, sell in South America, and collect profits in Ireland — or wherever else it may choose.

Nor are its activities tied to any one particular currency. Of course, its books will be kept in one currency at headquarters, but it can hedge against currency fluctuations on a worldwide basis. It can speculate against the pound this week, move into Swiss francs next Tuesday, and hedge against the dollar the day after. Nobody knows to what extent the currency games of large multinationals contribute to monetary instability. Yet whatever deplorable results corporate currency speculation may produce, the corporate treasurers are merely acting in the best interests of the shareholders in protecting the assets of their corporations.

As a result of these advantages of multinational operations, there has been a subtle shift in emphasis. Multinational development is no longer a matter of setting up local operations to exploit products and knowhow of the parent company in foreign markets. It has increasingly become a tool for exploiting the benefits of multinationalism as such. Many corporations seek foreign acquisitions with existing products and competent management — going and profitable concerns — rather than companies to serve as bases for implanting the products of the parent company in foreign markets. Multinational expansion thus becomes less an extension of domestic activities into new geographic areas than another facet of growth through diversification with the added advantages that accrue from the games that can be played by an organization that stretches across many frontiers.

The changing focus in foreign acquisitions has been accompanied by a shift in management techniques. As long as foreign colonies were set up to exploit essentially domestic products and knowhow, it was only natural to send experts from the home office to run the new outposts. People who had won their spurs running similar operations in North Carolina or Iowa were given a crash course in the local language and then sent off to get things organized and to instill growth and profitability in the foreign venture. This method is still being used by the less sophisticated and by those who have no other choice, but it is not very satisfactory.

All too often the highly competent executives sent out to govern the new colonies have discovered that strange things happen when they try to mold the foreign company in the image of a successful operation back home. Methods that were a great success on the domestic scene may utterly fail to produce the expected results. Local people may seem to react quite irrationally to the incentives and rules that work like a charm back home. Local laws may prevent the dismissal of redundant people unless large indemnities are paid. Unions may wield large political power and prove remarkably difficult to deal with. Competitors and customers may look with horror and revulsion on seemingly normal business procedures. And local laws may appear bizarre and cause unexpected obstacles.

Engulfed in these unexpected problems, the exported manager still has to produce results or he will be shipped home in disgrace. And in addition there may be considerable personal frustrations involved in relocating to a strange country. As a result, the seeming glamour of a job in the corporate colonies can turn into a nightmare, even with increased status, high pay, cost-of-living allowance, overseas bonus, home leave, and attractive personal tax arrangements.

There is also the problem of the future. It is not worthwhile to send a senior manager abroad unless he is willing to stay for a while. To move him back after two years would probably be a terrible waste of his new experience, but if he stays too long he will find it difficult to get back into the mainstream of things back home. After five years in the colonies, he will find that the organization has changed, current thinking at the seat of power may no longer be familiar to him, and the restraints of the home office may be hard to take after years of considerable independence abroad.

And if the executive stays away from home much longer, he may not be able to return at all. He may have gone largely native and adopted local habits, becoming almost useless if brought back to the domestic organization.

These problems involved in sending domestic people overseas have had a considerable effect on management methods. Smart multinationals discovered that qualified domestic managers with foreign backgrounds found it easier to adjust to overseas assignments. At least they might speak the colonial language and have some knowledge of local customs. Thus started a minor brain drain in reverse as naturalized Americans were sent back to their countries of origin, and pretty soon a considerable number of American managers on overseas assignments spoke English with faint accents and the local language without a flaw. But the supply of foreign-born U.S. managers, or managers with foreign background or French wives, was somewhat limited. And since the native-born American manager encountered all sorts of problems overseas, a better solution to the problem of governing foreign colonies had to be found.

The answer was to train foreign managers in U.S. business practices so that the colonies could be run as much as possible by local personnel. Replacing American managers by local talent offered many advantages. Local managers were familiar with local conditions, language, and customs, tended to camouflage the foreign ownership of the local company, and were often less expensive. They did not need overseas allowances, cost-of-living adjustments, and home leave. And they did not have to be repatriated after a few years, or even after a few months, because they had had enough or because their families could not take it any longer.

As a result, control of local operations shifted increasingly to local people, reporting perhaps to a few temporary expatriates at a regional headquarters. But as the development of local talent progressed and management techniques became more formalized, the need for stationing people from the home country at overseas posts gradually diminished. Local managers took over, not only in their own countries, but sometimes in other countries and perhaps even at corporate headquarters. The management of multinational corporations can become multinational too.

Once appropriate management systems have been installed, even newcomers to the corporation can be rapidly taught to manage by the system. Any reasonably intelligent foreigner who understands English can learn, in a matter of weeks or months, how to deal with the parent company and grasp the incentives and penalties built into the system. And as long as he produces the ordained profits, he will enjoy a large amount of autonomy. Regular reports fed into the home office computer and periodic flying visits by emissaries from headquarters then suffice to keep the foreign operation on the straight and narrow.

All this has produced certain changes in the foreign acquisition objectives of multinational corporations. Companies with development potential but poor earnings or mediocre management are no longer in particular demand as bases for the application of American management and technical knowhow. These days, corporations tend to look for companies with good profits and competent management, preferably to be acquired at a reasonable price-earnings ratio. The important thing is that management stay on, learn the corporate system, and run the company for the new masters. The sale of his company may make the owner-manager a millionaire, but the buyer still wants him to stay on and become an executive, at least until some bright young talent can be developed to take over.

So the new trend in multinational operations is no longer the export of management techniques and product knowhow. The objective is now to acquire going concerns to enlarge the size of the parent corporation.

Growth from Within

Compared to the instant leaps to larger size produced by corporate cannibalism, growth from within may seem like a plodding, pedestrian form of progress. Yet the month-by-month growth achieved in the continuous struggle for improvement is an essential ingredient in any corporate growth strategy.

For the corporation which cannot or does not want to grow by merger and acquisition, growth from within is the only way to achieve the increase in size necessary to cope with the ravages of inflationary profit squeezes and the perils of competition by escalating resources.

But even for the quick-growth, merger-mad corporation, growth from within is important, not only to fill the gaps between profitable acquisitions, but also to exploit the potential of new acquisitions. Diversification by merger often provides a springboard for renewed growth from within when the scope for growth in the original field of activity begins to diminish. Having made the move into a promising new business area, the opportunities for further growth must be taken advantage of.

Moreover, mergers often involve victims that were not doing too well. Acquiring an ailing company by merger may produce attractive instant increases in earnings per share, but the transaction becomes unattractive if the ailments persist after the merger. The profitability of the victim has to be brought into line or the shortcomings of the new activity will drag down the stock price of the surviving corporation. And apart from structural changes and cost reduction programs, rapid growth from within may be necessary to turn the acquisition into an asset rather than a liability.

Growth from within is thus an important factor in the development of a corporation's activities. However, growth alone is of dubious value if it does not yield adequate profits. Bootstrap growth will not create great delight among shareholders or be conducive to management longevity if earnings diminish or evaporate in the process. The pursuit of growth thus requires a certain degree of judgment and circumspection and may involve compromises between growth rates and profits that have to be carefully weighed.

The implementation of a strategy for growth from within depends on the concerted efforts of all parts of the organization. Resources must be brought to bear where they will do the most good, products and market situations have to be carefully analyzed, and the overall effort focused on the most promising opportunities. And whatever detailed plan for the growth effort is adopted, its success will depend on the corporation's ability to enlarge its markets.

This market enlargement can come from only three sources. First of all, there is the growth of the market itself. The market may expand because entirely new products have been introduced that did not exist before, because customers are changing their buying habits, or as a result of increases in prosperity and population. Expanding markets may provide important opportunities and justify investment in large-scale promotion to exploit rapid market growth. Other markets may show small growth and provide just a trickle of new business, no matter how much money may be spent on promotion.

The second source of market enlargement is the creation of entirely new markets. Such markets may be created by selling products in geographic areas that have not been covered before, by adapting existing products to new uses, or by persuading customers to use products they have never used before.

However, the most important source of market expansion is the theft of market shares from competitors, or competition. Price cutting, the development of superior products, and stepped-up promotion are the main tools for taking away someone else's market shares. And all three of these methods require resources. Investment will be required to cut production costs, to design and tool up for new products, to finance heavy promotion, and perhaps even to subsidize losses incurred during a price war over market shares. And these investments must be worthwhile and show an acceptable return.

If existing markets are fragmented and there are many competitors in the field, a strong effort to capture a larger market share may be profitable. Smaller competitors can be outresourced, and with luck some of them may be driven from the field and their markets can be inherited. But if the market is dominated by just a handful of large companies, the return from price cutting, product improvement, and heavy promotion may be unattractive. In that case, money might be better spent on diversification into less crowded markets. If markets are young and expanding they will obviously offer a better scope for growth than if they are saturated and tired.

Then there are the problems of product emphasis. Is it worthwhile to battle for a larger market share for a major and profitable product, or should the resources be allocated to a new item, which may be tomorrow's winner? Should development efforts concentrate on replacements for obsolete existing products or on new fields that may open up entirely new markets?

These problems are difficult enough to resolve in a small company, where the choice of growth opportunities may not be wide. They become extremely complex in a large diversified corporation, where dozens of different markets and perhaps hundreds of product lines have to be considered. Obviously, the direction of growth from within cannot be left to chance and accident.

It is not enough to advise all hands that sales and earnings must increase by 12 per cent during the next calendar year. Nor is it practical to wait until the end of the year to see whether the growth objectives have been met. Growth from within, like any other corporate activity, has to be carefully planned and controlled. Once the plan has been established, compliance with the plan has to be monitored on a monthly or even weekly basis so that corrective action can be taken in time if any shortfalls develop.

This problem of focusing corporate growth in the most profitable directions, and of ensuring that these directions are pursued with zeal and diligence, has given rise to new management techniques. These techniques not only provide for detailed planning of growth objectives. They also extract growth and profit quotas from every nook and cranny of the corporate organization with the inevitability of a skillful Mafia extortion.

Usually known as "management by objectives," these techniques are quite effective and have been widely adopted. They involve mainly breaking down the organization into profit centers, delegating responsibility for results to the lowest practical level, and coordinating the activities of what may be hundreds of profit centers through detailed plans for each and every activity in the corporation. These plans are not imposed from above but worked out with the active participation of every manager down the line, and every manager then becomes responsible for fulfilling his particular profit quota. Progress and compliance with the plan are then monitored on a continuous basis so that any deviations can be corrected before they become major problems.

The system thus provides a framework of plans, procedures, quotas, incentives, and punishments which are highly effective as a means of attaining whatever growth objectives may have been established. Management by objectives has been developed into a compelling technique for running large and complex enterprises that could not be directed by traditional forms of organization. Moreover, the technique has removed to a large extent the bothersome problems and ambiguities of dealing with people. The new system deals not with people but with abstractions — numbers, targets, shortfalls, procedures, and formulas.

Unfortunately, in their more developed forms these management techniques, with their built-in compulsions for all levels of the organization, tend to become totalitarian. They become "management by soviet."

7. Management by Soviet

The Origins

Once upon a time, the American manager was a competent, hardworking man. His formal education may have been limited, and he may have acquired his experience by working his way up through the ranks of the organization. He may have been somewhat lacking in grace and culture, and he probably had a one-track mind, fixed permanently on business matters. In fact, the stereotype of the blunt businessman, interested in business and business alone, was the object of much derision. Yet with all these shortcomings, the American manager of yore had one supreme virtue. He really knew his business.

If he ran a fertilizer company, he did not need a committee to tell him when and where he should build a new plant or how much it would cost to build and operate. He needed no expensive market studies to find out how much plant food he could sell at what price and to whom. Nor did he need voluminous justification reports and group involvement to limit his exposure when major decisions had to be made. He knew what had to be done, and he was prepared to stake his job on his decisions.

Today, this kind of management has become obsolete. It has

been replaced by formalized management systems and a new breed of managers, skilled in manipulating the system rather than widely experienced in the specific activities of the corporation. Management has become a game of numbers, of quotas and plans, played by detailed rules and under almost irresistible incentives. The players have to master the system, but they no longer have to possess any particularly deep knowledge of production, marketing, or any other specialized area. Nor do they necessarily have to be intimately familiar with the products and operations of the corporation.

Professional managers can thus move with some facility from one company to another, from chewing gum to drugs or aerospace. The particular skill of these managers lies in working with management systems, in managing by the book and dealing with numbers. And of course they have to possess the political talent to advance within the system and to climb up through the organization chart.

Management by experts has thus been largely replaced by management systems and bureaucratic administration, which has opened the door to top-level jobs to gifted amateurs. Since practical experience is no longer indispensable, there is no longer any particular need to spend twenty years acquiring this experience. Bright young professional managers can do the job just as well or even better than grizzled old-timers.

This profound change in management practice is mainly the result of the increasing complexity and diversification of the modern corporation. As long as companies are of moderate size and operate only in a limited business area, the traditional manager has no particular problem in running the show. He understands what is going on and knows what has to be done. But when a corporation reaches a certain size and becomes diversified, expert knowledge in one or two fields is no longer sufficient.

A manager with thirty years of practical experience in all

phases of the fertilizer business is bound to have some trouble managing a corporation which makes not only fertilizer, but packaging materials, firearms, sporting goods, and heavy chemicals. The expert in pharmaceuticals will be at some loss to cope with cosmetics, candy, fast foods, and airline catering.

An exceptional manager will, of course, be able to master these complexities after a while. But exceptional men are hard to find, and their long experience in one particular field, acquired over many years, will be largely wasted when they move into a top job in a diversified company. Moreover, there is hardly time to wait until the expert in electronics finds his feet in consumer goods, textbooks, and clinical laboratories. The stock market–based incentives which determine the personal fortunes of management demand immediate results.

Since the effective management of large and diversified organizations has become too complicated even for highly experienced traditional managers, the function of management has to be simplified. It is therefore necessary to fragment the corporation into smaller components. To start with, a diversified corporation is subdivided into divisions. Each division operates in its own field of activity, almost as if it were a separate company.

But even a division can be too large and too complicated for effective management. It is thus broken down further into departments, sections, groups, and profit centers. Responsibility for profit and loss is then delegated down the line to the profit centers. The manager of even the lowliest profit center then becomes responsible for running his operation as if it were a separate small business, responsible to his superiors only for the final results.

With this arrangement, the corporation becomes in effect a holding company, with hundreds of small units operating more or less on their own, each unit being small enough to permit effective management. The advantage of this type of organization is obvious. The person closest to a particular operating problem becomes responsible for solving this problem. His business is small enough to permit effective control, and he is in a better position to deal with the problems of his profit center than an executive two or three levels higher up. The concept of the small business within the large corporation thus offers considerable attraction.

However, in a corporation with hundreds of profit centers some sort of coordination and control over the teeming masses of small business activities are obviously necessary. Not only will there have to be a certain standardization in the business methods employed throughout the corporation, but it is also desirable that each profit center apply its efforts in directions which are most beneficial to the corporation as a whole. This tends to put certain restraints on the freedom of each manager to pursue the activities of his particular organization as if he were an independent business. And these restraints can become rather narrow and bureaucratic.

There is also the problem of management quality. A senior manager can be chosen with care, and if necessary given extensive grooming, to make certain he will fill the requirements of his exalted position. Training hundreds of managers for individual profit centers is a different matter. They have to be trained quickly and adequately, and no matter how many seminars they attend, this training can never be thorough enough to enable them to cope with all possible problems.

It therefore becomes necessary to condense whatever may be considered good management practice into a form that can readily be absorbed by reasonably skilled or even semiskilled managers so that they may perform their functions to the satisfaction of their masters. And finally, each manager, no matter how low his station in the corporate pyramid, must have powerful incentives to succeed in his job so the corporation may gather the maximum earnings from each profit center.

All this has led to the development of unusual organization structures, operating methods, and coercive systems to extort the last nickel of profit from every corner of what may be a complex diversified organization. These new techniques are usually called management by objectives because each manager, be he in charge of a multimillion-dollar division or a minuscule profit center, is given specific objectives against which his performance is continuously measured.

However, management by objectives has a tendency to degenerate into management by soviet for three reasons.

First, some of its techniques bear a striking similarity to the Russian model, with five-year plans, profit quotas, and faceless bureaucrats second-guessing the operating managers, and often a yawning gap between the unlimited responsibility of the manager and the very limited authority he is given.

Second, the need for protection from exposure to danger compels each manager to involve those around him in all major decisions, and this means that committees, or soviets, are created at all levels of the organization.

Finally, the coercions of the system are almost irresistible. The manager meets his quota or else. He is under an almost totalitarian compulsion.

As management fashions go, these methods, which were originally evolved for large and diversified organizations, are spreading. Management by numbers and by system is easier, requires less experience, and can be taught to semiskilled managers at a fraction of the cost and time needed to develop old-fashioned managerial skills. And as the philosophy of management by soviet filters down the line from the top corporate levels, traditional managers are gradually being replaced even in the lower tiers of the organization. Their places are being taken by sharp young systems manipulators with their own operating codes.

The Principle

Decentralization, delegation of responsibility, detailed planning, controls, and compelling incentives are necessary to run any large and diversified business organization. When the complexity of a task exceeds the limits of human capability, the task has to be split into smaller parts, and some mechanism to coordinate the activities of the parts has to be established.

However, after a while the functions of organizing and coordinating tend to assume a life of their own, and what started out as a perfectly reasonable concept can be carried to unreasonable excess. This is what often happens to management by objectives.

Once authority is delegated downward, some method to hold together what would otherwise be a fragmented organization becomes necessary. Disparate activities have to be directed to yield maximum benefits for the whole organization. This means plans, controls, incentives, and standardization of business procedures. Management practice has to be formalized to eliminate as much as possible the problems of human frailty and insufficiency even at the lowest managerial levels. And once the best management procedures have been reduced to detailed and easy-to-use handbooks, management is no longer an unreliable empirical art but an almost foolproof game of numbers. With proper standard procedures, almost anyone can become a reasonably efficient manager.

The advantages of the new management systems were so obvious that the new techniques swept like wildfire through the corporate world. No longer were corporations dependent on experienced managers who had the knack of getting things done through people and who could run complex organizations at the same time. Teaching bright people to manage by system was easier and less costly than finding people who knew the business and could cope with complicated organization structures.

This fact opened the way to the executive suite to anyone with political skill and the ability to understand procedure handbooks and read figures. Management by soviet can be handled by corporate lawyers, distinguished party members, political commissars, or young business school graduates, as the case may be. Eastern and Western methods of administration have become strikingly similar.

Once corporate managements understood the attractions of the new systems, someone had to work out the details. Sometimes this was done by underemployed staff people within the organization, who became experts in the new cult by attending seminars directed by promoters of the new technique. Management by soviet obviously appealed to staff people. Bureaucrats like to organize activities into orderly patterns and to set up formalized rules and procedures. They abhor the seeming disorder of case-by-case decisions, with all the human ambiguities that often cloud the issues.

Where staff people failed to jump in on their own, management consultants were happy to sell the new system, packaged to specific client requirements, and to help the people within the corporation to get the new method off to a good start. Either way, the originators often became important personages within the corporate organization. They became the experts, the high priests of the new religion. Their roles ranged from being missionaries of the new cult, converting the poor backward traditional managers, to deciding important questions of dogma and advising top management on what to do next. Properly played, these roles could lead to highly paid senior positions and to considerable influence behind the scenes.

Once these methods were installed, the nature of management changed and so did managers. The general-purpose professional manager can now handle almost any upper-level job.

The president of the corporation may well be a distinguished personality whose previous experience consisted in running an accounting group or a corporate legal department with thirty men, boys, and secretaries. At first glance, this may seem absurd. How is a man with this limited background going to run a billion-dollar corporation that employs twenty thousand people and makes a variety of sophisticated products?

Actually, the head of the legal office or the man in charge of the corporate financial staff may have a much broader view of the activities of the corporation than an experienced operating manager, whose previous experience may have been limited to one particular division of the corporation. He may not be closely familiar with production costs and market structures, but he may know a great deal about the problems of the corporation at the board level. And he may know exactly which closets contain what corporate skeletons. This knowledge can be most helpful in moving from a staff position to the top job. As far as detailed operating knowledge is concerned, he can always ask a specialist.

Moreover, under management by soviet, the president does not actually have to manage the corporation alone. In fact, he may do very little managing on his own. He will carefully avoid taking any major decisions in lonely agony. If he did, he would become vulnerable to criticism whenever a big mistake was made. For this reason, it is preferable to spread responsibility around, and this is why important decisions are usually taken collectively by what might be called the supreme soviet.

A soviet, in Russia, is a council or committee consisting of representatives drawn from various groups. A soviet takes joint decisions and also sends its own representatives to the next higher soviet in the organization.

In similar fashion, the president of a typical corporation will create his own soviet. This usually consists of a number of senior executives in charge of specific functions, such as production, marketing, finance, administration, and research.

These distinguished and usually expensive people do not run the corporation, nor do they actually manage the nitty-gritty activities in their special fields. Their function is to establish policies in these fields and to make certain that these policies are complied with. They also advise the president in matters concerning their particular area of expertise. However, their main purpose is usually to constitute the supreme soviet, which sets major corporate policies by group decision.

All this does not necessarily imply that the members of the supreme soviet are specialists in their chosen fields. But they have their own staffs of experts to fill in any gaps which may exist in their specialized knowledge. It is obvious that this concept can be expanded to the point where even the senior assistants of the functional specialists at the top level have more political acumen than deep knowledge of their alleged specialty.

The parallel to government organizations springs immediately to mind. Cabinet jobs are generally handed out to deserving politicians even though their background may in no particular way qualify them for the assignment. They run the show, but rely on underlings to whisper the pertinent answers and to prepare appropriate guidelines and position papers. Nor do assistant or deputy secretaries of government departments need to be experts. The political penetration of a major government department may be several layers deep. The same goes for certain corporate staff functions.

Group decisions at the level of the supreme soviet are of particular importance because corporate staff members are a likely source of candidates for the president's job. It is therefore essential that all members of this group be implicated in all major decisions. If a mistake is made, they will all share in the guilt. If the president is fired, no one can step forward to claim the throne with the argument that he knew all along the decision was stupid, and produce documentary evidence to prove his foresight.

This does not mean that the supreme soviet under the dynamic leadership of the president will boldly march in where angels fear to tread and display heroic decisiveness. The need for group consent and the potential danger of an opposition block disagreeing with the president will induce everybody to move with considerable circumspection. As a result, major decisions may take considerable time and when finally hammered out may be loaded with compromises to limit exposure of the group. Gone are the days when American corporations were renowned for their ability to reach sound decisions rapidly. Management by soviet can be a sluggish process when matters beyond the realm of standard procedure have to be dealt with.

While the supreme soviet deliberates on grand policies in what may be an atmosphere laden with internal power politics, and while corporate staffs develop and enforce their directives, someone has to get on with the job of making a profit. This not unimportant task is performed by an operating organization directed by line managers responsible for producing their preordained profit quotas. At first glance, this part of the organization looks very much like the traditional corporate command structure, but there are several important differences.

The old-fashioned corporation was organized more or less along military lines. Executives reported to their superiors, just as lieutenants report to captains, captains to majors, and so on. Orders were passed down the line, reports percolated upward, and the final responsibility for results rested with the top man. The performance of the managers or officers down the line was then judged mainly on the basis of whether or not they executed orders from above with efficiency and dispatch.

Management by soviet is different. Responsibility for results is no longer concentrated at the top. Managers become responsible, not for carrying out orders, but for attaining results. But while the line manager has unlimited responsibility for results, his authority may be quite limited. But responsibility without corresponding authority can be very frustrating.

Quotas and Five-Year Plans

The life of the operating manager revolves around his quotas, the debt he owes the corporation in terms of profits. Of course, they are never called quotas. They are referred to by polite euphemisms like "objectives," or "profit commitments." But whatever they may be called, they define the specific profits which must be reached, or better yet, exceeded, by each part of the organization if the manager wants to hold on to his job.

Profit quotas are worked out on an annual basis. Every year the whole corporation goes through the lengthy ritual of preparing a new five-year plan. This reflects the latest estimates of market conditions, costs, investment opportunities, and expected profit for each profit center. But the plan also reflects the profit levels which corporate management considers necessary to the overall corporate strategy.

Since the five-year plan is revised every year, there is some room to maneuver, at least as far as the long term is concerned. But the first year of the plan represents the operating budget for the coming year, and this must be met no matter what happens.

The five-year plan is usually called the forward plan. The origin of this particular cliché is somewhat obscure, and its meaning is not particularly striking. Neither backward nor lateral plans would make much sense, since a plan usually applies to some future rather than a present activity. It must be assumed that the expression is the result of the usual bureaucratic tendency to coin pompous words for quite simple and straightforward activities.

The similarity to the five-year plans of Russian origin is

obvious. The main difference is that the American forward plan is based on profits while the Russian model deals with production quantities of boots, fertilizer, or caviar. Also, the American plan is updated every year and is thus more flexible than Russian planning practice.

In either case the problem of guessing what the future may bring during the later stages of the plan remains the same. How can a line manager who is preparing his piece of the plan in 1977 foresee what economic conditions, technical changes, and opportunities might prevail in 1982? Lacking a reliable crystal ball, he has to guess and hope for the best.

The preparation of the forward plan each year involves reams of figures on sales, costs, investments, personnel requirements, and profits for each of the next five years. This amounts to making complex guesses in great detail and then working out precisely what the ultimate result of these guesses might be. It can be argued that adding up thousands of individual guesses is not necessarily more reliable than taking a deep breath and making a global estimate of the overall results.

But there are actually two very compelling reasons for developing the forward plan step by step, profit center by profit center. For one thing, the fact that the plan has been compiled from hundreds, or even thousands, of individual forecasts and hopeful thoughts lends it an air of precision and respectability which a simple overall guess would never attain. More important, the compilation of the grand plan from large numbers of individual estimates means that every manager, down to the last tiny profit center, is implicated. The manager made his own forecast and now he has to meet his own forecast. The plan has grown from the grass roots upward. Nobody can claim that the plan is not realistic or unduly harsh since every manager has contributed his little piece of personal forecasting to the amazing structure. This is collective responsibility at its best.

Nevertheless, the problem of predicting the future, not for

next week or next year but five years ahead, remains. This problem is illustrated by the following incident.

A large corporation had decided to adopt the forward plan concept to keep up with fashionable management practice. A hitherto obscure staff man was appointed as the roving apostle. He became Mr. Forward Plan and traveled widely to indoctrinate every part of the organization, down to the last colonial outpost, in the blessings of the new method. Wherever he showed up, all management activities were suspended for a day to let the managers soak up the new wisdom. Everyone was marched into the conference room, and Mr. Forward Plan explained the new intellectual breakthrough with kindly condescension. The presentation was largely inspirational and worded in simple terms so that even the most backward manager would appreciate the merits of the new path to profit and happiness. Practical matters were pretty much glossed over, but grandiose clichés and impressive buzzwords were trotted out in profusion. The conferences were not exactly revival meetings, but they came fairly close.

Then an awful thing happened. Over lunch a manager wanted to know how he could possibly forecast sales and profits even three years in advance since existing products were becoming obsolescent and there were no new products in the development pipeline.

The reply was classical in its simplicity. Mr. Forward Plan suggested that this case clearly called for acquisitions, either of products or of companies. Since corporate policy specified a net return of 15 per cent on all investments, the manager simply had to assume that the holes in his plan would be plugged with investments of an as yet unknown nature which would yield 15 per cent. All he had to produce was an estimate of how much corporate money he required to attain the necessary profits; that would be the missing link in his forward plan.

By now, other managers had woken up from the pleasant

euphoria engendered by the inspirational speech and the luxury lunch. An argument developed, and finally a small concession was wrung from the planning expert. It was agreed that forecasts based on new acquisitions, or as yet undefined new products, would not be binding to the same degree as forecasts based on the expansion of existing business. In other words, hopeful pipe dreams could be marked as such and did not represent a firm commitment.

Alas, this fine distinction was soon lost in the shuffle. The planning expert moved on to better things, and his verbal concession went unremembered except in the minds of the suffering managers. A plan is a plan, and the corporation expects everybody to meet his personal profit commitments.

But the plan does not consist only of the sum of all the guesses and wishful thoughts of the managers down the line. There are also inputs from above. If the plan, as originally compiled, does not meet the desires of top management, this fact will be conveyed in no uncertain terms to the masses who toil in the nether reaches of the corporation. And that is where the squeeze comes in.

The manager of a small foreign subsidiary of a large corporation was faced with a serious but not atypical dilemma. His business was in a rapidly shrinking market, and the only thing that had so far prevented disaster was substantial exports to Poland. If these sales continued, which was by no means certain, business would be adequate, but there would be no growth. And if they did not, which was about equally probable, the situation would become dire since the small company had no other products of any importance.

A plan based on receding sales and the possible ultimate extinction of the subsidiary was obviously not acceptable to the parent corporation. The solution was to forecast large sales to Russia during the later years of the plan to fill what would otherwise have been a most unsightly gap in sales and profits.

Since no equipment had ever been sold to Russia before, and since the Russians had never shown the slightest interest in buying this equipment, the forecast of large future sales was nothing but wishful thinking. However, it kept headquarters quite happy and bought time for the management of the subsidiary. Perhaps a miracle would happen; the Russians might buy some equipment after all, or perhaps some other market could be developed later on. Whatever happened, the optimistic forecast gave local management time to look for other jobs if it became obvious in a couple of years that the plan could not be met.

Apart from the problem of predicting future events, the forward plan involves a staggering amount of work. Each operating unit has to work out not only detailed forecasts, but also explanations, strategy definitions, and justifications for whatever course of action it proposes. Meetings have to be held to coordinate this effort, first within the unit preparing the plan, and then with higher levels of management.

As the plan takes shape, there may be lengthy hassles and interdepartmental negotiations until the plan for a particular operation is deemed satisfactory and is transmitted to the next higher level. By an extended process of coordination and negotiation, the plan slowly works its way up the line until it is finally submitted to the supreme soviet. All this takes time and a great deal of management effort. The preparation of the plan may start in the spring and finally be approved late in the fall. The cost of preparing an exhaustive forward plan can be very large in terms of managerial time.

But the plan usually does not progress smoothly from level to level inside the corporation. Parts of the plan may be sent back down the line for improvement if they do not appeal to the higher echelons. And if the overall plan, gleaned from hundreds of sources and assembled piece by piece, is not satisfactory to top management, further negotiations may follow, and certain changes may have to be imposed. These changes then have to be incorporated at various levels of the organization — estimates must be revised, figures fudged, assumptions shaded, situations reappraised — until finally a plan acceptable to top management emerges.

This plan is then duly approved and becomes the law until a new plan is adopted twelve months later. During the interval, the plan will govern all actions of the corporation, from headquarters policy to the employment of janitors and messenger boys. Everything is settled, and there is a brief respite until the next plan has to be developed a few months later.

As far as operating managers in the corporation are concerned, there are two basic planning strategies. The choice between these two strategies depends on whether a productive operation or a service department is involved.

Service departments may be essential, but they do not generate profits. Their contribution to the plan is limited to expenses. And these expenses are bound to escalate from year to year to provide for the increases in activity and personnel inherent in any bureaucratic organization. Also, overstating the expected cost provides a hedge against cutbacks that might be imposed from above. Needless to say, the next higher management echelon will be tempted to add to the contingency factors of the lower service cost centers. The cumulative safety factors built into service department budgets may thus provide a substantial cushion.

This procedure, which is not uncommon to organizations devoted to spending other people's money, like military establishments, government agencies, and welfare organizations, means that annual expenditures are subject to automatic escalation. And once the money has been allocated it will have to be spent. If expenditures do not reach the forecast level, it will become obvious that the budget was set too high, and there is the danger of cutbacks the next time around.

The problem of the operating manager is different. His plan

is made in terms of profits rather than expenses. If he submits an overly optimistic plan he may be an instant hero, but he will be in trouble later on if he fails to meet his objectives. Prudence would thus recommend the submission of a conservative plan with profit quotas which can be attained without undue difficulty.

Unfortunately, top management generally does not cherish conservative plans. Headquarters wants to see dynamic growth, which will be reflected in increasing profits and price-earnings ratios. The operating executive will therefore be encouraged to set himself more challenging goals and to submit a good rather than a safe plan.

This line of argument can be very persuasive. If the manager yields to pressure from above and later fails to meet his targets, that will be his own personal problem. The people who talked him into inflating his profit objectives will not share the blame.

On the other hand, the line manager who proves obstinate in the face of pressure for higher profit targets obviously lacks the proper frame of mind. If he cannot get the right results with all the means the corporation places at his disposal, there must be something wrong with him. His superiors may well begin to doubt his ability and start looking around for someone who can do the job in a more satisfactory manner.

There are some unusual ways to cope with this dilemma. One particularly gifted manager submitted an outrageously optimistic plan and immediately started to build a large team to accomplish the great things which had never been done before. His dynamic approach so impressed headquarters that he was promoted to a vice presidency. The rest was easy. As the disastrous results rolled in, he blamed his successors for their dismal failure to meet his rosy plan. Heads rolled, but the reputation of our hero remained almost untarnished. It took another six years before corporate management finally got wise and told him to go play somewhere else.

Clearly, such an approach to planning requires great skill, audacity, superb timing, and a good deal of luck. The less gifted manager has to live with his problem and try to make the best of it. Like his Russian counterpart, he may try to underbudget if at all possible. If he is too cautious, he may lose because his plans are too pessimistic; if he errs in the other direction, he will be in trouble when he fails to meet his quota.

Corporate life can be hell.

Collecting the Rent

Once the forward plan has been established, management becomes as simple as collecting the rent on a piece of slum property. The task is merely to make sure that everyone pays what he is supposed to, or else.

From the top down, every level of management sees to it that all subordinates comply with the plan and deliver the agreed-upon profits. The commitment to profit is total, and the methods to enforce compliance tend toward the totalitarian. Woe be it unto him who fails to produce his proper contribution to the prosperity of the corporation.

The ultimate results of the collective effort to meet planned profit quotas will become evident when the books of the company are closed after the end of the year. However, by that time it will be much too late to correct any shortcomings. It is thus essential to keep close track of operating results throughout the year so laggards can be smartly pushed back into line.

For this reason, the performance of each and every profit center has to be reported and analyzed continuously throughout the year so as to catch as early as possible any tendency to fall behind. Remedial action can then be taken in time to ensure that overall profit objectives will be met at the end of the year. Detailed reports have to be submitted up the line on a monthly, or even weekly, basis. In their simplest form, these reports may show sales, manufacturing costs, operating expenses, and pre-tax profit. However, as reporting procedures become more refined, additional meaningful information may have to be included. As in any other bureaucratic organization, the refining of procedures is a continuing process as the headquarters staff develops needs for additional pertinent data.

As the system gathers momentum, there will be demands for such items as cash flow statements, analyses of sales by product, reports on order backlogs, receiveables, and personnel. Moreover, projections of earnings, sales, and various other interesting statistics may be required on a monthly basis.

All this information is extremely useful as a tool for judging the performance of each department, section, and profit center. Moreover, it compels the individual manager to watch his own operation closely, look out for dangerous trends, and become aware very early on of the need to change his course of action if results are not proving satisfactory. However, the collection and processing of all this information consumes a large amount of time and effort.

Corporate management is not very interested in historical information, produced two or three months after the event. It wants to know what is happening "at this point in time," as the bureaucrats like to put it. Progress reports must therefore be prepared and submitted within days of the end of the reporting period, or they will be of only limited practical value.

The need to produce comprehensive reports quickly can only be met if there are enough people to do the job. The preparation of a progress report can become a major activity. A small European subsidiary of a diversified U.S. corporation at one stage employed no less than seventeen people in its accounting department. Since total employment at the time was about sixty and only around a dozen workers were actually involved in manufacturing activities, the size of the accounting department was quite amazing. Yet all the accountants were very busy, mainly in producing reports.

In fact, the small company prepared close to three hundred progress reports of one kind or another during each year. There were monthly highlights, detailed monthly progress reports, even more detailed quarterly reports, and a variety of other documents, all of them reflecting refined reporting techniques designed for much larger operations.

Closer inspection revealed that not all of these reports were actually required by corporate headquarters. In fact, almost half of them were permutations of the headquarters reports for the use of local management. They were not strictly necessary, but the local executives felt that as long as the data had to be compiled anyway, they might just as well have the information converted into local currency, for their own purposes, too.

The cost of reporting procedures in this case was completely out of proportion to the size of the small company. Eventually the reports for local consumption were abolished, but all appeals to headquarters for relief of reporting requirements went unheeded. Although it was generally agreed that in this particular case the cost of reporting was ridiculous, there was simply no practical way to change the system.

This is obviously an extreme example, but the cost and waste involved in highly developed reporting procedures can be staggering. Yet these reports are indispensable tools for controlling the diversified activities of a major corporation.

Unfortunately, the cost of progress reports goes beyond the effort required to prepare the information and then consolidate it at the higher levels of the organization. Someone also has to read and process the reams of data so painstakingly compiled. This keeps considerable numbers of staff happily employed in making profound analyses and interpretations based on neat and logical figures rather than on the messy realities of actual business problems.

It also creates a terrible temptation for operating managers to work by numbers rather than through personal knowledge of what is going on. Numbers are easier to deal with than people and real-life problems, with all their annoying ambiguities. The availability of huge amounts of detailed numerical data keeps many a line manager safely ensconced in the comfort and dignity of his office when he should be out on the shop floor or in the field. It also opens operating management positions to people whose abilities lie more in the realm of data interpretation than in technical knowledge or managerial skill.

All this must be similar to Russian practice. However, we have made a major breakthrough in the exploitation of five-year plans and profit quotas as tools of bureaucratic administration. We use computers. And computers may be one of the worst things that ever happened to American management. Because they process large amounts of numerical information very rapidly, they play a dominant role in the formalized management-by-numbers game.

In modern business the computer has become indispensable in many functions, such as accounting, record keeping, payroll processing, inventory control, and production planning. It also permits the rapid processing of research data and the evaluation of complex mathematical models that otherwise might require years of human work.

But experts and computer salesmen were not slow to point out that computers could also be highly effective management tools. Thousands of lectures, seminars, and publications have extolled the wonderful things computers can do for managers. Yet in management's delight over instant access to huge amounts of information, there may be a slight tendency to overlook the basic limitations of the computer.

The computer works on numbers alone. It does not reason, except on a rudimentary programmed basis. Nor can it take into account the nonnumerical motivations of people which may cause market changes, labor problems, imperfect decisions, or clashes of interest. The computer is logical, man is not — at least not all of the time. Yet management, by definition, is the art of getting work done by imperfect, fallible, and sometimes emotional and illogical people.

This difference is sometimes forgotten as managers take decisions on the basis of numerical abstractions. The robot becomes the oracle for management decisions. Keeping the computer happy can become the ultimate goal in running the corporation.

The practical application of this philosophy is simple. The forward plan with all its ramifications is fed into the computer. As progress reports from every part of the organization arrive at headquarters, they, too, are fed into the computer for comparison with the plan. Information on shortfalls or negative variances may thus be on the desks of the headquarters staff even before the operating managers have had time to work out credible alibis. Searching questions flow down the line while staff bureaucrats at the head office express concern and sorrow over unsatisfactory performance. Since the afflicted manager will probably not be present to explain his side of the story, his reputation may easily become tarnished.

If the negative variance is substantial, things may become pretty hectic. There may be an unseemly scramble to identify scapegoats. Sharp reprimands and calls for immediate remedial action will flow down the lines of corporate communications while carefully phrased explanations percolate upward as everyone runs for cover.

The guilty manager will not fail to assure his superiors that corrective measures are being implemented at once. These measures often center on mass firings, euphemistically called cost improvements, and or any other actions that offer any promise of restoring compliance with profit quotas. At this point, the afflicted manager must be ruthless. Failure to collect the proper profit from subordinates is unforgivable. Reluctance to take drastic action, no matter what the reasons for the shortfall, merely shifts the problem to the next higher level of management. If that happens, the lenient manager may well find that he himself has now become the object of remedial action.

Being fired is something that happens to hundreds of managers every week all over the country. It is not nearly as unpleasant as being stood against a wall with a firing squad in attendance. Nor is it quite as unattractive as participating in one-way group travel to Siberia. Even so, it causes problems and is best avoided whenever possible.

This explains the considerable preoccupation with the avoidance of risk among corporate managers. This attitude fosters certain safety mechanisms, ranging from the technique of writing very careful memos for the record to limit possible risk exposure, to the proliferation of soviets at all levels of the organization to share the burden of important decisions. In the interest of personal security, these group decisions must not only implicate the peers and possible rivals of the manager, but preferably also his superiors.

The decisions reached by group consent within the appropriate soviet may waste a great deal of everybody's time. They may be neither particularly efficient nor particularly logical, nor reflect much in the way of courage or decisiveness. But they protect the individuals involved.

Security is a group decision.

Passing the Buck

Any totalitarian system has a tendency to sharpen the instinct for self-preservation. When survival becomes a matter of avoiding conflict with the system, people will adopt patterns of behavior that reduce the risk of such conflict.

Management by soviet is no exception to this rule. The dangers that stalk the unwary manager who fails to produce as

planned, or otherwise violates the rules of
cient to lead to a strong preoccupation w'
safety.

One important safety mechanism is ս.
responsibility downward through the organiza.
ager passes as large a part of his own responsibilities ս.
to his underlings, and each of them does likewise.

This delegation of responsibility may be worked out in considerable detail. Each manager may receive a formal document,
prepared with loving care by the head office staff and signed by
his superiors, which defines exactly the extent of his responsibilities. As a result, he knows exactly where he stands, what
his duties are, and how he is to conduct himself. His responsibilities will be as broad as circumstances permit and will cover
every aspect of his job.

Few managers complain that this system places too many
decisions into the hands of possibly less competent subordinates. On the contrary, they are usually delighted, since delegation implies a convenient supply of scapegoats. If the local
manager in Kalamazoo falls down on the job, it will not have
been the fault of the area manager in Chicago to whom he
reported.

There is another important aspect to delegation. The responsibility of the individual manager, as defined by his formal
charter of delegation, may be very broad. But his authority,
even within the limits of the forward plan, is much more narrow. An operating manager may have unlimited responsibility
for a multimillion-dollar division. Yet when he needs a new
piece of machinery worth $70,000, he may still require specific
approval from higher authority, even though the purchase of
this item was included in the forward plan. If an investment has
not been listed in the plan because its need was not foreseen, the
same manager may have to obtain head office approval if the
cost exceeds $10,000.

The limitation placed on the authority of line managers varies from company to company. But it is not unusual that in a billion-dollar corporation even the supreme soviet cannot approve an investment exceeding $100,000. Approval for larger investments must be obtained from the board. Since the board is probably infested and largely controlled by corporate officers, this referral may seem a pointless and time-consuming exercise. However, it complies with the overall system. It also protects the inside directors by implicating their outside colleagues in the decision.

Approval for major investments requires detailed written presentations to justify the transaction. The form of these capital appropriation requests is usually spelled out explicitly in the procedure books which govern all activities of the sovietized corporation.

The purchase of a new machine not included in the forward plan may require the submission of several pages of closely reasoned justifications. The proposal to build a new plant or to buy a small company may involve a whole book of exposition, statistics, market studies, forecasts, and profit projections. To stand any chance of success, the facts, figures, and explanations will have to prove conclusively that the recommended course of action is essential to the interests of the corporation and its shareholders.

The preparation of a request for investment money for a major project may keep half a dozen people busy for weeks and require countless meetings of various soviets. Some of these meetings may actually be necessary and fruitful, others serve mainly to enlist political support from various parties.

When the presentation is completed, the document is signed by the originator and sent up through the appropriate channels. If the project is modest in scope it may actually find its way to the desk of someone who has the authority to approve it.

More likely, the proposal will have to travel all the way to the head office for approval by top management. However, before submission to the supreme soviet, it will be scrutinized by various staff experts, any of whom may voice grave doubts, criticisms, and opinions. Since these lesser actors at the corporate court are in no way responsible for ultimate results, they have the opportunity for much innocent fun. Among themselves, the staff people may even succeed in killing the project simply by piling up enough doubts and objections to make a positive decision impossible. Or they may score enough points to make major changes necessary.

Once the staff has run out of profound comments and objections, the proposal can be submitted to the supreme soviet for approval or for referral to the board. At either level, the debate of the project offers much scope for political gamesmanship. The vice president for personnel may voice his concern over whether union problems have been given proper attention. He does not say they have not, but he wants to go on record in case labor problems arise. In the same spirit, the vice president for transportation and materials handling may chime in with reservations concerning his own specialty.

At that point the man in charge of corporate research may enthusiastically endorse the project even though it does not relate to his own field. He simply has a feeling that the president has already made up his mind — he likes the project, perhaps because the corporation needs some good publicity. This incursion upsets several members of the supreme soviet. Of course, they are not stupid enough to show their resentment or actually attack the project. But they produce more meaningful questions, suggest more areas that should perhaps be looked into more closely, and generally drag down the discussion. A deadlock threatens. The president could, of course, take a decision and settle the matter then and there, and maybe he does. But he may also be reluctant to march off alone in view of the lack of enthusiasm of most of his lieutenants.

At this point an ambitious young member of the group wonders casually whether the proposal is really in keeping with the latest in-depth study of the long-range objectives of the corporation. That does it. Everybody scurries for cover. Security is avoidance of risk exposure. And everyone will remember that young Charlie is somebody to be reckoned with. That, after all, was Charlie's intent when he deftly flashed his rapier.

The proposal then goes back to the originators for amendment in light of the very pertinent comments made by the various distinguished members of the supreme soviet. There is just a hint of a reproach because the people who originated the project obviously did not do all their homework. After some frantic revision and fudging of forecasts to make the proposal even more irresistible, the routine is repeated. This time there may be no more political points to be scored at headquarters meetings, and the project may finally be approved.

This scenario is, of course, an exaggeration. It fictionalizes what actually happened in one corporation, which is probably an exception. Most corporations are bound to handle appropriation requests in a more factual and efficient manner. Yet even so, management by delegation does not lend itself to particularly rapid decisions. Nor is there any guarantee that the decisions so laboriously arrived at will necessarily be sound.

Whatever happens, the involvement of all the high-priced help in the upper levels of the corporate hierarchy does not in any way absolve the originator of a project from guilt if things do not work out. In that case, the alibi at headquarters is simply that the originator grossly misled his superiors when he presented his proposal. In fact, the whole routine is specifically designed to absolve the upper ranks and corporate staff from any particular responsibility. All the impressive signatures on the authorization to proceed will not help the line manager when the project rolls over and dies.

The astute manager is fully aware of this problem and will

take his precautions before he commits himself to a project. He will identify the people who thought of the idea and have their original recommendations on record in his files. He will delegate the responsibility for preparing the proposal as far down as it will go. If disaster should occur, he too wants to be among those who were grievously misled.

And as the project gathers momentum, he will implicate as many people as possible. Not only his subordinates, but also his peers and superiors must become involved. He will carefully note any glimmer of opposition and devote much time to dealing with this opposition. Can it be ignored? Must it be negotiated away, perhaps by means of compromises affecting the project? Should the whole project be dropped to avoid political repercussions? To cope with these problems, the manager who originates a major project will seek as much help and comfort from his superiors as he can get. He may know exactly what ought to be done and how, but he certainly does not want to do it alone. The more people he can actively involve, the better he will sleep at night.

Before finally committing himself to the proposal, the manager will then have to weigh carefully the factual and political implications of the inevitable differences between his own views and those of his own entourage, his superiors and the headquarters staff, as well as the conclusions of the expensive market study he bought from a consultant who plays golf with the president. The result of these deliberations may well be a carefully balanced compromise to achieve minimum personal exposure on the part of the manager. The proposal for the new project will no longer reflect the personal views of the originator. It will be based on as broad a consensus as can be achieved to implicate as many people in the organization as possible. Any other course of action would be reckless.

The danger of becoming overly implicated in a new project

is not lost on those who may be reluctantly drawn into complicity in preparing the proposal. Many memos will be written to limit individual exposure, and many meetings will be held that are likely to abound with grandiose clichés and sophisticated double-talk, as everyone present hedges his bets and limits his risks.

If the project succeeds, there will be many to claim part of the credit for the great achievement. But at the slightest hint of failure, the proper role to assume is that of an innocent bystander or victim of fraudulent information.

Bureaucrats and Fads

To coordinate the activities of a far-flung corporate empire requires the services of a staff bureaucracy. Corporate staffs issue directives, draft position papers, monitor reports from operating managers, and generally provide for corporate law and order. All these functions are necessary, even though they may on occasion be carried to extremes. But the importance of the head office bureaucracy goes beyond these obvious functions. As we have noted, the staff people often play a role of considerable importance behind the scenes.

By definition, the perfect staff member is a self-effacing person who stays in the background and works quietly and efficiently for others. There is little glory in a staff job well done. Someone else stands in the limelight and collects the applause.

Yet the staff people are also human, and in the corporate environment of compelling motivations, they too tend to develop ambitions. These ambitions find various outlets.

There is the natural desire to enlarge activities and obtain a larger budget to hire more people. To attain these Parkinsonian objectives, staff people must put on display their unique abilities and their large contributions to the success of the corporation.

One way to do this is to search diligently for errors, omissions, policy violations, shortfalls on quotas, and failures to comply with standard procedures. And every time a diligent staff member succeeds in uncovering yet another misdemeanor or crime, he can let the world see what a great and essential job is being done.

Of course, not all staff people set out on conscious crusades against the faults of others, but the compulsions of the system in which they operate tend to push them in this direction. They then become the monitors of good behavior and the arbiters of proper attitudes, doing their part to keep everyone on the virtuous path of good performance and clean thinking. The Russian secret police apparently perform similar missions with similar objectives.

As a result, the staff is not always very popular with line managers, yet is treated with great care and respect. Staff people are often closer to the seat of power than managers, and they also tend to be carriers of popular opinion at headquarters. Their individual and collective thinking may influence their superiors in the supreme soviet, and their wrath may cost the operating manager dearly.

The reputation of a perfectly capable line manager may easily become tainted by a casual staff comment over lunch or by a couple of snide remarks at the conference table. And the investigation of a particular activity by staff with negative prejudices, culminating in a confidential report to the head office, can do a great deal of damage, particularly if the hapless manager remains unaware of the specific nature of the criticism.

Since a good reputation at headquarters is a precious asset, managers will be as cordial as possible to staff members, no matter what their personal thoughts may be. This cordiality tends to grow with the square of the distance that separates the

manager from the location of the head office. The more remote
his location, the less he will have the chance to mend his fences
at corporate headquarters.

The manager of a small office in Germany with less than ten
employees on the payroll knows perfectly well that the visit of
a staff man from New York to review personnel development
programs is an absurd waste of time and money. Yet unless he
happens to be the brother-in-law of the president or a nephew
of the main shareholder, he will keep these heretical ideas
strictly to himself. He will meet the emissary at the airport,
spend hours with him at the office, trot out all the appropriate
clichés, and display the kind of corporate thinking that will
look good in the report the staff man will produce when he gets
back home. He will take the man to lunch, to dinner, and if need
be to a nightclub, and will listen with rapt interest to the tall
tales about the heroic deeds accomplished by the personnel
people at headquarters.

He may even go further. He may send a personal note thank-
ing the man who wasted his time for his visit, culminating in
the brazen lie that the meeting was most worthwhile. He may
even suggest that the performance be repeated at regular intervals to provide crucial inputs on an ongoing basis.

And he will do the same thing for the man who comes to
inspect security arrangements, or public relations policies, or
research-related activities in what happens to be a sales office,
or for anyone else who happens to show up in search of meaningful activity and company-paid foreign travel. The manager
has no choice. Staff people not only write reports. They also
talk. And either activity performed in a spirit of hurt feelings
or outright hostility can be costly.

On the other hand, a well-cultivated staff member can be
of great help to the operating manager. He can provide val-
uable inside information on shifting power constellations at

the head office, suggest proper timing for delicate projects, identify potential enemies and suggest ways to overcome their animosity, put his finger on people who are not doing so well and whose friendship might be better shunned, and help in many other ways. Getting along with the staff is important and a staff man's friendship is worth its weight in martinis and roast beef.

But staff people have another important function. They are the preachers, and sometimes even the prophets, of new management fads. These fads may be supposedly infallible new methods for problem-solving, decision-taking, or organizing the day's activities, and they may go all the way to sociological quackery and psychological gimmicks guaranteed to make workers work harder, become more efficient, or fall desperately in love with the corporation.

Sometimes these fads are promoted with great vigor throughout the corporation only to be quietly dropped into oblivion a few months later, either because they did not seem to work, or because a new intellectual toy has come along. In other cases, the fad lingers on, perhaps in bastardized form, and becomes part and parcel of the usages that govern the acts of the corporation.

The origins of such fads are hard to trace. Maybe the chief executive officer heard about a new technique from a colleague in another corporation or read about it somewhere. Or somebody inside the company was exposed to the gimmick at a seminar and was sufficiently impressed to start a campaign to adopt it. Most probably, however, the new patent medicine was discovered by a member of the corporate staff looking for new meaningful activities for his department.

Once the idea gains momentum, the scenario is fairly predictable. A committee is formed to assess the possible impact of the new fad on the corporation's ongoing activities and long-range objectives. The conclusions of this evaluation are likely to be positive for two reasons. The members of the committee may sense an opportunity to get involved in something new, which might yield benefits in terms of status. They also know that top management greatly welcomes new techniques which will help make management more effective. The committee then prepares a plan for implementation.

This usually involves the services of an outside expert in the new witchcraft. The expert may merely come in and head some inspirational seminars to explain the poignancy and effectiveness of the notion to various key people. After drinking from the fountain of wisdom, the enlightened few then go out and spread the new faith throughout the corporation.

A more skillful expert will not be satisfied with a fee for just a few seminars. He will point out that the new technique is powerful medicine and must be applied in exactly the right manner, under carefully controlled conditions. If the corporation buys this spiel, the expert can collect fees for months, or even years. He will analyze the conditions within the company, set up controlled experiments on his hapless human guinea pigs, study the results in depth, and then tailor the treatment to fit the particular requirements of his victims.

Whatever the procedure, every manager in the corporation is expected to adopt the new gimmick with enthusiasm. And the managers usually do so or pretend to, no matter how madly inappropriate the fad may be. Criticism or, heaven forbid, outright refusal to comply would mark the manager as an outsider who does not seem to fit in with the team. So everybody goes along with the game.

A few years ago the management of a large corporation became madly infatuated with a new technique called PERT, a sophisticated method for planning the sequential development of complex activities, such as building a ship or developing a spacecraft. PERT is actually useful in planning the production of large numbers of items of differing complexity which must be available for assembly at certain particular times.

As it happened, this particular corporation made pills and paper and metals, and at first glance it was hard to see how PERT would be particularly applicable. However, the president apparently felt the new technique would solve many of his problems.

An overseas manager was at headquarters about that time and had a meeting with the president, during which he expected to discuss a number of urgent operating problems. But the president showed little interest in these mundane matters, and instead delivered himself of a glowing eulogy on PERT. The manager, who was mainly involved in running a number of subsidiaries and sitting on the boards of affiliated companies, tried to explain that PERT was perhaps not all that useful to his particular work.

He caught the shadow of annoyance that furled the brow of his master and quickly changed his tune. Not only did he, then and there, embrace the concept with enthusiasm. He went further. In his hotel room that night he drew up a sophisticated, totally meaningless PERT chart to which he referred conspicuously at all the meetings during the rest of his stay at headquarters. When he returned to his office overseas, he produced a large and very complicated chart, which was prominently displayed and referred to whenever possible in the presence of emissaries from the head office. The chart had no meaning but it served its purpose. It proved to headquarters that the manager was intelligent, obedient, and chock full of the right sort of attitude.

A few months later the manager returned to the head office for another updating. PERT had mercifully been forgotten. The new fad was a book called something like *Management Squares,* which was urged on the manager by the president himself. The book was looked at, found to be of no practical use, and displayed prominently in the manager's office until it, too, was made obsolete by yet another fad.

The preoccupation of corporate managements with new fads and gimmicks is quite understandable. They are nothing more than attempts to synthesize management knowhow to supplement the inadequate numerical abstractions on which management by soviet is based. They reflect the hope that perhaps somewhere in one of these fads the magic secret of effective management may be found.

The range of these fads is vast. Name any problem, and somewhere there is a new method guaranteed to solve it. And most of the solutions seem to involve the manipulation of people — making them smarter or more cooperative, imbuing them with positive thinking, getting them to work harder, making their work seem more fulfilling, teaching them to cope with conflict situations and to assert themselves, conditioning them to become happy and productive little ants in the corporate antheap. Any and all of this is grist for the mills of management theoreticians, consultants, psychologists, sociologists, motivation engineers, and other witch doctors who can come up with a catchy formula to arouse the interest of corporate managements.

In the stone age of management, the manager was supposed to be not only technically competent, but also skilled in the art of getting things done by other people. The fragmentation of management means that dealing with people has become a synthetic function plied by specialists, rather than by the numerically oriented new breed of managers. Hence the search for the magic formula, easily learned and practiced by the unskilled, for dealing with the people in the organization.

Unfortunately, none of the magic formulas has so far succeeded in distilling the quintessence of effective management with a human face. Implanted on the totalitarian structure of management by soviet, they tend to remain fads, and the compulsion to use them merely adds to the pressures under which operating managers have to meet their quotas.

And so the search continues.

8. Corporate Stakhanovites

Rewards

No management by soviet would be complete without its Stakhanovites. Stakhanovism goes back to the thirties and originated in Russia. A coal miner by the name of Aleksei Stakhanov apparently succeeded in getting his team to increase daily coal production to seven times the normal volume. The Soviet government considered this outstanding achievement worthy of special reward. And from that time, Soviet workers who managed similar feats of production have been called Stakhanovites and have received special honors and privileges.

In Russia, Stakhanovites tended to be burly fellows who exceeded their production quotas while driving a tractor, operating a lathe, or whipping a gang of road workers. They received not only tangible rewards, but also medals and publicity to encourage others to follow their fine example.

We also have Stakhanovites, but they are somewhat different. They do not receive medals and government-sponsored publicity. They may not even get their picture into the company magazine. But their rewards are just as compelling. Our Stakhanovites are not tractor drivers or shop foremen. They happen to be executives who wear well-made suits and live in attractive homes in the right kind of suburb. Of course, they are never called Stakhanovites. We label them overachievers, go-getters, men who will go far, potential top managers.

Their rewards are cash and stock options, which may be more costly to the organizations they work for, but are also more effective for greed is a more powerful motivation than vanity. Moreover, these tangible rewards enable our Stakhanovites to buy the status symbols of their own choosing; and therein lies another strong incentive.

In many foreign countries, managers receive part of their rewards in company-paid status symbols. This can mean company cars, chauffeurs, company villas, and perhaps even servants. The company supplies the status that goes with the job, and this provides ready identification of the manager's importance in the company.

By comparison, the status symbols provided by American corporations tend to be skimpy and internal. There are differences in office size and location, furniture quality, and other subtle symbols of status, but these can be interpreted only by those within the corporation. To outsiders, friends and neighbors, these symbols are meaningless.

This does not mean that external status symbols are unimportant. The executive still has to display a standard of living that reflects his position, but he has to pay for his status symbols out of his own pocket. And since there is no precise definition of what symbols are appropriate to his status, he has to make his own choices. These choices will be influenced by the level of ostentation of his colleagues in the corporation and of his neighbors, and by his own — and his family's — vanity and compulsion to keep up with or to surpass the Joneses.

This need to buy appropriate and perhaps excessive status symbols creates important economic pressures and motivations for the American executive. As the young executive starts his climb up the corporate ladder, he becomes exposed to these pressures. His salary increases with each promotion, as does the company's demands on his personal time. He has to entertain business associates, and, American customs being what they are, some of this entertainment must be done at home. The executive must thus have an abode suitable for such entertainment. A two-room walkup in a low-cost housing development will probably not suffice, no matter how original its décor.

This means moving into the right sort of place in the right section of town and getting the right sort of furniture to provide at least an adequate ambiance for business-related social gatherings. And the stage for entertaining in the proper manner must be set more or less concurrently with the promotion to an important position. The status symbols have to keep pace with the executive's job; they cannot be acquired several years later when he has saved up enough money to afford them. This means that the advancing young executive may have to borrow to finance the trappings of status.

He could refuse to go along with this custom and continue to live in the clapboard house inherited from his parents in what may meanwhile have become a somewhat run-down neighborhood, and if he is a genius in research or otherwise indispensable he may actually get away with it. Otherwise, his reluctance to abide by the social requirements of his position is bound to cast a shadow over his prospects for promotion, for his failure to follow established custom marks him as an outsider and sets him apart from his peers. To avoid this problem, he may have to live slightly, or even considerably, beyond his means to keep up with the unwritten laws of corporate social behavior.

But these are not the only demands corporate customs make on the financial resources of executives. In the course of his career, the executive may be promoted to jobs at different locations to broaden his experience. Or he may change companies to speed his ascent to the higher levels of management. This means pulling up stakes and moving to another town, another state, or even another country.

The corporation will pay for his moving expenses and may even provide an indemnity for the miscellaneous and sundry costs involved in settling at the new location. Unfortunately, the actual cost of the move usually exceeds even the most lavish indemnities. Between the new curtains, redecorating, and getting rid of his old house, the executive may have to make considerable investments out of his own pocket or with the help of his friendly bank. And the more frequently such promotions and relocations occur, the heavier the financial load becomes.

This need not bother the executive too much. Given time, raises, performance bonuses, and stock options that pay off, he will be able to liquidate his debts. And so, in the best American tradition, he lives just a little beyond his means. The practice is habit-forming, and pretty soon he may become rather dependent on the next raise to maintain solvency.

He is now hooked. He has to make more money, earn more incentive awards, and get more promotions simply to make ends meet. He has to meet his quotas, outdo himself, achieve like mad, so he can make more money. Success becomes a requirement of economic survival. And as his income mounts, each additional slice in net income is harder to attain because the government confiscates an ever-larger portion of pretax earnings.

The fact that the executive may travel and do a great deal of entertaining at the company's expense does not help matters. The man who has lunched on several martinis and lobster at the best restaurant in town and charged the expense to the company may look with a jaundiced eye at the hamburgers his wife has prepared for dinner. After three weeks on a business trip in Europe, taking the family to a big night at the ice cream parlor tends to be rather a letdown. As the personal standard of living tries to keep up with expense account habits, personal finances are bound to suffer.

The executive could easily solve these personal problems by applying the technique of a good corporate cost reduction drive to his life. He could move to a less expensive residence, stop buying costly status symbols, drive an old compact car, and drink cheap liquor. Unfortunately, these visible signs of economic retrenchment would be interpreted as indications that he feels insecure, no longer exudes confidence in his own success, and may, in fact, be on the skids. His image in the eyes of his peers and his superiors would suffer, and a tarnished image is not helpful in improving one's chances for further promotion.

As the executive moves toward the higher reaches of corporate management and the tax man becomes greedier, stock incentives become increasingly important. They offer the chance of paying off debts, financing the next deluxe vacation, putting the kids through college, or perhaps even building a personal fortune. And a small personal fortune offers a glimpse of some independence from the corporation and the compelling and urgent need for that next paycheck. Thus is born the unique preoccupation of the American manager with the price fluctuations of his corporation's stock, which we discussed in Chapter 3. For these price fluctuations determine to a considerable extent his personal fortune, or even his continued solvency.

The American Stakhanovite may not get much in the way of company-paid status or public recognition, and he may suffer heavily from the dire effects of progressive taxation on his salary. But stock-based incentives offer the chance of large rewards with considerable appeal to what may be self-imposed economic necessity and greed.

But financial rewards are not the only incentives to compel the manager to meet his profit quotas and be a good Stakhanovite. There are others.

Fear

A man who is serene and happy has little reason to change, and a happy manager would be unlikely to make heroic efforts to increase the glory and the profits of his corporation. Contentment does not provide much in the way of motivation.

But contentment is not the only obstacle to getting people to exert themselves beyond the immediate call of duty. Even the average man, with his share of ambitions, worries, and frustrations, may need more than just the prospect of material gain to overcome laziness and inertia so that he will perform to the limit of his capacity. The carrot is not enough. It also takes the stick to extract the full performance a man is capable of producing.

With management by soviet, the art of motivating people has been developed to an unusually fine pitch. Once caught up in the system, the executive has to work very hard and turn in an outstanding performance just to stay in the same place. But staying in the same place may not be enough. The executive has to go up or out, as the brutal saying goes. The manager continually has to surpass himself and his rivals.

This is why most managers put in working hours that would have been considered exceptional in the age of early industrial sweatshops. As the weak fall by the wayside, the others step up the pace in the hope that the next promotion or the next unique accomplishment may bring some relief from the pressure. It hardly ever does. And there are no unions to negotiate humane work hours for managers.

Management by soviet — in Russia or Rhode Island — is based not only on incentives but also on fear. Insecurity and the danger of exposure are always present, no matter how skillfully the manager tries to cover himself by spreading responsibility and by obeying the golden book of corporate procedures down to the last word.

There is the ever-present fear of failing to meet quotas and objectives. There is the fear of being sacrificed as a scapegoat on the altar of expediency to protect someone else. There is also the fear of being fired, or pushed aside, because of changing power constellations, reorganizations, or mergers. The fear of being done in by aggressive subordinates. The fear of getting tired, of losing initiative, of becoming deadwood.

And there is very little the manager can do to allay these fears. He has to produce, or else. He has to be better than his rivals, and he has to do better than he did last week. Like tomorrow, the goal always keeps sliding away from him. His great deed of today merely escalates the degree of performance expected from him next week.

Hardly ever can an executive decide that he has gone far enough, reached a comfortable position, achieved a job he likes which provides him with sufficient rewards to take things a little easier. He has to try for the next higher job, even if he knows it will not suit him, and perhaps even in the firm knowledge that he will fail when he gets there.

If he stops and settles down, he will block the avenue of promotion for those below him. Corporate policy usually requires that every manager train his successor. If he fails to do so, he is not doing his job properly. The corporation will not be able to promote him because there is no one to take his place.

But if he complies with personnel development policy he may be digging his own grave. Once a younger man has been trained to take over, the incumbent faces obsolescence. He will have to move up or risk being replaced by his own trainee. He simply cannot win.

As long as management required extensive practical experience, this problem was not too serious. The supply of trained candidates was limited because of the time required to accumulate the necessary experience. But with new management systems, any bright young college graduate can be taught the ropes of systems manipulation and be given some brief exposure to the requirements of a particular job. With the right training and perhaps a couple of years of on-the-job experience in different departments, he — or she — is ready to challenge managers twice his age. Since practical experience has become secondary, the young challenger may be capable of just as good a job as the older man he replaces.

As a result, younger managers are taking over, and seasoned executives are no longer in great demand. If they lose their jobs after forty — when they should be getting to the peak of their performance — they may find it difficult to get new jobs. They have no choice but to hang in there and scramble to stay ahead of the young challengers.

Unfortunately, every corporate organization tapers toward the top. Not every department manager can become a vice president. Not all executives can move to higher jobs, no matter how diligently they exert themselves, even if the company is subject to frequent reorganization and hierarchic churning. The pressure from below and the lack of openings at the next higher level are enough to drive men to drink, and they often do.

These pressures affect not only the middle layers of management; they go right to the top. Even the president is not always out of the reach of danger. His subordinates may also aspire to attain the top job before they themselves fall prey to ambitious underlings busily mining their positions from below. With all the court intrigues and power plays at the head office, the chief executive officer may have his share of worries, too.

In this environment of danger and fear, executives sometimes tend to form mutual protection associations with almost feudal overtones. This is not really surprising. In the Middle Ages the same motivations caused people to band together in similar fashion under leaders who offered protection in return for alle-

giance and obedience. The leader then organized defensive measures, led his followers into battle, and distributed any spoils
that might accrue.

The same motives sometimes cause managers to rally around
a promising leader who looks like he will be going places. They
provide him with loyal support in corporate battles for many
of the same reasons that the medieval villagers pledged their
obedience to their lord. Sometimes these allegiances are temporary and fall apart after a while. Others can last for years,
particularly if the leader is consistently successful and moves
his faithful retainers along as he climbs up the corporate pyramid with their help. Some strong leaders even take their main
vassals along when they change corporations. They thus assure
themselves of a core of loyal henchmen who can be placed in
strategic positions in their new setting.

But the feudal system has its dangers. When the leader is
beheaded, his loyal supporters may also be hunted down. Quick
changes of allegiance may save the day and stave off the odious
task of mailing off reams of résumés, but many an executive has
had to change jobs because he bet on the wrong leader.

When the leader of a feudal league moves toward the top,
taking his retainers along with him, the rest of the organization
will soon realize what is happening. Hundreds of clandestine
meetings will take place at all levels of the organization as
disturbed executives try to weigh the dangers of the intrusion.
Depending on their personal appraisal of the situation, the
threatened managers may try to join the gang, organize opposition leagues, or blend into the scenery in the hope that the
hangman will overlook them when the gibbet is set up.

If the leader makes it to the top, his loyal retainers will get
key positions from which they can exert a large measure of
control over the corporation. If the group has very strong
bonds, its members may even work out a timetable for the
succession to the presidency. This shows either a mutual loyalty

of admirable proportion or indicates that the vassals know so much about the dark deeds performed during the epic climb to the top that mere vice presidencies would not be sufficient reward for their discretion and loyalty.

Other leagues lose their coherence when the leader has attained the summit. He may no longer need his devoted servants, or he may even have to purge the group because some of his followers become too ambitious.

Nothing disappears faster than a league whose leader has fallen by the wayside.

As the internal power constellations in the corporation change, the powerful and aggressive league of yesterday may suddenly find itself in the role of the entrenched establishment, fighting off the threat of a new gang bent on wresting control from yesterday's usurpers. These political struggles contribute substantially to the fear and insecurity of the organization men. A slightly paranoiac disposition can actually be a useful asset to executive survival, since danger lurks everywhere.

Even the perfect manager has little security. He may meet or exceed all his profit quotas year after year, follow all regulations, comply with every last wrinkle of standard procedures, play his politics with skill, get along with everybody, and still be wiped out. One day an emissary from the head office may come to see him with the polite suggestion that he should really consider early retirement. After all, the manager once mentioned that he would like to write a novel or raise horses. Oozing sincerity and friendship, the man from headquarters suggests that the proper time to follow these inclinations is now. As the message sinks in, he may add wistfully that he wishes he could do the same.

His mind reeling with shock, the stricken manager knows at once that resistance is useless. There is no higher court and no right to appeal. If he follows the pointed suggestions, he will leave with full military honors and the corporation will make it worth his while. He will be paid off, be allowed to keep his options, and be remembered as a nice guy who met with a regrettable mishap. If he is obstinate and fights he will leave anyhow, but the circumstances of his departure will be far less cordial. The mere fact that he dares to question the wisdom of top management will at once turn him into a disloyal scoundrel. He will leave under a cloud, and this may cause problems when he starts looking for a new job. And whatever financial settlement he may be able to extort will be sure to be less generous than if he plays the game properly.

Having perceived all this in a flash, the victim is bound to inquire about the reasons for his dismissal. His mind races through past accomplishments, mistakes, personality conflicts, unfortunate utterances, in search of the event that tripped him up. The executioner immediately reassures him. His performance has been exceptional. He has done a great job, and everyone knows it. The president himself is most upset about the whole matter and has requested that the severance be handled with consideration and in the most generous manner. Everybody involved is truly sorry and prepared to help in any way possible. The problem is that an organization change is under way to adapt the corporate structure to cope with the problems and challenges of the future. Most regrettably, this change has eliminated the executive's position, and there just does not seem to be any other job within the corporation which would do full justice to the executive's outstanding talents.

All that remains, then, is to negotiate the terms of separation, the price the corporation will pay for the victim's letter of resignation. It could have been worse.

For one thing, top management has tried to be polite about the whole business. They could have just sent him a letter through the personnel department. Or they could have told him that his job was needed for a member of the president's personal entourage as a suitable reward in recognition of past accomplishments and as a basis from which to move on to better things. Whatever the reasons and the dismissal technique may be, the executive is out, and for good. He may discover six months later that his successor is making a complete mess of things, or that the people who fired him were in turn fired shortly after his own departure. This may provide moral satisfaction, but it will not get the victim reinstated.

The cost of such political turnovers can be very large as experienced managers are removed to make room for political appointees. Yet the waste of experience and talent involved may not be the only cost. Some management reshuffles can mean substantial out-of-pocket expenses for the corporation without yielding any discernible return. This is what happens when a senior manager cannot be fired because he is too prominent and privy to too much confidential information. Since he cannot simply be dumped, he will have to be neutralized. This may involve the payment of his salary for years to come, the creation of an impressive but meaningless position, even certain changes in organization and the relocation of personnel so that the man who cannot be fired is left in expensive but effective isolation. An operation of this sort performed at a regional headquarters overseas can cost a multinational corporation something like a million dollars in shareholder money.

The fact that a manager who is doing an outstanding job can be made to resign or be shunted out of his position into an expensive dead end greatly increases the insecurity felt by his remaining colleagues and tends to aggravate their consumption of martinis or tranquilizers.

Corporate Addiction

Greed and fear have been important motivating forces throughout history, and they remain potent factors in modern management systems. But they are not the only factors. An important additional inducement is required to compel highly intelligent people to accept the unrelenting stresses imposed by totalitarian management systems.

This motivation is an almost complete devotion to the corporate spirit, an addiction to the organization. This addiction keeps the hard-pressed manager within the system, just as it does the functionary in a totalitarian party, or any other member in a tightly knit organization.

A good manager displays a devotion to the affairs of his corporation that goes far beyond the dictates of greed and insecurity. He will literally live, and sometimes even die, for his job. His work will often take precedence over his family life. He will spend a great deal of his spare time on activities relating to the corporation. He will take a briefcase of work home at night and on weekends, entertain business associates, play golf with business contacts, and get involved in community affairs to brighten the image of the corporation. He will travel anywhere at the drop of an interoffice memorandum and move to any location the corporation chooses for him. His whole style of life will be patterned on the written and unwritten laws and demands of the corporation. His commitment to corporate life is total.

Of course, the executive may complain and grumble. He may talk about quitting the rat race and enjoying life. But even if he has the means to drop out without becoming a welfare case, he hardly ever does so. Mere loyalty to the corporation is not the answer.

Corporate propaganda departments may excel in the art of

preaching faith and loyalty and devotion to the company for the benefit of employees at all levels. But senior managers are too blasé to believe this kind of inspirational drivel. They may sneer at the idea of total loyalty to the corporation and point out that they have worked for five different companies over the last seventeen years. Properly relaxed, they may become very expansive indeed about the shortcomings of their corporations and the crimes and imbecilities committed by their superiors. But they will rarely quit to take up farming, or teaching, or to lead the quiet happy lives they keep dreaming about. The alibis for this seeming contradiction are manifold.

There is the crucial job that could not be done by anyone else. There is the idea of changing the system from within. There is the promotion that should come about any day now; it would be stupid to quit at this point. Maybe in a couple of years, but not right now. There are also the material factors. The good life that one gets used to and that could not continue without the monthly paycheck and the profits from the current set of stock options.

But even when material considerations are not of overwhelming importance, dropping out is not easy. What would family, friends, and associates think of an executive who quits during his peak earning years to settle down somewhere in the country and contemplate the universe? Success is the measure of a man's worth in our society. To abandon success casts doubt on a manager's ability or mental balance.

Moreover, dropping out is largely an irreversible process. A forty-year-old executive could presumably become a hippie if he made some effort. But once a hippie, he would find it extremely difficult to get back the vice presidency he so foolishly resigned two years earlier.

And so the manager goes on fighting and climbing for all he is worth. Actually, no matter what he may mumble after the fifth martini, he does not really want to quit. He is only fooling himself and perhaps his family. Yet he cannot really explain, to himself or to others, exactly what keeps him firmly caught in the corporate fold.

This strong and seemingly irrational attachment to the organization comes about because the corporation provides the executive with certain intangible comforts and fulfills certain emotional needs which perhaps few people within the organization clearly realize. The fulfillment of these needs keeps the harassed manager in the corporate treadmill. Belonging to the organization provides an identity, an importance, even a purpose in life.

The peasant in a medieval village may have been miserable in many ways, but he knew who he was and what his place in life amounted to. He worked, he fed his family, he obeyed his lord, and he went to church. His objectives were simple and clear. And if his life was hard and unpleasant, there was always comfort in the belief that his merits might be more fully rewarded in a vividly imagined posthumous existence than in the grubby despair of this world.

Our universe is different. We live in a world of change and uncertainty. We live in cities where neighbor knows not neighbor, and we belong to huge nation-states the destinies of which are almost completely beyond our influence. We are exposed to a chaos of conflicting ideas and swamped by oceans of irrelevant information. And all the time we hope to exploit this mass of confusion, of seeming opportunities and menaces, to our own benefit. And we may be haunted by the thought that our existence may be devoid of any purpose and meaning. Our spiritual beliefs no longer offer much solace; in our age of technical progress the creed of our fathers has a tendency to wear rather thin.

Hence our need to build a synthetic universe in which we can feel snug and important, a world that provides us with a clear identity, a purpose in life, and a yardstick against which we can measure our accomplishments.

The corporation can provide us with all these things. In a desert of anonymity, it allows us to associate with peers of similar background, status, and ideas. Our place in life is clearly defined by the box in the organization chart that bears our name. We can judge our own importance, not only by the modest trappings of status provided by the corporation, but also by the status symbols our rewards permit us to acquire and by the caliber of the people around us, the men who work for us and the men we work for. And we can identify with our work to such an extent that our contribution to corporate profits becomes a major accomplishment, and the negotiation of a major deal becomes a milestone in our life.

As long as we work for the corporation, our status follows us wherever we go. The branch office in Paris, or the local representative of the corporation in Kenya, will know exactly who we are and treat us accordingly. We know who we are and so do the people around us.

The corporation also provides us with clearly defined goals and rules of conduct. A glance at the organization chart shows the path to follow to promotion and other rewards. Stock options promise future blessings for the faithful. The manual of standard operating procedures provides unambiguous guidance on how we should go about our work.

Even the dreaded profit quota becomes important in this context. It shows exactly what is expected of us. A good superior will not fail to point out that the harsh quota imposed on a manager reflects nothing more than the company's belief in his outstanding ability. Everything is clearly defined in terms of black and white, in words, numbers, and computer printouts. And therein lies much comfort.

Finally, belonging to a powerful organization lends us a feeling of power and importance, be that organization a corporation, a military establishment, or the party in a totalitarian state.

The corporate organization thus fulfills to a remarkable degree the emotional needs of its managers for belonging and self-identification. The result can be a strong subconscious belief in the corporate way of life, which can take on almost religious overtones.

The corporation will provide comfort and sustenance for its loyal servants and their kin. It will reward hard work and success with salaries, bonuses, and deferred compensation. It will protect those who toil diligently. And it will punish transgressions against its laws, graven not on stone tablets, but inscribed in handsomely bound manuals of standard procedures.

Thou shalt meet thy profit quotas. Thou shalt respect and honor thy superiors. Thou shalt believe in the innate wisdom of the chairman, the president, the board, and the corporate staff. Thou shalt live in a manner befitting thy station in the corporation. Thou shalt not speak ill of the corporation, its products, or its servants. Thou shalt devote thyself with all thy heart and soul to the glory and growth of the corporation. Blessed be those who abide by these commandments, for they shall receive promotions, salary increases, status, bonuses, and stock options.

Utter rubbish, exclaim thousands of practicing executives from all levels in the organization charts of American corporations. We do our jobs because they have to be done and we can do them. We enjoy our work, not to mention our rewards.

Yet many former executives who have been cast out of the corporate paradise will tend to agree. Only they know the trauma of suddenly finding themselves out in the cold, bereft of the material and spiritual comforts of corporate life. They may be wealthy and enjoy expensive sunshine while they fiddle with their hobbies and try to keep busy. They may claim that they cherish their enforced idleness. But they know perfectly well that their separation from corporate life was not a liberation from drudgery and fear. It was also the sudden collapse of a way of life.

Gone are the comforts of the daily office routine. Gone are the assistants and secretaries who handled tedious details and provided protection from the intrusions of petty problems and undesirable visitors. Gone are the meetings, discussions, arguments, even the intrigues of interoffice politics. Gone are the business friends and luncheon companions, the expense account, and the quick and easy business trips.

There are no longer any clear goals and challenges and tight schedules. There are no longer any quotas and commitments, and they are sorely missed. There is no longer the excitement of working on complex and important deals. Even the enemies and the people who had to be watched are gone. Life has become dull and tedious.

The retired manager types his own letters, licks his own stamps, dials his own telephone. When he travels he is no longer an important representative of an important corporation; he is just another tourist. If he gets into trouble, he no longer has access to the resources of the corporation to bail him out. He is strictly on his own.

No wonder retired executives are particularly prone to heart attacks during the first few months of retirement. The change of pace, the lack of stimulation and purpose, can be quite literally killing. Some executives who have lost their jobs are unable to find another position because the shock process proved too great. They simply go to seed, shattered by the experience of being fired. To the diligent executive, the corporation is more than a source of bread and a place to work. It is a purpose in life.

Yet a manager may change corporations many times. He may leave because he is disgusted, by popular request, or simply because somebody offered him more money. How can he believe in the corporation when he is ready to leave for an $8000-a-year increase? The explanation is simple. The manager does not resign from corporate life, but only from a particular corporation where his talents were not sufficiently appreciated. After the change, he will serve his new corporation with the same diligence and devotion he displayed at the old one until he quit or was fired.

The fact is, life outside the corporation is simply unthinkable for many harassed managers. And so they stick with their jobs until they are hired away or premature death, retirement, or some other disaster forces them to leave the material and emotional comforts of the corporation.

Happiness is a place on the organization chart.

9. The Consequences

A Total System

Management by soviet and Stakhanovism have created a corporate environment of total profit commitment. Because lower-level managers in the corporation are personally liable for results, from the division vice president down to the lowliest sales supervisor, decisions that may have far-reaching consequences may be taken far down the line by people who can see a problem only from their own narrow point of view and who are under a strong compulsion to meet their profit quota. Many of the acts for which large corporations may be blamed are not necessarily the result of a fiendish "public be damned" decision at the board level. They may simply reflect a measure taken in desperation by a lower-echelon manager with his back to the wall, hoping to solve what might otherwise be an unsolvable problem of quota compliance.

What manager can be expected to sacrifice himself on the altar of business ethics by opposing a course of action that will generate profits — for the corporation and for the manager — because he feels that this course of action might conflict with the interest of the public? And how can a manager, caught up in his daily activities and subject to certain pressures, objectively judge the broader consequences of what may seem a routine decision?

Even if the conflict between corporate and public interest were clear-cut, the decision would be heavily weighted in favor of the corporation. And usually the conflict is by no means a matter of good and bad or black and white, but of shadings and nuances.

A new food product may meet all the applicable requirements and regulations. Its introduction on the market would be perfectly legal, fill a genuine need, and yield large profits. Yet there may be a small shadow of doubt about possible adverse effects which might occur in a small percentage of the user population. And perhaps this small shadow is only perceived after a substantial investment has been committed to the launching of the product.

The manager is now faced with a formidable dilemma. Perhaps the new product causes eye pains in a few people. How important is the part of the population that will be affected? How many of these people will be smart enough to stop using the product? How many will go on using it anyhow? And if they do, what will happen to them? Will the pains stop when they cease to use the product, or will continued use over years cause blindness? Should the product be killed before it kills someone? Or were the people who complained suffering from an eye disease before they started using the product? It might take months or years to determine the answers to these questions. But the product cannot be held in limbo while a detailed research program is undertaken. Someone somewhere in the corporation has to take a decision now with incomplete data and under pressure. The investment is committed; the machine of production and promotion is rolling along.

A cautious manager might decide to abort the project: stop everything, write off the investment, and start looking for a new product. If he does so, he is not likely to get any particular credit for this heroic act, and he may look very foolish if a competitor then sweeps the market with an identical product. And he will look very foolish indeed if it is subsequently discovered that the product was perfectly harmless while he has thrown away a million dollars in corporate investment.

Unless his convictions are very strong, the manager has little choice. He will protect himself as best as he can, establish a clear record to prove that he has taken all reasonable precautions, and make certain that his superiors will be fully implicated, just in case the small doubt should turn into a major disaster. And having done so to his satisfaction, he will introduce the product and hope for the best.

The problem is the same in many fields. Who can objectively decide at which point the danger to the few outweighs the benefit to the many? What is the proper ratio of lives saved and diseases cured versus the potential danger of a new pharmaceutical product? To what extent must product design protect the user from the results of gross negligence and stupidity? The judgment is difficult at best. And in the case of the manager fighting to meet his profit quota and earn his bonus and stock options, objective judgment may become almost impossible.

Yet if mistakes are made as a result of negligence, ignorance, or desperation, the consequences can be serious. There may be product liability suits, bad publicity, and crusades against corporate abuses, and the result may be new laws, rules, and regulations to improve corporate ethics, punish corporate waywardness, and make the corporations more responsive to the public interest.

It makes no difference that the defenders of the public interest may be a vociferous minority with extreme views. Once they have created enough commotion, politicians and government agencies will espouse their cause and pressure will be brought on the erring corporations to mend their ways. Sometimes these reforms will be reasonable and useful, and sometimes they will be very costly and of doubtful merit. Whatever their value, the cost of these reforms will inevitably have to be paid by the customers and the public.

The campaign for improved safety in automobiles has presented us with all sorts of bells, buzzers, and gadgets to make our cars safe at any speed. Yet none of these gadgets has changed the mentality of the Model 10,000 B.C. *homo sapiens* or his inclination to do stupid things when upset, under the influence, or otherwise in the raptures of his ego-bending power machine. The safety features may occasionally prevent an accident and perhaps more frequently alleviate the consequences of human error, but no array of electronic sensors, optic, acoustic, or tactile warnings, or reinforced bumpers will provide an adequate substitute for human judgment and patience behind the wheel. Man, not the machine, has a tendency to be unsafe at any speed.

Nor did the scandal involving charitable contributions to foreign political figures by U.S. corporations necessarily improve the ethics of this imperfect world. Because the practice of "buying orders" is now frowned upon in the United States, it may provide foreign countries with a certain advantage in markets where kickbacks, bribes, and suspect commissions to intermediaries are the accepted way of doing business. It also leaves the American corporation interested in these markets with a rather awkward problem. It can deplore the poor ethics of the market, refuse to engage in questionable practices and lose the business, or go after the business and hope that whatever compromises may be necessary can be suitably camouflaged.

The problem with public indignation, bad publicity, and the resulting laws and regulations to curb corporate misdeeds is that they do not really change things. If a scandal breaks, the management of the afflicted corporation, anxious to preserve the company's reputation and the allure of its stock on the market, will be forced to act. Public statements will be issued, agonizing reappraisals will be held in the boardroom, culprits will be fired, new corporate policies to cope with the situation will be issued, and perhaps even the chairman may tender his resignation.

But in the end, all these measures merely pile additional restraints on the managers down the line who have to meet their profit commitments. If the new rules of the game involve additional costs or the loss of some business, the manager involved may have to raise prices, making all his customers pay for the new policy, shift his activities to another business area where the new restraints do not apply, or cheat on the rules.

In fact, the manager is locked in. Between forward plan, profit quotas, standard procedures, and policy decisions from above, his options may become very narrow. He is under unrelenting pressure to meet his goals and objectives. Either he does his part or he will be replaced by someone else who will. Short of throwing in the towel and dropping out, he has to comply with corporate objectives, and this applies not only to the lower management echelons, but also to the people at the top. Once the course has been charted, even the captain may find it difficult to change direction unless he has very compelling reasons that can be sold to the board, his peers, and to his lieutenants.

The board of the corporation may solemnly declare that past misdeeds will not recur and order all hands to govern themselves accordingly. But there is no way to change the system of plans, quotas, and regulations to ease the problem of meeting profit objectives under the new conditions.

Total management tends to become a totalitarian system.

And from the collective compulsion to act in accordance with the objectives, procedures, and policies of the corporation or suffer the consequences, a way of thinking develops which may be quite different from that of the people outside the corporation. Personal ethics may subtly shift as managers try to comply with what they perceive as the demands of the organization. Under the compulsions built into the system, managers may gradually condition themselves to accept, support, commit, and even plan acts which may seem perfectly normal within the framework of corporate thinking but which might be rather difficult to explain to outsiders, or to a congressional committee or a court. The spirit of the corporation thus gathers it own momentum, which may be almost impossible to resist. And compliance with the demands of the organization may develop patterns of thought and action that would seem strange to outsiders.

Lieutenant Calley could probably bear this out. So could the Watergate plumbers.

Of course, corporate compulsions have some limitations. No matter what their antagonists may say, corporations by and large operate within the law, are subject to some outside restraints and influences, and are run by people who would be horrified by the thought of unethical behavior or criminal intent. Unfortunately, ethics cannot be readily measured in absolute terms. And, barring outside restraints, corporate ethics become the ethics of a particular corporation and of the people who manage that corporation.

The individual has no choice but to accept and comply with the demands of the organization and its ethics or to drop out.

The Impact of Growth

Not all corporations employ the more extreme forms of growth strategies and totalitarian management. Not all major corporations are able to grow through skillful mergers and colonial expansion. And not all corporations with rapid growth strategies are successful in attaining their objectives.

Some of the fast growers run into problems. They may lose

momentum and settle into a less glamorous existence. They may become stable, stolid corporations with modest growth and equally modest price-earnings ratios. Others may have to retrench and perhaps spin off earlier acquisitions that contributed little beyond publicity and instant profits per share at the time of the merger. Still others may find themselves overextended to the point where they themselves become candidates for acquisition.

Yet the basic incentives and mechanisms for rapid corporate growth remain. Wherever possible, growth strategies will be pursued with alacrity as a matter of profit and even survival for both corporations and their managements. And where some companies fail to achieve their growth targets, others will succeed.

The trend toward concentration of corporate power becomes quite evident if we consider the importance of the largest corporations in relation to the overall economy.

In 1961 the combined sales of the ten largest U.S. corporations amounted to $56 billion, or just under 11 per cent of the gross national product. By 1974 the sales of the top ten had risen to $234 billion, or almost 17 per cent of the GNP. In relation to the overall economy, the importance of the ten largest corporations had increased by more than half.

Interestingly enough, the top ten in 1974 were the same companies that had made up the top ten in 1961, although the order of size had undergone some changes. This stability is not too surprising; the top ten are fairly sedate giants rather than fast growers. They are not madly diversified, and because of their very size they stick out like sore thumbs and are watched with concern by the federal trust-busters. Not for them the quick merger that increases size by half at the stroke of a pen. They have to tread softly, or public outcry will demand their dismemberment. They have to grow largely from within. Still, they show substantial growth in relation to the economy.

During the same period, the second ten largest corporations more than quadrupled their combined sales, from $19.5 billion to $92 billion. Their growth in relation to the GNP amounted to more than 75 per cent. However, this group includes not only sedate giants, but also two rapid-growth companies. Between 1961 and 1974 the sales of IBM increased from $1.7 billion to $12.7 billion. And ITT did even better, growing from $930 million to over $11 billion during the same period. This corresponds to an average annual growth rate of 21 per cent. These two companies show what growth strategies can accomplish.

IBM and ITT may be conspicuous by their size, but they are not the only rapid-growth corporations. Among the lower ranks of corporate size are many other companies that try to emulate, with greater or lesser success, the example of the illustrious growth leaders. Some of these less visible growth companies may ultimately manage to join the elite of corporate giants.

A sustained annual growth rate of 20 per cent will double the size of a company every four years. A $2 billion company that maintains this growth rate through mergers, overseas expansion, and growth from within will reach $12 billion in ten years and $31 billion five years after that. And the field from which these future giants may emerge is quite large. In 1974 there were more than two hundred corporations with sales above $1 billion.

If the trend toward accelerated growth persists — and there are certainly enough incentives for it to do so — the effects of the continued concentration of corporate power can be foreseen without much difficulty. In 1961 the sales of the fifty largest corporations represented around 20 per cent of the GNP of the United States. Thirteen years later, this figure had grown to 30 per cent. Ten years from now, this figure may well be around 45 per cent. But this percentage understates the importance of the top fifty corporations because it does not take into account the secondary business generated by these corporations —

the activities of suppliers, subcontractors, distributors, and all the other companies and people who feed and depend on the giants.

The implications of this concentration are staggering. Yet an economy largely dominated by perhaps three score very large corporations is not necessarily a terrifying prospect.

We may complain bitterly about the vast economic power of giant corporations. But, as we have seen, we tend to show a distinct preference for the products of large corporations, and this preference is not entirely due to promotional brainwashing. It is, to a large extent, a matter of trust. We know what to expect if we are dealing with a large corporation. The product may not be exciting or unique, but it will be standardized and backed by the manufacturer. There will be a service organization and spare parts, and if we have a major complaint we can get redress from the head office. We trust the large company and its reputation.

If we rent a car, we patronize one of the large rental establishments rather than Joe's Garage, which is a couple of dollars cheaper, because we have no idea of the quality Joe might provide. And if there is a problem, the large outfit will know how to cope; it will provide another car, and have other locations if the thing breaks down en route. We are in the hands of a large organization and help is only a phone call away. Joe does not provide these services. He has no nationwide reputation to defend and he may not be able to help even if he wants to because he has only three cars and the other two are not available.

The rooms in hotels operated by large chains may be of dreary uniformity but they offer one vast comfort. We know exactly what to expect and how much we will pay when we make our reservation. And this beats the adventure of staying at a small hotel in a strange town whose standards of comfort and cleanliness we cannot assess in advance and whose rates may be based on a spur-of-the-moment appraisal of the customer.

So we patronize large corporations rather than take our chances on small competitors who may offer similar goods and services. This preference is the main reason why there are large corporations to start with. And there is no particular reason why this preference should change, even if corporate concentration becomes far more pronounced than it is now.

The customer would still have a choice between competing products because the law says there must be competition. However, the nature of this competition will be modified by several factors.

Competition is only worthwhile for the corporation if there is a reasonable chance that its market share can be enlarged, by outresourcing smaller competitors, for instance. In a business area dominated by a handful of large companies with similar resources, we have shown that genuine price and product competition is not a promising road to a larger market share and higher profit. In these circumstances, it is preferable to engage in symbolic competition based on minor product differences and heavy promotion. Market shares may then shift slightly because one competitor has a more attractive package for his product, or a more compelling advertising campaign, but there will be no unseemly tooth-and-nail struggle over market shares.

However, there is another important consideration which can inhibit real competition, even if there are smaller competitors who might succumb to an attack from their bigger brethren. Once the number of competitors becomes small, it becomes necessary to ensure the survival of all competitors to preserve the image of competition. There is little doubt that General Motors and Ford could wipe out American Motors, and perhaps even Chrysler, if they made a concerted effort. However, this would be a fatal mistake because four competitors are desirable from the point of view of complying with antitrust rules. Three competitors might not suffice, and if only two were left, they would have to be broken up to restore competition. To avoid this problem, the stronger competitors must make certain that the little fellows can survive.

Finally, competition may also be modified by the relationships which may exist between diversified competitors. Just how fiercely can two companies compete in a particular field if they collaborate in others? How strongly can the fast food divisions of two corporations battle over market shares when other divisions of the two companies are in a supplier-customer relation, operate joint ventures in the Near East, license products from each other in pharmaceuticals, and perhaps have other common or related interests in other fields? In an environment of high corporate concentration, where large diversified companies have many interfaces, dog-eat-dog competition is bound to be the exception rather than the rule.

This is not a revolutionary development. Even now, real competition is a matter of carefully judging the chance of success in terms of increasing profits rather than a heedless out-and-out battle. And when competition no longer offers the chance of worthwhile rewards because competitors are too strong, or too few, then growth urges must be channeled into new fields.

Built-in Inflation

Everybody deplores the inflation that saps the purchasing power of our money. Yet nobody seems to be able to cure the disease. As we watch the erosion of our money from month to month, economists provide convoluted explanations while governments announce new strategies and utter reassuring statements to becalm the disturbed populace. Yet inflation seems to respond neither to scientific patent medicines nor to political hocus-pocus.

What causes inflation? Union blackmail? Excessive corporate profits? The boundless urge of consumers crazed by advertising to buy the good things in life, regardless of cost? Too much government spending? Too much government interference with business? Too much socialism? Too much money? Shortages of raw materials exploited by their owners? The list of conceivable causes is almost endless.

Yet one cause of inflation seems to be largely overlooked. This is the inflation built into an economic system based on competition through resources, a competition that appears to become more pronounced as the concentration of business activity progresses. Growth strategies and totalitarian management systems may actually be significant factors in creating inflation and economic instability.

In the absence of competition, there are no restraints on the corporate urge to maximize profits, and prices will be high. Conversely, competition can be expected to result in lower prices as competitors vie for the favor of the customers. But competition is not a natural state of business. It occurs only when there is conflict over market shares. But to launch an attack on market shares of other companies, the aggressor must be convinced that the effort will provide increasing profits, or the exercise will be pointless. The aggressor must therefore have some concrete advantage over at least some of his competitors. The advantage may be a superior product, better service, a better sales organization, or a better image. But to compete on price, the aggressor must have a better cost structure, which will permit him to undersell his competitors and still increase his profit.

Operating on a worldwide scale, a corporation might attain lower costs by producing in an area where labor is very cheap and raw materials plentiful and inexpensive, by paying no taxes, and by engaging in all sorts of interesting schemes to cut down on administrative and distribution costs. However, a company operating in a developed country in a legal fashion has more limited options. It has to do business like everyone else, pay taxes and comply with whatever regulations apply to its activities. To gain a cost advantage over competitors is then a matter of reducing the cost of people and materials.

People can be replaced by investment in machinery and equipment in shop and office as long as the volume of business is large enough to make the investment pay off. As investment increases, labor costs tend to become smaller in relation to total cost. However, once the investment is made, the corporation becomes vulnerable. The investment is based on a certain volume of production, and this volume must be reached or exceeded to pay for the investment.

If the target volume cannot be reached, the cost advantage bought with the investment will be lost. In a recession, the corporation may have to raise prices so it can survive the reduction in business volume. And it has to be more responsive to union demands for higher wages to avoid having its assets idled by a strike.

Because corporations with large investment may have to accept wage increases in preference to having their assets idled by strikes, the steady escalation of wages has become a normal expectation. Companies that cannot afford wage increases will price themselves out of business and their market shares will go to the survivors. And the steady increase in wages continues, whether business is good or bad.

As long as these wage increases can be compensated by growth and additional investment, their inflationary effect can be swept under the rug. But not all corporations can grow all the time to justify additional investment. Wage increases may thus have to be compensated by other means. And among these other means is invisible inflation, a phenomenon economists never seem to mention. When prices increase and this increase can be measured by numbers and shown in statistics, the increase obviously represents inflation. Invisible inflation, the deterioration of products and services caused by efforts to maintain or enlarge profits, does not show up in any statistics, yet its role in our economy is nevertheless important.

For example, if the cost of producing an oak table increases by 50 per cent because of wage and material increases, the small cabinetmaker has no choice but to pass this increase on to his customers. The result is inflation in the price of oak tables.

But a large corporation can hide the effects of labor and material cost increases. It can spend money on research to develop new techniques using new and cheaper materials, then invest more money in a new plant with sophisticated machinery, and finally make another investment to promote the new product in the mass market.

The new table may be made out of reclaimed sawdust, third-grade plastics, and the cheapest fasteners that will just suffice to hold the pieces together. It may almost look like an oak table, though in fact it is a piece of sophisticated junk. However, its price is lower than that of the original oak table. Inflation has become invisible.

This kind of invisible inflation has been with us for many years, as manufacturers tried to absorb rising wages through what are euphemistically called cost improvement programs. And the large competitor is in a far better position to develop and sell through mass brainwashing the junk that hides inflation.

As discussed earlier, annual model changes are a convenient method to introduce the progressive downgrading of products. This may involve substituting cheaper materials, changing design elements, making the product difficult to service in the interest of manufacturing economics, and replacing worthwhile functions by original but useless gadgets. Yet few customers really seem to mind. They have been carefully conditioned to start lusting after the new improved model as soon as it appears in the dealer's showroom.

And thus for many years competition for market share, increasing investment, and invisible inflation have helped to hide the effects of wage increases on the economy. While prosperity grew, everyone was happy. Unfortunately, however, this prosperity carried some destructive seeds.

Wage increases originating in high-investment, high-productivity businesses tend to spill over into activities that, by their nature, are not amenable to productivity improvement as a result of investment. Since the higher wage cost cannot be buried, it has to be passed on to the customer. This price increase affects the cost of living and in turn prompts demands for further wage increases to maintain the purchasing power of the workers.

But even in high-productivity operations, there are certain limits beyond which the effect of wage increases can no longer be hidden. When the range of possible material substitutions has been exhausted, when further modifications to reduce product cost are impractical, and when the return on investment to improve productivity becomes unattractive, invisible inflation must turn into highly visible inflation.

And the same is true when it becomes impractical to enlarge the volume of activity because the market is becoming saturated and the battle for a larger share in it no longer promises any additional profits. And this happens when there are no obviously weaker corporations left from which market shares can be alienated. Real competition will not disappear altogether when this stage is reached, but it will be reduced to skirmishing for limited objectives rather than for large chunks of the market.

And finally, when perhaps four or five corporations virtually control a market among themselves, real competition will have to be largely abandoned to protect the weaker of the remaining competitors and to preserve the image of competition.

When competition becomes unprofitable because there are no more market shares that can readily be captured, the incentive for price reductions is removed. But the compulsion to increase profits built into totalitarian management systems remains, and the pressure for wage increases continues. So also does the threat that a strike could paralyze costly assets and play havoc with earnings and stock option profits. There is no other solution. Wage and profit increases must be paid for by higher prices. And, as we have seen, when volume falls off because of a slack in demand or a recession, costs increase and prices again will have to be raised so the corporation may survive.

Inflation is inevitable when cost reductions are exhausted and no further growth is possible and becomes rampant when business declines. There is only one practical remedy: more growth. But growth from where?

Growth from Where?

We have seen that corporate strategies based on stock market incentives and the coercions of totalitarian management systems make continued corporate growth unavoidable. And in an environment of growth, no corporation can afford to stand still. If it does, it risks being overtaken by more resourceful competitors bent on stealing market shares in the pursuit of their own growth objectives.

But when growth in any particular field slows because the market is not expanding, and competition for increasing market shares becomes uneconomical, further growth can only come from cannibalism and diversification, the lateral sprawl into new fields. But once a major acquisition in a new field has been made, antitrust laws usually prevent additional mergers in the same field. The next merger must then be consummated in yet another business area.

But not all areas of diversification are attractive. Some may already be dominated by other diversifiers with large resources, and the newcomer would find the battle to establish a foothold in the new market too costly. Or the competition for potential merger victims is too severe to permit a profitable deal. Or the business itself may be static or recessionary and offer little opportunity for growth and profit beyond the leap in size and earnings per share produced by the merger itself. These considerations may eliminate diversification into fields closely related to the original business of the corporation.

The ideal target for such diversification is a business that is largely in the hands of small enterprises but which is amenable to organization on a large scale. Such fields offer large opportunities. Not only will acquisitions be relatively easy, but once a bridgehead has been established, the intruder will be able to deploy his resources to take away market shares from the small established businesses. By setting his own standards and objectives, the intruder can then impose his own operating mode on the business, which small competitors, operating on what may be a local basis, will find impossible to match.

This sort of thing has already happened in some fields which have traditionally been the province of small operators. It has happened in hotels, restaurants, and other service activities. And no doubt the trend will continue.

This threat to small businesses is not necessarily the result of a malicious design to wipe out small enterprises. It happens simply because the entry of a large corporation determined to acquire an important slice of the market changes the rules of competition and escalates the minimum practical company size. The large corporation merely follows its growth objectives by exploiting opportunities for profitable competition. Unfortunately, this competition may wipe out not only those small competitors who were marginal to start with but also small firms that were doing quite well before the intruder spoiled the game.

Our laws solemnly decree that competition must be maintained. But they afford no protection to the small enterprise whose market share is the objective of large corporate competition, and which may be driven to the wall by changes in the market structure when large companies enter their field in search of growth opportunities.

But what happens when all the more promising fields of diversification have been conquered by large corporations, and only activities offering little interest to the giants are left in the hands of small enterprises? What happens to growth companies when there are no profitable avenues of growth left? Will they turn on each other and pursue battles for market shares without regard to profitability? Or will they settle down and accept the fact that no further significant growth is practical?

In fact, some growth companies get stuck even now. Their own business may be in saturated markets that permit little growth because competition is devoid of any real profit potential. They may lack the resources to diversify or the price-earnings ratios that will permit profitable mergers into new business areas. Or they may be regulated, and the regulators may frown on expansion into other fields. And growth from colonial expansion may not be possible. In such cases, the corporation has two choices. It can accept defeat, become a humdrum also-ran on the stock market, and try to make the best of a basically unattractive situation. Or it can attempt to create artificial growth and rely on its size, prominence, and the number of jobs it provides as security when artificial growth leads the company into difficulties.

The commercial air transport industry is one example of a successful strategy of artificial growth. In the fifties air travel grew by leaps and bounds as people became travel-conscious, international business expanded, prosperity grew, and passengers abandoned slow surface transportation. Traffic increased substantially from year to year, and airlines were a genuine growth industry.

In the sixties the real growth of airline traffic began to level off. Further diversion of passengers from surface transport was no longer possible, and there were natural limits to the expansion in business and vacation travel. Yet the airlines continued to behave like a growth industry, assuming traffic would go on increasing and ordering more capacity. Since the opportunities for real growth were limited, the airlines proceeded to create artificial growth to fill their aircraft.

This was accomplished through special fares for people who were unwilling or unable to pay full fares. The conditions for these special fares were carefully set so that business travelers — most of whom do not pay for their own tickets anyway — and other people in a rush would always pay full fare. But tourists willing to put up with certain inconveniences could enjoy substantially cheaper travel. The reasoning behind this pricing policy was that the cut-rate travelers would fill otherwise empty seats, so whatever they paid in reduced fares would be almost pure profit for the airlines.

The sale of a product or a service at discriminatory discounts to certain classes of customers is unusual in other lines of legitimate business, and is in fact even illegal in certain countries. No car manufacturer could get by with selling products at a special discount to people who belong to affinity groups, or buy a package consisting of a car, 500 gallons of gasoline, a refrigerator, and a TV set, or who agree to use the car only on alternate weekends and at lunchtime on weekdays for nonbusiness purposes. Yet the airlines, with the consent of their governments, have succeeded in developing special promotional fares with great success. The result has been a veritable jungle of special rates accompanied by an expansion of traffic that has

largely hidden the reality that the real full-fare growth of the
airline business fell off years ago. And as special fare business
developed and prospered, the supposedly incremental business
became more and more important, and the airlines began to
suffer from disappearing profits.

Yet by this time, the strategy of artificial growth had largely
accomplished its purpose. The airlines had grown to be large-
scale employers. The demise of a major scheduled carrier would
be bad news to too many people to be ignored by the government. Foreign airlines are often government-owned, and the
injection of public funds to cover losses and to keep the scheduled carriers going is no particular problem. Yet even in the
United States, where airlines are privately owned, the government could not just sit there and watch a major company go
under, although help would have to be provided in a more
discreet manner.

Thus the public may ultimately have to pay for the artificial
growth strategies of some corporations. In fact, the public has
been paying some of these costs all along.

In the case of the airlines, artificial growth has aggravated the
problems of traffic congestion in the air and on the ground, and
this congestion has made necessary large investments in airports and traffic control systems. The cost of coping with air-
traffic growth is mainly borne by the taxpayers, as are the
attendant noise and pollution.

It may be argued that the airline business is a special case and
bears little similarity to other corporate activities. Airlines,
after all, are government-regulated, and international fares are
fixed by the International Air Transport Association to eliminate unseemly price competition. And since the fares for each
route are established by the unanimous consent of the airlines
involved, fare levels reflect the needs of the weakest and least
efficient competitors.

This provides a considerable degree of protection for the

airlines, permitting them to pursue growth strategies even when there is little real full-fare growth possible. At the same time, there is a semblance of competition projected by advertising that implies differences in service quality when virtually none exist.

It is of interest to note that artificial growth can be infectious. The growth of the airline business has led to a tradition of equipment replacement that continues even in periods of low prosperity. Future traffic is estimated in great detail, and optimum configurations for handling this traffic are developed, thus creating new markets, or at least the illusion of new markets, for airplane manufacturers. It is immaterial that the investment in yesterday's airplanes may not be recovered for years to come, or that the advantages of the new equipment may be minor in relation to its cost.

New products can then be developed by the airplane manufacturers to meet the new markets forecast by the airlines. Yet the cost of this development comes very high, and the market is limited; recovering the investment may take years at best, and the risk is enormous. Apart from Boeing and McDonnell Douglas, the industry leaders, it is doubtful whether any manufacturer of commercial airplanes has made an honest profit building airliners over the last fifteen years. Yet three U.S. companies and five European manufacturers compete in a business that under normal circumstances could sustain perhaps two competitors.

The reason for this competition is that European governments are subsidizing the development of airliners in the hope of breaking the virtual monopoly of U.S. manufacturers in the commercial air transport market. Since the market is too narrow to support that many manufacturers, the subsidies for the development of costly new equipment serve to support an industry that has become overgrown. Concorde is perhaps the most striking example of such government subsidies.

Airlines and the aerospace industry show what can happen to growth companies with limited diversification and flagging markets once they reach a certain size and too many jobs depend on the maintenance of that size. The collapse of a large corporation with extensive ramifications among thousands of suppliers and subcontractors which might affect a few hundred thousand voters is politically unacceptable. The government has to find ways to protect the very large corporations. Though it may not be able to provide more artificial growth, it may have to save the company from the consequences of artificial growth in past years. And the cost of these activities will have to be borne by the public.

Maintaining Jobs

Reasonably full employment is necessary to ensure political stability.

People who are gainfully employed, have money, and own cars and color TV sets are far less likely to go out into the street to revolt against the established order than the desperate who lack jobs and are stricken by abject poverty.

Maintaining jobs and some measure of prosperity is thus a major objective of any government bent on staying in power. And here lies a fundamental contradiction between government objectives and the facts of life of a modern economy.

Governments need work for everyone. Corporations want to grow, and this implies conflict over market shares and competition and involves the replacement of labor by investment to reduce production costs. The resulting increase in productivity then permits wage increases, the mainspring of prosperity. But increasing productivity through investment means more production for a given number of workers, or fewer workers for a given production volume. Maintaining or enlarging employment while productivity increases imposes the need for growing markets, or at least growing market shares. As long as markets can be made to grow rapidly enough, full employment, rising productivity, stable prices, and increasing wages can coexist. Prosperity reigns.

But competition and markets have their limits, and no amount of promotion will change this fact. We may buy two cars and replace them every two years, but few people can be persuaded to buy a new car every six months, or three television sets every year, no matter how far artificial obsolescence and limited life design may be developed. And if a recession occurs, or even threatens, people will cut back on new purchases and demand decreases.

When this happens, production costs increase because of the reverse relationship between volume and cost, and in the interest of maintaining profits, or even survival, corporations will have to lay off people and raise prices if at all possible. Unions will continue to press for higher wages, but there will be unemployment and inflation until demand can be restored.

Yet even without a recession there is the problem of saturated markets, because an advanced industrialized society with high productivity as a result of large investment has a tendency to produce more than it can consume. Some mechanism must therefore be found to dispose of the excess production in a constructive manner. The traditional mechanism is exports, which permit growth beyond the requirements of the national market. Exports provide an enlarged production base, which justifies investment to provide higher productivity and higher wages. Prosperity, as the examples of Germany, Japan, and Switzerland have shown, lies in large exports.

But exports require the exploitation of a certain advantage in foreign markets. The advantage may be technology and superior products, lower cost, or a better marketing organization. Conversely, the foreign market must be able to use and pay for

the products. Simple products with low prices resulting from
cheap labor can be sold almost anywhere. But there may not
be much of a market for electronic data-processing systems
among the lesser African nations or for washing machines in
the Brazilian jungle. High-technology products require markets
with a certain technical infrastructure. Mass-production goods
require mass markets of a certain affluence. Export markets for
industrial products are not unlimited.

But even so, the volume of U.S. exports tends to be comparatively small. Germany and Switzerland export more
than one fifth of their gross national product. By contrast,
the United States exports only about 7 per cent of its GNP,
and a substantial part of this consists of agricultural products, which do not play an important role in stimulating
investment to increase productivity and prosperity through
noninflationary wage increases.

This low export volume may seem strange for a country that
is a leader in many technologies. However, the owners of these
technologies tend to be multinationals whose technical advantages are exploited not through exports, but rather by local
production abroad. Yet even the mononational U.S. corporation tends to focus its efforts mainly on the large domestic
market rather than on faraway countries. The medium-sized
Swiss or German machinery manufacturer knows that his prosperity will depend on creating products for exports, not just for
the narrow local market. If business is bad, he will fly to wherever his markets may be and cut his prices to the bone to drum
up orders. His U.S. counterpart will probably react differently.
He will follow the dictates of his forward plan. If there is a
slump, he will not fly to Rio or Vienna to get business; he will
try to meet his profit quota by domestic promotion and, if that
does not work, by cost improvements, which means by laying
off people.

When exports are not sufficient to soak up excess production, other means to cope with the problem have to be found. This is where the government comes in. There are two aspects to the role of the government in solving this problem. One is the creation of artificial markets to provide for economic growth and employment. The other is the removal of workers from production activities.

It is obviously not possible for a government to purchase a million automobiles a year to stimulate the economy and then to dump the vehicles into the ocean to serve as breakwaters. Government purchases must appear plausible, even if their main purpose is the simple consumption (and disposal) of productive capacity. In fact, the art of producing plausible waste has been developed to a fine pitch by the governments of countries with mature economies.

First, there is defense. Vast amounts of money are being spent on development and procurement of ever more sophisticated military equipment, and this keeps a considerable segment of industry gainfully employed in manufacturing products that do not have to be sold in commercial markets. But defense requirements also absorb a part of the working population in essential but fortunately unproductive activities. Soldiers who drill, clean rifles, drive jeeps, and sometimes even engage in combat do not glut the labor market or produce yet more needless ball-point pens, window awnings, or washing machines. Two million people taken off the job market and paid to protect the country while wearing out expensive equipment can be a considerable asset in solving the problems of a modern economy.

Space programs also are helpful in soaking up manpower and industrial capacity to produce plausible waste. Since space programs are not suitable for mass-production techniques, they tend to be very labor-intensive. A good program can keep hundreds of scientists and engineers and thousands of technicians busy for years as the frontiers of technology and science are advanced for the benefit of mankind at the expense of the taxpayers. Also, space activities and military development programs may provide technical by-products that can be applied to commercial product areas where the cost of innovation might otherwise be prohibitive in relation to the return on investment. Electronics, aircraft design, medical research, and many other fields have all benefitted from space activities.

But space programs have another advantage. They produce throwaway products which can be neatly disposed of. The results of years of research and costly toil are launched and disappear. Only a small part of what started off as a giant contraption may return — the capsule — and this can be donated to museums to delight the curiosity of the multitudes since it has no further practical use.

Governments can also use their resources to stimulate markets. Export financing, subsidies on exports and foreign aid to be spent on products of the donor nation, can create significant export markets for domestic producers. And government spending at home on a variety of programs can help to provide business, profits, and employment.

Yet, even so, the problem of excess productive capacity and employment may remain. Every year our educational systems spew forth millions of young people for whom employment must be found. To employ them all in productive activities supported by high investment could cause a glut of products for which there is no market. To leave them unemployed and roaming the streets is an invitation to anarchy and rebellion. The state, in the interest of its own survival, must find a solution.

Lengthening the educational phase is one possibility. The more kids can be persuaded to go to college, the more young people can be kept off the labor market, at least temporarily. But the process cannot be stretched out indefinitely. Entry into the working force at thirty or forty is hardly practical.

Another method, suggested by some European governments,

is early retirement. In practice, this means chopping the working population from the top to make room at the bottom. This may impose some hardship on older people, but it can be argued that they have had their time at the horn of plenty and should now move on. Such a solution is attractive because older people are less likely to organize disturbances to protect their income. However, some sort of a social security scheme, financed by beneficiaries and employers, is indispensable to this kind of employment strategy. In the United States, the number of senior voters is too important to permit similar measures, and the current trend is toward later retirement, even at the cost of higher unemployment.

Other ideas have been proposed by concerned governments. One European government is trying to revive artisanal production, and subsidies are being given to unemployed workers who want to start their own business. Unfortunately, this notion presumes that there is a market for goods painstakingly produced by artisanal skills, but paid for at wage levels largely set by high-productivity mass-manufacturing operations. If a mass-produced item of adequate quality can be bought for $20, the market for a handmade product of similar quality at twenty times the price tends to be highly limited.

Much scorn is heaped on sprawling and inefficient government bureaucracies, but these organizations can also play an important part in soaking up manpower. The activities of some government agencies may seem madly irrelevant and devoid of any practical use to many a citizen, but they nevertheless provide gainful employment for what might otherwise be idle hands. Seen from this point of view, bureaucracies, and particularly inefficient bureaucracies, can perform an important service to the national economy that is probably not sufficiently appreciated by the population at large. The U.S. government alone employs almost three million people in activities that fortunately produce nothing that has to be sold in a commercial market.

However, the problem of manpower remains. Corporate objectives require the minimization of labor through investment as a tool for cost reduction to increase market shares and permit wages and salaries to rise as a result of higher productivity. Governments for their survival need full employment and prosperity. As long as markets expand, these two contradictory requirements can be reconciled after a fashion, or at least glossed over. But when further expansion and productivity increases become impractical, or when recessions occur, the state has to intervene.

The state has to create employment and fight inflation or risk collapse of the political system. It has to subsidize exports, create artificial markets, protect corporations, step up unemployment benefits, raise taxes, go deeper into debt, disburse money to the poverty-stricken, devaluate its currency, and risk insolvency. Any of these measures may spell disaster in the long run, but they are infinitely preferable to open rebellion. And as governments become more desperate, the measures they adopt will become more drastic and the need for scapegoats more urgent. Somebody has to be blamed for the crisis.

Unfortunately, large corporations make plausible scapegoats.

10. Is There a Remedy?

Curbing the Giants

The private citizen may be concerned over the economic power of the corporate giants. Economists may worry about the disappearance of real competition when business fields become dominated by just a handful of large corporations and the conflict over market shares is no longer profitable. And governments may be in jeopardy when markets become saturated and wage increases can no longer be hidden by business growth, and when large corporations with high productivity created by large investment eliminate labor-intensive small companies and aggravate unemployment. But not very much can be done about the increasing corporate concentration.

There is no practical way to change an economic system which is based on competition by resources. We cannot reduce corporate size and investment to restore business to artisanal levels. The change would be too drastic and the results would probably be disastrous.

Necessities and luxuries we now take for granted would become unattainable as the economics of mass markets and large investment disappeared. Wages would plummet because productivity would drop to artisanal levels. Unemployment and inflation would soar to levels that would make our present problems look like minor annoyances.

Replacing the corporate economy with small businesses would be madness. And so far all attempts to replace the shortcomings of the capitalistic system by something better have led to anarchy or to totalitarian systems with artificial economies and low standards of living. Tampering with an economic system is a perilous game. The consequences are too unpredictable, and the process is usually irreversible. Once the system is shattered, there is no way to put it back together again.

But perhaps some limited measures could be taken to curb the excesses of corporate concentration and to limit the power of corporate giants. Curbing big business is bound to appeal to large sectors of the public and attract the fancy of political leaders bent on scoring points with the electorate.

Various measures along these lines have been proposed. Large corporations could be broken up into smaller companies to reduce their power and to restore competition. Or perhaps they should be nationalized and run by the government, representing the public interest. Or perhaps industrial democracy should be established, giving workers a broad influence on corporate decisions. Finally, there might be more regulations to prevent abuses based on corporate size. But though all of these measures may seem attractive, they would not be likely to cure the problem.

If the government were to dismember excessively large corporations, General Motors and Ford might be obvious candidates. These corporations are very large and between them control a very large part of the automotive market. Under government pressure, the two companies could presumably be brought to accept fragmentation, and their place would be taken by perhaps ten smaller companies. The public would no doubt rejoice. A victory for competition would have been won and a signal blow against monopolistic business struck. Or would it?

Instead of four manufacturers there would be twelve, who presumably would compete fiercely for market shares to the benefit of the public. More jobs would be generated through the duplication of functions which that had formerly been centralized. Everybody should be happy.

And nobody should be happier than Chrysler and American Motors. Their big competitors would be gone. What would be left after the fragmentation would be companies of roughly similar size operating under similar conditions. Yet, in fact, the situation of the two smaller companies might have become distinctly worse. Under the present arrangement, the giant competitors cannot afford to lose the two smaller companies to preserve the image of competition in the automotive industry. If there were twelve companies in the business, this protection would be gone. The demise of a few of the smaller companies would no longer bring the antitrust policemen running. Survival of the smaller competitors would no longer be guaranteed.

But breaking up the giants would cause other problems. Anyone who cares to compare financial statements will notice that the smaller car makers tend to be less prosperous than the two giants, and in a bad year their business may become pretty marginal. This is not because the smaller companies are inept, but because their scale of operations is smaller. Making and selling cars at an annual volume of $5 billion or $10 billion is less profitable than doing the same thing at $30 billion or $40 billion.

After the giants had been broken up, everyone would be in the same situation. Yet each of the twelve companies would have to make a profit to survive. Two marginal competitors out of four is possible, but a major industry consisting of twelve marginal companies does not make sense. It would thus be necessary to improve profits at the new low volumes. This implies higher prices.

There would not be any other solution. The new companies could not reduce wages. They would have to promote their products on a nationwide basis. They might have to pursue technical development with diminishing returns to compete with each other. And all this would cost money, even though the size of the business had become smaller. Yet the new companies would have to make a profit.

The result of the attempt to restore competition among smaller companies would thus be an increase in car prices. This would not exactly be a pleasant prospect, but perhaps the public would be prepared to make this sacrifice in the interest of the common good. Unfortunately, the sacrifice would be useless. The problem would not have been solved.

All men are supposedly created equal, but as life goes on their equality becomes less and less perceptible. And our twelve equal car companies would not be likely to remain equal for any length of time. The fragmentation of the automotive business would create competition and problems of survival. To cope with this situation, each company would strive to increase its resources in order to become more competitive and more secure. Growth once again, would become a major objective, and five years after the split there would certainly be substantial differences once again in the size of the car companies. Some managements would be more successful, others less so, but all of them would make every effort to improve the situation of their company by rapid growth.

Since too much growth in the car business would be likely to lead to a repetition of the breakup trauma, growth would have to come from diversification. The more aggressive companies would thus be forced to expand into new fields that offered opportunities for rapid growth. And there would be nothing to prevent them from spreading in any direction they chose to become diversified giants.

The result of the fragmentation of the automotive industry is fairly obvious. The sedate giants of today, which cannot grow too quickly lest they attract undesirable attention, would be replaced by a pack of hungry and aggressive smaller companies bent on diversification and rapid growth. Would this make sense? By the same token, would it be desirable to break up AT&T, or the oil giants, or Sears, Roebuck? Probably not.

But what about nationalization?

Government ownership of large businesses exists in many industrialized countries of the Western world. Telephone services, utilities, railways, and even airlines are state-owned in most European countries. The British government is in the coal, steel, and aviation business; the French government owns banks, oil companies, and automobile and aerospace manufacturers, and the Italians have state-owned industrial trusts. The U.S. government is in the utility business and could conceivably take over some of the industrial giants and run them for the public.

But nationalization has some drawbacks. Banana republics may be able to confiscate companies, particularly if they are owned by foreign capitalists who ruthlessly exploit the local populace. But the same procedure would meet with stiff opposition in the United States. Consequently, the government would have to pay for the companies, and this would tend to get expensive.

At current market prices, the cost of buying the four largest corporations would run to about $75 billion. If the top ten were to be nationalized, the government would have to shell out around $120 billion in taxpayers' money. The sheer size of the transaction would involve protracted argument — this is not a deal that could be accomplished by presidential fiat or administrative order.

The first problem would be the selection of the companies to be nationalized. What would be the critical measure to trigger nationalization? Sheer size? Any organization with more than $10 billion in annual sales? Or any corporation that controls more than 30 per cent of its market? Would the top thirteen be enough? Or the top thirty-one? Or would it be better to nationalize by industry? All aerospace companies or all automobile makers? Or all energy companies?

The argument could rage for years. Whole divisions of the finest lawyers and armies of lobbyists could spend a great deal of time haggling with congressional committees, economists, and presidential advisers to settle this question. Whatever criteria for nationalization were finally adopted would necessarily involve hardships and injustices. And smart managers and skilled lawyers would inevitably find loopholes and develop new corporate structures to get around the law.

There is also the question of what happens to smaller enterprises that are suddenly faced with competition by state-owned corporations with virtually unlimited resources. Nationalized companies hardly ever go bankrupt. They may lose money, but their losses are taken over by the government, which places privately owned competitors at a terrible disadvantage. The only way for them to overcome this problem is to grow quickly and get nationalized.

The logical outcome of fighting corporate size by nationalization is state ownership of entire industries. There would be a Federal Automotive Corporation, a U.S. Communications Corporation, and perhaps a National Retailing Administration. The implantation of government bureaucracy on large corporations would no doubt create more jobs. It would also raise the direct and indirect cost of the products and services provided by the nationalized industries. Inefficiency would have to be paid for through higher prices or higher taxes to subsidize losses. There are enough actual examples around to prove this point. There must be few, if any, nationalized corporations in the world that are efficient, competitive, and not a burden on the taxpayer.

Once a large corporation is nationalized, the growth urge can continue unchecked. Relieved from any worry about profit and survival, the nationalized giants could concentrate their efforts on expansion. And anyone who has ever considered the ability of government organizations to spend other people's money on a breathtaking scale can foresee the direction of future events. The Department of Industry would soon acquire spending habits akin to those of the Pentagon, where billions in public funds are committed to all sorts of projects deemed to be of national importance, and where the magnitude of the money involved has largely lost any real meaning.

Nationalization is obviously no real solution to the growing concentration of business and resources. If anything, the problem would become worse as faceless bureaucrats directed huge and growing government corporations that operated largely outside the constraints of normal business practice.

Worker participation or industrial democracy has been suggested as a means to make corporations more socially responsible. The general idea is that the participation of workers in setting corporate objectives would somehow provide a counterweight to the presumably asocial behavior of corporate management and owners, and reward workers for their role in creating corporate prosperity. The introduction of such schemes may provide governments with political support among workers and unions, but they are unlikely to solve the problem of economic concentration and corporate power. It mainly means that workers and their unions acquire a stronger influence over corporations; they can not only strike but also participate in management. Social responsibility then translates mainly into concessions to the special interests represented by labor unions. Yet the interests of labor unions are not necessarily identical with those of the public as a whole. The need to comply with management growth strategies and totalitarian profit extortion systems as well as with vastly enlarged union power will not curb corporate concentration or result in cheaper products and services, as the population of the United Kingdom must have discovered by now.

This leaves regulation as the last alternative of direct government action to control corporate growth. We have already seen that most of today's giants are not rapid-growth corporations. Freezing their size would not really change very much, but would permit smaller companies to catch up and attain whatever size limit the government might impose. The growth of the largest corporations would be inhibited, but concentration would nevertheless continue. Freezing the size of all corporations would obviously not be practical. If no one could grow, there would be no conflict over market shares; competition would be eliminated. Nor would it seem practical to limit corporate growth rates by government edict.

The solution, if there is such a thing, must lie elsewhere. Yet while none of these measures shows much promise of solving the problems posed by excessive corporate growth, this does not mean that they may not be adopted by harassed governments. Plausible action may become a political necessity, even though the action may ultimately prove to be ineffectual or self-defeating.

But perhaps other solutions to the problem may be possible. We cannot prevent corporations and their managements from taking advantage of the opportunities of their operating environment. But perhaps this environment can be modified in a manner that will inhibit excessive corporate growth and make corporations more responsive to the interests of the broad public.

To attain this would require different incentives for corporate management. We would have to change the rules of the game.

Changing the Rules

Since corporate growth strategies have been developed as a reaction to the threats and incentives of the environment in which corporations operate, it is conceivable that this environment could be modified to deemphasize the advantages of rapid growth and large size.

This process does not have to be a matter of direct interference with the activities of large corporations, but rather of changing incentives to reduce the benefits now accruing to corporations and their managers from rapid growth, mergers, diversification, and totalitarian management.

And since stock market speculation plays such an important part in both shareholder attitudes and management objectives, certain changes in taxation, for instance, might have some beneficial effects on corporate strategy. The purpose of these changes would be twofold.

They could make investors more interested in long-term stock ownership rather than in quick capital gains and thus compel them to take a more active interest in the affairs of the corporations whose stock they own. Second, they ought to reduce, or eliminate, the role of stock price fluctuations in managerial compensation plans.

The first step would be the elimination of the lopsided tax treatment of dividends, which are in fact taxed twice, and of capital gains, which enjoy reduced tax rates if the stock is held for more than a relatively short period. Movements to exempt dividends from taxation are already under way as this is being written, and this measure should go a long way to make continued ownership of stocks more attractive. It would also help to encourage the purchase of stocks that are not expected to show a rapid price increase in the near future.

By contrast, the preferential tax treatment of capital gains makes little sense when applied to the typical stock market transaction. The argument that capital gains tax treatment encourages investment applies only to the purchase of newly issued stock. The speculator who buys stock from another speculator is not investing in the corporation.

Consequently, preferential capital gains rates should be limited to special cases — to newly issued stock and to used stocks that have been held for a long time. Short-term stock speculation should be subject to ordinary tax rates. A scheme along the following lines might be considered. Stock in new companies, where the risk is particularly large, should be exempt from all capital gains taxes, and losses should perhaps even be deductible from ordinary income. This would greatly encourage investors to place money with small young companies, rather than playing large established favorites where the risk is small.

Newly issued shares of existing corporations should be free from capital gains tax if held for a certain period, say two years. This would make the purchase of new stocks attractive. At present, corporations dislike selling new stock because this dilutes earnings and so depresses the price of the stock and affects management options. Instead, corporations prefer to borrow money on the financial markets. The result is a strong competition for financing — with the advantage going inevitably to the large corporations — along with high interest rates and gloomy prophecies by experts about impending capital shortages. Finally, capital gains resulting from the trading of old stocks between speculators should be fully taxed at ordinary income tax rates for perhaps three years. If held longer, the stock should then benefit from a declining tax rate on capital gains. Thus, a stock held three years and a day might be taxed at 80 per cent of the ordinary income rate, at 60 per cent after four years, with stock market profits tax-free if the stock were held more than seven years.

Stockbrokers would greet such measures with heartrending

wails, but the effect on investors and corporations might be rather salutary. In fact, the whole spectrum of investor interest would shift. Daring high flyers with volatile stocks would lose a great deal of their attractiveness as investors scrambled for issues in new companies, new issues in existing corporations, and solid stocks worth holding long enough to obtain the reduced tax on capital gains. And because the investors would be locked in for a while if they wanted to profit from reduced taxation on the fruits of their speculation, even the large masses of small shareholders would be bound to take a more active interest in the activities of the companies they have invested in. They would want to be sure their stock would be worth something when they finally got ready to sell it. The fast stock rise triggered by a profit from a quick merger would lose its charm as stockholders looked ahead to what would happen in five or seven years.

Needless to say, tax reform should also include measures to curb the excesses of stock-based incentive schemes. In fact, it would be a good idea if managerial compensation could be altogether divorced from stock market games. Recent changes in the tax laws have removed some of the tax shelter aspects of stock options. Unfortunately, the result is bound to be new schemes to alleviate the impact of taxation on options — such as options convertible into phantom stocks, which provide executives with stock benefits without their needing to actually own the stock — and probably an escalation of options to compensate the recipients for the higher tax burden. As a result, management attention is likely to remain firmly riveted to the stock market.

Yet even here solutions are possible. One solution would be to eliminate all stock-based incentives in favor of tax-free management dividends. A certain part of the net after-tax profit of the corporation would be allocated to deserving managers, either on a temporary or permanent basis. This would be distributed like a dividend, and since dividends would be tax-free, the benefit to the recipient could be substantial. This benefit would not involve stock ownership and would depend directly on the performance of the corporation rather than on the market price of its stock.

If the manager wants to play the stock of his own corporation, let him do so with his own money and under the rules that apply to any other shareholder. He would still have the benefit of his insider information, but at least he would not be aided and abetted in his speculation by corporate compensation procedures.

The idea of a management dividend scheme has another useful advantage. Since the scheme would be financed out of net profits, shareholders would be bound to take a strong interest in the nature and size of the awards to deserving managers. It would be their money that is being doled out, which is rather different from the prevailing idea that stock options cost the corporation nothing. This new awareness might impose some rather important restraints on managerial greed.

These measures, which are merely speculations as to the kind of action that might be taken to modify the present growth-generating corporate environment, are by no means radical. They would not interfere with the normal conduct of corporate business. They would not cause panic in the streets — except perhaps briefly on Wall Street — and they would not contribute to an economic crisis. And they would seem to be vastly preferable to the more drastic actions advocated by reformers and enemies of big business.

Of course, there might be other and more direct measures that could be taken into consideration to curb the excesses of corporate growth. There could be special taxes on mergers to eliminate instant increases in earnings per share in the aggressor corporation. All sorts of permutations of this scheme are possible, ranging all the way to the extreme of taxing net assets of merger victims as income to the surviving corporation. Judicious application of the tax clout could be an effective means for discouraging the continued sprawl of diversified corporations to the detriment of their monobusiness competitors.

But taxation is only one of many aspects of the corporate environment. Control is another, and this is where shareholder power could play an important part.

Shareholder Power

The owners of a corporation should have some measure of control over its destiny. Yet under current usage, the rights of shareholders are symbolic, not real. The small shareholders with two hundred or two thousand shares to their name have little means to make their influence felt, even though they may collectively own an overwhelming majority of the shares of a corporation. Control rests with the insiders, management and perhaps some shareholders who dominate the board because they happen to own large blocks of stock.

Giving all the shareholders effective rights would not only be a matter of fairness and justice. It could also be a means of making corporations more responsive to the desires of a fairly broad section of the public. And this could go some way to curb certain corporate abuses that provide plausible targets for advocates of more drastic reforms. Strengthening shareholder power could thus be a useful objective of corporate strategy.

There is no reason to fear that an improvement in shareholder rights would enhance the power of dominant insiders, since they already have all the power they can use. The goal would be to give an effective voice to all the people who own stock and who are now deprived of any means to express themselves.

To start with, all shareholders should know who actually

controls the corporation. This means public disclosure of the largest shareholders and their holdings. The names of the ten largest shareholders, or of anybody who owns more than one per cent of the stock, and the number of shares held should be revealed. This would give even the small shareholders a clear idea of the big fish that may be floating in the same puddle. It would also provide them with a means to judge to what extent certain corporate actions may reflect the interests of these large shareholders and insiders.

Then, the small shareholders should have voting rights that permit them to express their views in a more meaningful manner than the present procedures, which virtually guarantee unanimity of voting on certain important issues. The key issue, of course, is the election of the board of directors. With current procedures, the shareholders either approve the official slate or withhold their vote. This is absurd. Voting implies a choice, so the shareholders should be given a choice. They should be able to vote for or against specific board members. Cumulative voting has been proposed as a means of doing just this.

In cumulative voting, the shareholder does not cast one vote for the official slate of director nominations or lodge his protest by abstaining. Instead, he casts as many votes as there are seats on the board and is permitted to accumulate these votes for just one, or several, candidates on the list. Thus the shareholder can cast ten votes for one candidate who happens to appeal to him. The shareholder is, of course, still limited to the candidates that have been nominated by the board, but at least he has a choice in voting, even though the choice is limited.

It is amusing to read the reaction of the board of one large corporation to a proposal for cumulative voting. After listing the proposal, the proxy statement sent to the shareholders contained the following passage:

THE BOARD OF DIRECTORS IS OPPOSED TO
THIS PROPOSAL.

The most equitable method of voting shares on proxy matters is one vote per share. If in the election of directors
through cumulative voting, a share is assigned a greater number of votes, it becomes possible for a few large holdings
voting as a block to elect one or more directors representing
special interests or particular points of view. The shareholders of the Company have on a number of previous occasions
rejected proposals to adopt cumulative voting. They
reaffirmed thereby, as does management now, the principle
of electing directors who will represent the interests of all the
shareholders.

Management recommends that you vote AGAINST this res-
olution.

Of course they do. They do not want anyone meddling with
perfectly comfortable procedures. After all, the board knows
best what is in the interest of all the shareholders. If the shareholders decided not to rubber-stamp the board's wise proposals
for electing itself, where would it all lead?

Apart from that, the argument of the board is pure nonsense.
Of course, cumulative voting permits the pooling of votes to
elect directors representing special interests, for instance, those
of the small shareholders. The owners of 10 per cent of the stock
band together and elect 10 per cent of the board to represent
their particular point of view. And is that not exactly what
voting is supposed to be all about?

By contrast, under the time-hallowed forms of corporate
board elections, chances are that half the board members represent the interests of management and the other half large shareholders, bankers, big creditors, and the corporation's outside
legal counsel. This leaves the smaller shareholders, who may
own 95 per cent of the stock, without any representation what-
soever. Is this "more equitable"?

Cumulative voting may have its drawbacks, but at least it gives every stockholder a choice. And this choice implies that not all nominees may be elected, or at least it should. But the large mass of lesser fry among the shareholders should not only have the right to a meaningful vote. They should also be able to introduce their own nominees if they so desire. In practice, this means that any shareholder should be able to present himself as a candidate. Obviously, certain rules and requirements should be established to discourage frivolous candidacies. The candidate should have to file a formal statement giving his background and qualifications to permit fellow shareholders to judge his suitability for the job. He should also submit a formal undertaking to the effect that he is familiar with the obligations and responsibilities of board membership and that he will perform his functions in a proper manner if elected. And perhaps he should have to place a certain number of shares on deposit. If he is not elected, the shares will be released, but if he becomes a director they will be held as a guarantee for the proper discharge of his functions until he retires from the board.

This may sound like an invitation to corporate anarchy, but it is not. The election of the board is a right of the shareholders that has been usurped by management. It should be restored to the rightful owners. If the shareholders then decide to elect noisy crusaders, bearded guitar-twangers, or little old ladies, so be it. It is their corporation.

It is also their money that is invested in the corporation, and this makes the election of candidates from the lunatic fringe rather unlikely. On the other hand, enough shareholders might feel that a strong management contingent on the board represents primarily management interests and that the outsiders proposed by the board are hardly representatives of the broad mass of shareholders. Given voting rights and open nomination lists, they could do something about this particular problem. With these or similar changes in election procedures, the shareholders would finally have a chance to express their views. The silent corporate majority would have a voice.

But shareholders should also have other voting rights. They should be asked to approve, or reject, the annual incentive awards to senior executives. Thus we might be spared the obscene spectacle of a corporation foundering under poor management while the culprits happily award themselves large performance bonuses even though earnings drop to disaster levels. The threat of shareholder disapproval would go a long way to curb management greed.

In the case of management dividends, suggested before, the matter would be relatively simple. Shareholders would approve a certain percentage of net earnings for management rewards; the payments would then depend on net profits rather than on management greed and board collusion.

In certain foreign countries, the shareholders are asked to approve the financial results of the company and the conduct of the board members. Both approvals may be largely a formality, but they nevertheless serve to keep management and board on their toes. If the board members are not absolved by the shareholders, they could presumably be held personally liable for errors or misdeeds committed while in office. As long as all the shareholders have genuine voting rights in the board election, these measures may not be necessary; the owners would be able to elect a new board if performance were not satisfactory. Under the present system, they do not have this option unless they own big blocks of shares and are wealthy enough to organize a proxy fight.

But there are other measures that could cause corporate managers to avert their gaze from stock market quotations and devote their attention more fully to their primary job of managing the corporation.

One such measure relates to mergers. Whenever a merger is

proposed, the shareholders should receive not only the usual legalistic explanation, but also pro forma financial statements that clearly show the effect of the transaction on both the companies and the fortunes of the owners. The fact that a seemingly attractive merger owes its attractiveness chiefly to the exploitation of the owners of the victim might cause the shareholders to sit up and take notice. And this might make mergers with the primary purpose of creating instant profits for the surviving company out of the hides of the victim's shareholders more difficult.

In this context, it might also be useful to reveal the identity of the major shareholders of the two companies to both sets of owners. This would enable the small shareholders to judge whether the merger might be arranged for the convenience of financial interests with substantial holdings in both companies. This sort of thing does sometimes happen.

And to avoid the obvious loophole of mergers through corporate subsidiaries, there might be a law that all mergers, spinoffs, and similar transactions involving major portions of corporate assets must be approved, not only by the management and board of the parent companies, but also by the stockholders. The sale or merger of a subsidiary is too important to be left entirely to the discretion of management.

Finally, something ought to be done about the archaic voting procedures themselves. These procedures obviously date from a time when companies were smallish, local affairs and shareholders could attend meetings without much difficulty. When corporations have millions of shareholders, such meetings become absurd. Shareholders who cannot attend the meeting — which means 99 per cent of them — vote by proxy; somebody else votes their shares. And the somebody else happens to be a member of the board. The proxy may contain voting instructions or may be left blank, in which case the recipient may vote at his own discretion. Together with the limited voting options, this procedure places an undue bias on the whole voting process. Board members appointed to vote on behalf of absent shareholders are not likely to vote against their own interests, even when these interests conflict with the interests of the shareholders.

There does not seem to be any valid reason why absent shareholders should not be able to vote directly by mail, without the interposition of a board member. Nor should management power be amplified by blank proxies. Shareholders who are too lazy to express their views should not be able to delegate this function to a representative of management interests. By the same token, shareholder resolutions should not have to be presented in person at the meeting, a process that largely eliminates resolutions from owners living far away from corporate headquarters. They should be just as valid if they are presented by mail. The owner of five hundred shares who lives in Europe should have the same rights as the shareholder who lives in the same town or works for the corporation.

Once the voting is over, the exact results should be communicated to the shareholders. So many shares were voted for, so many against, a particular proposal, and so many were not voted at all. At this point the small shareholder can tell how many others voted the way he did.

Obviously, these suggestions are merely examples of what might be done to provide all shareholders with full voting rights. Such measures would not provoke economic disaster, the collapse of corporations, or protest marches by newly unemployed board members. But by giving all the shareholders a voice, they might help to impose some outside control over corporate boards, which now reign with almost unrestricted power. And since shareholders, in the United States at least, represent a broad cross section of the general public, shareholder power would tend to make even very large corporations more responsive to the public interest.

From the corporate point of view, a change along these lines might be vastly preferable to more drastic reforms, more government regulations to curb corporate power, or the introduction of union power into corporate management in the guise of worker participation.

More Government

We have suggested the possibility of certain modest changes in the corporate environment. The purpose of these suggestions is to remove some of the incentives for fast growth and diversification in the hope that this might slow the race toward larger corporate size and the increasing concentration of corporate power while retaining, by and large, the advantages of our economic system. But measures along these lines are unlikely ever to be carried out. They are doomed from the start. The reasons are not hard to find.

For one thing, too many vested interests are involved. Managements will hardly be delighted at the prospect of losing their independence and seeing their stock-based incentives disappear. Large shareholders are not about to give up their insider status without a fight. The security industry is not about to welcome measures that cut down on stock market gambling and encourage long-term investment. And speculators, large and small, will fight tooth and nail for preferential tax treatment of capital gains. They want to make money from playing the stock market, and they could not care less about how the corporations are run, since their stock ownership is strictly a temporary matter.

But what about the eternal crusaders, anxious to strike their well-publicized blows against big business? And what about the politicians in search of a plausible cause to endear them to the electorate? And the champions of free enterprise, untrammeled competition, and the public interest? Would not a corporate reform movement to curb the excesses of diversification and concentration appeal to them? Probably not.

Changes along the lines suggested above are not likely to attract any large following. Crusades and revolutions require the image of bold action rather than quiet reform. Behead the king, assassinate the wrongdoers, break up the evil corporations. Let there be blood and violence as the noble aim is achieved and the guilty are punished.

Modifying the corporate environment is a lost cause for many reasons. It is perfectly normal for a government and its leaders to support important corporations and millionaire shareholders or oil tycoons quietly and effectively in the guise of protecting commercial freedom and in appreciation of past and future campaign donations. It is something else to stand up and espouse the cause of shareholder rights in a public place, even if the shareholders whose rights are in question are masses of minicapitalists rather than millionaires. "Capitalist" has become a word with ugly connotations, and there is little glory in championing the cause of an unpopular minority.

It is politically far more expedient to fight big business with increasing regulations, to speak loudly in favor of restoring competition, to crusade noisily against corporate misdeeds, and to curry favor with the electorate by bold action and ambitious programs to protect the public interest against the detested corporate monsters.

It is beside the point that these measures may be utterly ineffectual and that increasing regulation may penalize small business more than the giants. And so we can expect to see more regulation and more powerful regulatory bodies as the government machinery clanks into high gear to protect the citizens from the evils of large corporations. We may see very large corporations dismembered to increase competition. And the general effect of this government action to please the voting masses will be to make business activities more cumbersome

and costly and to increase the critical size below which a corporation cannot survive.

But this kind of regulation will not solve the problem because
it deals with the consequences rather than with the causes of
excessive corporate growth. And the remedy of ever-increasing
government regulation may be worse than the disease it is
supposed to cure.

The Wrong Problem?

History shows that we are always late in reacting to changing
conditions. And very often our reaction is neither appropriate
nor effective. Of course, we sense the changes around us. We
know that no two moments in life are exactly the same. Our
whole existence is a matter of continuous adjustment to change.
Unfortunately, by the time we wake up to the implications of
a certain change, decide that something ought to be done, and
have figured out what we should do, the world has moved on.
Thus we tend to solve the problems of yesterday rather than
those of today and tomorrow. And very often our solutions are
not solutions at all, but merely minor adjustments to buy time,
to squelch annoying symptoms, rather than effective action to
solve the basic problems.

The time lag in responding to change and the nature of the
response appear to depend on the suddenness with which a
problem appears. A drastic change is bound to produce a fairly
rapid reaction. The man who is suddenly fired from his job is
likely to do something about his situation then and there. He
will start looking for a new job, print résumés, call his contacts,
have a nervous breakdown, get drunk, or even commit suicide.
His reaction may not be appropriate or useful, but it will be
prompt.

Slow, insidious, creeping change is much harder to detect

and to cope with. Things may get just a little worse every day, but the difference from one day to the next is never important enough to trigger real action. The smallness of the daily change offers much scope for wishful thinking and procrastination. There is always the hope that the trend may be only a temporary setback that will reverse itself in due time, or that the inevitable disaster will not really happen, or will only happen in the distant future, and there is plenty of time to do something tomorrow. There may also be the convenient thought that premature action may be more dangerous than waiting to see how things develop.

Man's ability to rationalize inaction can be remarkable. An executive promoted to a meaningless job may successfully pretend to himself that the crumbling of his empire is but a temporary, transient reverse, rather than face the awful fact that he is on the skids and doomed; and his illusion will be carefully fed by those who are busily greasing the skids.

If an individual's reaction to changing circumstances is slow, the reaction of a large group of people or a complex organization may be even slower and may lag five or even fifty years behind the events that sparked the change. By that time an acceptable solution may no longer be possible. The response to the problem may then have to be limited to futile gestures, pseudo-solutions, minor changes to attenuate symptoms, substitutions of artificial problems which are amenable to solution in place of the unsolvable real problem, and fervent hope that the real problem might somehow disappear before a catastrophic upheaval becomes unavoidable.

And there lies the problem of coping with corporate concentration. Astute measures may be able to slow the trend to rapid corporate growth, but they cannot eliminate the results of decades of corporate expansion. Short of drastic measures that would upset the whole fabric of our economic system, there is no practical way to eliminate the concentration of corporate power, which many people perceive as a menace.

But is corporate giantism really such a meance? Corporate growth is the logical outcome of competition in an economic system in which price reductions and product improvements require mass markets and large investments. This economical environment may be inherently unstable, but it has nevertheless brought to the Western world a mass prosperity that has never before existed in the history of mankind and that is far in advance of any other economic system. And large corporations have played a key role in creating this prosperity by offering products at prices which could not be attained by small-scale industrial activities, and by being able to pay wages far in excess of what the small competitive company so beloved by economists could ever afford.

Giant corporations may dominate many sectors of the economy, but the customer still has a choice. He can choose between the products and services of different giants, or he can refuse to patronize the giants if he really considers large corporations a menace. He can withhold his business or buy from smaller companies. Yet this does not seem to happen. We like to buy from large corporations, even if there is a choice available. Otherwise there would be no corporate giants. And anyone who feels that corporate profits are excessive is free to buy a few shares and participate in the allegedly huge profits extorted from the public.

Modern management methods may be totalitarian and shareholder rights a polite fiction, leaving large corporations almost entirely under the control of their managements. But even here the individual has a choice. As a manager he is free to leave and do something else if management by soviet does not appeal to him. As a disgruntled shareholder he can sell his stock and invest in real estate, savings bonds, or even in small businesses.

This is not to say that all is for the best in the best of corporate worlds, but simply to suggest that even in an economy dominated by a few very large corporations, the public would still have certain choices. And choices are becoming more and more scarce in our modern world.

Giant corporations have often been likened to states within states. By the same token, states can be compared to supercorporations. And the menace of these supercorporations may, in the long run, be far more serious than the threat to the public interest of the large multibusiness, multinational corporations because the state offers its citizens no significant choices.

The business of the state is protection. The purchase of this product is compulsory at prices unilaterally fixed by the seller. The citizen has no choice of how much protection he wants and how much he wants to pay for this protection. He has to buy the whole package, or else. The analogy to certain other protection rackets immediately springs to mind. In the beginning the state provided protection mainly against outside enemies and crime. But as time went by, governments found that the good citizens needed, wanted, or at least put up with protection against all sorts of other dangers, misfortunes, and discomforts. The protection business was susceptible to growth, and from this growth potential developed the manifold activities of the modern state, with its teeming bureaucracy and escalating expenditures.

As the protection business of the state grows, the activities of government agencies interfere more and more with the lives of the citizens and the pursuit of corporate affairs. The modern state provides protection not only against enemies without and crime within, but also against unexpected disasters, poverty, sickness, old age, pollution, unemployment, unethical business methods, and even against the citizen's own stupidity. The fact that this protection may be very costly and not always very effective is beside the point. The state has the monopoly and the citizen pays or he goes to jail.

The growth potential of the governmental protection monopoly is almost unlimited. Propelled by the urges of bureaucrats to enlarge their jobs and importance and by the ambition of politicians to improve their reelection prospects by sponsoring plausible measures to improve the protection of the citizens, the state protection business is a leading growth industry. And as this growth progresses, the governments of free democratic countries are developing into Big Brother organizations wielding ever more power through complex webs of agencies and regulations. And this structure remains virtually intact no matter which set of political leaders may be elected.

In fact, the right to elect the government may be more symbolic than real. Candidates are usually nominated by party organizations and do not necessarily represent the choice of a large segment of the population. The voters then have the right to chose between nominees, or rather between the images projected by the candidates and their backers during the election campaign. Nor are the candidates under any particular compulsion to fulfill their campaign promises once they are elected. The only redress for disappointed voters is to cast their ballots for the other lot when election time comes around again.

Yet the fact that there are elections has some important consequences. It is only natural for any elected official to want to hang on to his job and to be reelected. This must be one of his main motivations. This means pleasing the largest number of voters possible. And since the less affluent usually outnumber the wealthy, there is a built-in bias toward Robin Hoodism in any democracy. The tendency is for robbing the rich and helping the poor. A poor man has the same vote as a multimillionaire, and since there are few multimillionaires compared to the large masses of people with low or no income, political judgment dictates that the numerous votes of the lower-income classes should be courted. Egalitarianism has thus become a political goal, no matter what its ultimate consequences may be. The fact that the rich may be more helpful with campaign contributions does not restore the balance. Universal suffrage has a built-in slant toward socialism and against capitalism.

And this is where large corporations are vulnerable. They make convenient and plausible targets for crusades to protect the voter. Big, bad business is a popular issue even though we happily buy its products and services at prices that good little companies could never match. And since corporations cannot vote and would be crucified if they attempted to influence the votes of their employees, their only means to stem the tide of criticism is to exert subtle or not so subtle influence on government officials, for which they are promptly castigated if the dark deed becomes known.

No such restrictions apply to labor unions, which are free to endorse political candidates and suggest that their members vote accordingly. Nor do corporations have much chance to prevail against the votes of the almost three million civilian employees of the federal government who are free to express in the voting booth their vested interest in bigger government and larger jobs for themselves.

But corporate giants are also vulnerable for another reason. By their size and economic importance they rival the monopolistic supercorporation that is the modern state. In an age of ever-increasing government influence and spending, and of politically sponsored egalitarianism, the multinational corporation may well become the only organization that preserves a certain degree of freedom from government rule. It is not inconceivable that multinational business giants may thus preserve certain freedoms of choice which may no longer be available to individuals and mononational business enterprises.

The existence of corporate giants may provide, twenty years hence, the only practical alternative to the all-pervading state, as did the church hundreds of years ago. Choosing life in the absolute environment of the giant corporation might then be an alternative for those who find the encroachments of the absolute state too stifling. And seen in this light, the survival of large corporations may well provide some sort of an escape from the power of the modern bureaucratic nation-state.

However, in order to survive, the large corporations will have to develop new strategies to cope with public distrust and the inroads of the government agencies. Merely acquiescing in more government regulation may have its short-term advantages but will ultimately spell the complete submission of the corporation to the bureaucracy of the government.

On the other hand, there are certain measures which might involve short-term inconvenience and cost, but, in the long run, they might ensure the survival of corporate life as we know it. One is corporate reform to curb the more flagrant excesses of growth strategies, totalitarian management systems, and managerial stock market games. Another is the creation of broad public interest in the corporate cause. This might well involve corporate support for tax laws designed to curb stock speculation and to encourage long-term stock investment, and giving the teeming masses of small shareholders a real voice in corporate affairs. When millions of shareholders become vitally interested in the fate of the corporations whose stock they own — because that is where their money is and will be for years to come, since selling the stock would cost too much in taxes — corporations may suddenly find themselves aided and abetted by an important segment of the population, and this might change the aspect of political crusades to a remarkable degree.

Finally, there is education. Our children are taught that capitalism is a derogatory word. Nobody bothers to explain that capitalism, while not perfect, has some rather important advantages not only for fat cat capitalists, but also for the ordinary citizen. When corporations are accused by the mass media and vociferous minorities of dastardly behavior, corporate managers make lame apologies instead of boldly standing up to defend their course of action. Why should corporations have to bear the blame when politicians, at home and abroad, solicit campaign contributions or outright bribes?

And when are experts who really ought to know better going to stop bemoaning the evils of corporate concentration and pining for the never-never days of real competition with lots of small businesses? Educating the public about the realities of our economic system will take more than glossy full-page institutional advertisements, and it might well be worthwhile.

As it is, there are obviously excesses in corporate growth strategies and operating methods, as there are in any other human activity. But to destroy large corporations, or regulate them to death, would probably not be a very reasonable solution. The corporate menace, if it really exists, may in the end be far more preferable than a state-run economy, or $20 light bulbs and $5000 refrigerators produced by competitive small companies.

DATE DUE
